MW01518318

HEALTH CARE ISSUES, COSTS AND ACCESS

SOCIOLOGY OF INTERPROFESSIONAL HEALTH CARE PRACTICE

CRITICAL REFLECTIONS AND CONCRETE SOLUTIONS

HEALTH CARE ISSUES, COSTS AND ACCESS

Additional books in this series can be found on Nova's website under the Series tab.

Additional E-books in this series can be found on Nova's website under the E-books tab.

HEALTH CARE ISSUES, COSTS AND ACCESS

SOCIOLOGY OF INTERPROFESSIONAL HEALTH CARE PRACTICE

CRITICAL REFLECTIONS AND CONCRETE SOLUTIONS

SIMON KITTO
JANICE CHESTERS
JILL THISTLETHWAITE
AND
SCOTT REEVES
EDITORS

Nova Science Publishers, Inc.
New York

NOTICE TO THE READER

LIBRARY OF CONGRESS CATALOGING-IN-PUBLICATION DATA
Sociology of interprofessional health care practice : critical reflections and concrete solutions / editors, Simon Kitto ... [et al.].
p. ; cm.
Includes bibliographical references and index.
ISBN 978-1-60876-866-0 (hardcover : alk. paper)
1. Health care teams. 2. Interprofessional relations. I. Kitto, Simon.
[DNLM: 1. Interprofessional Relations. 2. Patient Care Team. 3. Cooperative Behaviour. 4. Education, Medical. 5. Interdisciplinary Communication. W 84.8 S678 2009]
R729.5.H4S63 2009
362.1068--dc22
2009044338

Published by Nova Science Publishers, Inc. † *New York*

CONTENTS

PREFACE

As this important collection of papers makes clear interprofessional experiences in health and human services, encompassing education, learning, practice and care, need focal points in theory that promote research. Any approach to this task must involve a mix of health and human service professionals within and across the sectors of post-secondary education and service delivery.

Over the past 50 years it has become clear that there is an urgent need to develop a sound basis of scholarship for interprofessional experiences in health and human services. A need to examine the bases of these enterprises through various theoretical lenses provided by, for example, the fields of sociology, linguistics, philosophy, anthropology, economics, political science – each of which offer theories and experimental methods with which to explore the diversity of interprofessional experiences and from which a strong evidence base may be obtained. The sociological and psycho-social viewpoints expressed in this volume represent the first time a particular academic discipline has offered its unique view of the issues confronting the interprofessional experiences associated with health and human services.

Reviewed in this work are illustrations of how and why sociological ideas may be used to first develop models on which to base testable hypotheses of appropriate sociological theories, and second to show that data from tested hypotheses lend credence and acceptability to interprofessional experiences.

The chapters in this book set out to describe the reality of "being interprofessional" – rooted in a history of *perceived value* and the accumulation of *evidence based experience*. Thus, the authors develop an understanding of the complex relationships that obtain amongst and between perceptions of interprofessional experiences. This understanding is then used to develop models that allow measurement of change (the evidence base), as a function of collaborative and team-based experience. As yet, however, there is not a clear understanding of the impact of those changes as they are translated into practice.

Implicit throughout the papers is the rationale that if interprofessional experiences are not driven by theory it is difficult to know and measure what those experiences represent. The Law of Unintended Consequences then emerges i.e. findings derived from interprofessional experiences and understanding of their operational power remain moot, and a body of knowledge that might better inform interprofessional experiences does not develop and grow. Ergo, interprofessional experiences remains at the mercy of fashion and expediency. A sad lesson that has been learned from innumerable interprofessional demonstration projects in many countries is that good ideas about interprofessional experiences require explicit plans for sustainability and evaluation metrics that clearly demonstrate their added value i.e. impact on the systems of education and health and human services.

The work represented in this book demonstrates that, if the fields of interprofessional experiences are to succeed, then they face a task familiar to all other similar movements whose work ranges from theory to practice; that is, they must develop a theoretical framework based on principles that are coherent, generalisable, transferable and of continuing applicability, a framework which can then be developed into principles of practice that are evidence based and systemically possible.

Interestingly this book, through its many authors, points to a troublesome irony, that is whereas societies spend large sums of money on *professional* education and practice (the infamous silos), they as yet spend almost nothing on interprofessional experiences, which by inference are assumed to be vital to assuring the highest quality of care. This irony needs to be addressed in studies that will continue the work presented here.

It is to be hoped that those who read this book will be strongly motivated to take the materials herein and use them to build a meaningful, measurable and sustainable environment of interprofessional experiences which may then lead to profound system change.

John H.V.Gilbert, Ph.D., FCAHS
Vancouver, Canada

In: Sociology of Interprofessional Health …
Ed: S. Kitto, J. Chesters et al.

ISBN: 978-1-60876-866-0
© 2011 Nova Science Publishers, Inc.

Chapter 1

INTRODUCTION: A SOCIOLOGY OF INTERPROFESSIONAL HEALTHCARE

Janice Chesters, Jill Thistlethwaite, Scott Reeves and Simon Kitto

In recent years Western governments, plus an increasing number of health and social care practitioners and academics, have acted and written in support of the importance of increased interprofessional education, learning and practice. The UK government, for example, has invested heavily in developing shared or common learning and in developing interprofessional policy and practice guidelines. Similar movements can be found in other countries such as Australia, US and Canada. Much of the academic writing in the field describes the implementation of a variety of interprofessional alternatives to uniprofessional, orthodox Western biomedicine. The interprofessional 'solution' to perceived flaws in health care practice and delivery is often uncritically presented as 'common sense' and at times comes close to being an ideology or an emerging, perhaps soon to be dominant, discourse. While many of the contributors to this book are committed to interprofessionalism, they are united in the view that there is a lack of critical sociological analysis of the interprofessional phenomenon. We set out to redress this deficit by inviting sociologists and other academics and clinicians with an interest in critical enquiry to contribute to this edited collection.

The tools of sociological analysis, whether used by researchers and writers who call themselves sociologists or by members of other disciplines, have a lot to offer people interested in interprofessional education, learning and practice. Sociology has a range of lenses to study a field – from narrow and particular to wide and general and used at the micro, meso or macro level. Each lens and level can be employed with either a theoretical or empirical approach or both. Sociologists research and write as if the surface is what is important or argue that a more helpful reality is only reached when the depths of an issue are explored. Some sociologists argue that the world is at least partially real while some say it is almost wholly socially constructed by people thinking, planning and talking about things. All of these perspectives are partial and have addressed issues of professional power and practices, the relationship between health care practitioners and their patients, the various cultures of health care and the wide variety of meanings people have attached to the seeking of and provision of health and social care. All of these perspectives are useful and have an important contribution to make to the improvement of health and social care.

Sociology is a broad discipline and we made no attempt to limit an author's interpretation of what might constitute an appropriately sociological contribution. However, we advised that at the very least all the chapters should incorporate extensive critical reflection and offer some concrete or practical ways forward to better, more effective patient centred interprofessional health and social care practice. Reeves (Chapter 2) and Bainbridge and Purkis (Chapter 3) chose to be quite explicit in their approach; both called their contributions sociological and recognised the importance of the sociological canon to interprofessional education and practice. Other contributors were more implicit in their approaches but never the less engaged with the key sociological concerns of history, context, critique, conflict, power, structure, function, emotion and the key issue of the investigation of the diverse nature of the relationships between the social actors engaged in this field. We wanted partial, locatable, critical approaches and that is what our contributors have delivered. The key themes that emerged were team work, the dangers of stereotyping, professional socialisation, the quality and safety of health and social care and the importance of interprofessional education, learning and practice to health care service reform.

THE MEANING OF INTERPROFESSIONAL EDUCATION, LEARNING AND PRACTICE

The meaning of interprofessional education, learning and practice is contested. In the West interprofessional is often used interchangeably with multiprofessional, multidisciplinary and interdisciplinary and generally refers to collaboration or team work between various tertiary trained health and social care professionals. In the developing world, where access to any trained health professional is often severely restricted, interprofessional education, learning and practice is more often about the training and provision of 'bare foot doctors' or generic health care workers who can provide basic health care services at the village or community level. While both meanings are important all of the contributors to this book have concentrated on the field as it applies to Western or more developed economies. While the book is aimed at an international audience, the content and context is predominately concerned with Australia, the United Kingdom and Canada, the environments of the contributors.

While definitions in the field are fluid and contested, and have contributed to an on-going conceptual confusion about the nature of these interactive activities, we thought it worthwhile to provide the commonly used definition for a number of key terms. These definitions are increasingly recognised internationally and used explicitly or implicitly by the contributors to the book:

- Interprofessional practice (IPP): Two or more health/social care professionals working together as a team with a common purpose, commitment and mutual respect (Freeth, Hammick, Reeves, Koppel & Barr, 2005).
- Interprofessional learning (IPL): Learning arising from interaction between members (and/or students) of two or more professions. This may be a product of timetabled

interprofessional education or happen spontaneously in the workplace or education settings (Freeth et al., 2002).

- Interprofessional education (IPE): Occasions when two or more professions learn from, with and about each other to improve collaboration and the quality of care (CAIPE, 1997).

Interprofessional education, learning and practice are not new concepts. CAIPE (the Centre for the Advancement of Interprofessional Education) was, for example, founded in 1987 to promote and develop IPE. The World Health Organization published a report on what it then called multiprofessional education in 1988 (WHO, 1988) but even this seminal publication was preceded by educational activity in Australia. In the 1970s a University of Sydney initiative was developed in which students of different health professions were able to learn and work together in multiprofessional teams planning health care for community members (Piggott, 1975). This activity and another two similar initiatives at the University of Adelaide around the same time disappeared when funding was withdrawn. In Australia short term or pilot study funding has enabled then curtailed a number of interprofessional education and learning projects.

THE IMPORTANCE OF TEAMWORK

Learning together to work together, or at least to understand each other's profession, is seen as increasingly important in the complex world of chronic and acute health care delivery in many Western nations. In the USA another early example focused on developing collaborative 'interdisciplinary' learning and was pioneered in Ohio in the 1970s, where eleven health disciplines came together to learn both in the classroom and on clinical placements (Casto, 1994). However interprofessional education has never become firmly embedded as a long term integrated component of health professional curricula. The reasons for this failure are explored in various chapters, especially d'Avray and McCrorie (Chapter 9).

While interprofessional practice is not solely about teambased care and interprofessional education is not just about learning to work in teams, health and social care delivery in the twenty-first century is focused on enabling a team based approach. Best practice guidelines construct the team as ideally patient or client or family-centred. Patient centredness can be conceptualised in several ways. The patient can be considered as a key focus but not a member of the health care team. Alternatively patients and clients can value a well-functioning patient-health professional relationship. This one professional may then mediate their views, needs and wants to the wider team. If the patient or client is viewed as a team member then the relationship becomes more complex as the team will differ in composition from hour to hour or day-to-day. Moreover the focus on the individual patient-centred approach is very much rooted in the Western paradigm of individualistic care. A family or community-centred approach fits better with the collective perspective of many Eastern sociocentric cultures. In these cultures there is a stronger connection between the individual and their family, friends and community (Draguns, 2008). These differences have profound implications for team formation and practice.

The reasons why interprofessional practice is important are frequently stated – the increasing complexity of health service delivery, the ageing population, the rising numbers of people with chronic diseases and the shortage of health professionals in certain areas. Collaboration is a key attribute of working together rather than working alongside, with the setting of shared goals (including, where possible, those of patients and their relatives). The purported rewards are said to be that effective collaborative practice optimises health services, strengthens health systems and improves health outcomes (Barr, Koppel, Reeves, Hammick & Feeth, 2005; Malone, Marriott, Newton-Howes, Simmonds & Tyrer, 2007)

There is some evidence that collaborative practice decreases the length of hospital inpatient stays, reduces tension and conflict among caregivers and lowers hospital admission and mortality rates (Lemieux-Charles & McGuire, 2006; Mickan, 2005).

Also other evidence from the community suggests that collaborative care can increase patient and carer satisfaction with mental health services (Malone et al., 2007). However, much stronger intervention design and evaluations need to be undertaken before such claims can be verified.

In primary care settings interprofessional practice can be less formalised and more diverse. General practitioners often work alone or with practice nurses, rather than being co-located with other health professionals. Communication is reduced and effective chronic illness interventions generally rely on multiprofessional care teams with clinical and behavioural management skills. Not all doctors have the training nor time to provide all critical elements of care such as regulation of medication, self management support and intensive follow up (Wagner, 2000). Patient care teams in the community have the potential to improve the quality of care for patients with chronic illness if the roles of team members are clearly defined and explicitly delegated and if team members are trained for their roles. However the presence of a trained team may be of little help if doctors cannot share care effectively (Pearson & Jones, 1994) or if a general practice's lack of organisation limits the availability of staff to work in these complementary roles (Wagner, 2000).

MOVING FORWARD

Interprofessional education, learning and practice can be understood in a number of ways. From some perspectives achieving interprofessional health and social care teams can seem like a new social movement (Melucci, 1988). Individuals and small groups from across the world share values and practices that are in conflict with dominant health care codes. The old order is criticised and the new interprofessional way forward is presented as non-hierarchical, safer and more in tune with the needs of patients and health professionals (Cotgrove & Duff, 1980). The new way is shaped as a solution to a variety of health care crises around cost, patient safety, ageing populations and rising levels of chronic disease. But whatever their perspective the authors of this book are not mavericks and many are at the centre of relevant health and social care disciplines. However, while all of the authors demonstrate a commitment to producing evidence-based work it is true that none of them can be characterised as an opponent of interprofessional education, learning and practice. However the authors do reflect critically on interprofessionalism and bring the benefits of different perspectives and experiences in undergraduate, graduate and post graduate education and in hospital and community based practice settings. There is little doubt that many people working for the adoption of interprofessional practice pursue a quest for holism, harmony, or just better quality health care outcomes. In this book there is a fair bit of the quest and some feeling of at least an implicit commitment to a new health care order. But we believe this is all to the good.

THE CHAPTERS

Chapter 2
Reeves uses the notion of the 'sociological imagination' to explore and interpret interprofessional interactions and relationships. The sociology of the professions and of doctor-nurse relationships is specifically discussed. He also draws on an ethnographic study of an interprofessional placement for undergraduate health care students to demonstrate how a range of sociological theories can contribute to better interprofessional education and practice.

Chapter 3
Bainbridge and Purkis trace the evolution of Western health professions, such as medicine, nursing, pharmacy and physical therapy, into sociologically distinct cultures. They argue that a critical analysis of the delineation of the professions over time can help to inform the construction of better models of interprofessional practice. Five practical strategies for achieving interprofessional collaboration, while honouring specific professional traditions and expertise, are also presented and discussed.

Chapter 4
Coyle, Higgs, McAllister and Whiteford critically examine three aspects of interprofessional health care teams: why people choose to work with others rather than alone; the relationships between social groups and individuals and a specific case study of physiotherapists experience of practicing in teams. The complexity and fluidity of health care team practice is analysed. A key issue raised in this chapter is the importance of trust to team building and practice.

Chapter 5
Carpenter and Dickinson use the perspective of social psychology to consider the interprofessional encounter between health and social care students and health professionals. Empirical and theoretical evidence is used and the authors conclude that mere contact between health professionals or health students is not enough to overcome professional stereotyping. The chapter goes on to helpfully set out the requirements for effective interprofessional outcomes in five lessons and six recommendations.

Chapter 6
Curran and Sharpe introduce readers to the need for student socialisation into individual disciplines and into interprofessional practice and introduces several important educational concepts and principles needed for effective interprofessional practice.

Chapter 7
Radomski and Beckett report on advances emerging from international research on workforce learning that can help to improve interprofessional thinking and health care collaboration. Interprofessionalism is presented as a socially situated relational practice that is

arguably better understood as embodied, negotiated and reflective actions linking people, processes and artefacts. Using this approach provides an opportunity to re-envisage interprofessional health care education and learning.

Chapter 8

Chesters and Burley make the case for considering that interprofessional team based care may be failing due to a lack of shared health care goals. This chapter challenges health care teams to see that team work requires strong shared goals and a day in day out training to performance ratio. The authors argue that health care teams need to learn from sporting and other work force teams who train together for safer and more effective performances in dangerous and challenging environments.

Chapter 9

d'Avray and McCrorie ask what works in implementing interprofessional education and practice. The chapter documents and discusses common learning, problem-based, case-based and workshop learning and interprofessional learning in practice. The chapter analyses barriers such as the diversity of learning needs, gender, ethnicity and class, assessment and timetabling issues as well as appropriate skills and attitudes of teachers and facilitators. Overcoming these barriers demands contact, establishing social identity, organisational competence, implementation strategies and on-going interprofessional education and practice facilitation.

Chapter 10

Russell draws on the practical experiences of a medical anthropologist's developing and implementing first and second year community placements for medical students. Readers are asked to consider interprofessional health care training in community settings as intercultural experiences. The benefits of these intercultural interactions are listed and discussed in the context of a case study.

Chapter 11

Moran, Boyce and Nissen break new ground in considering how competition between students from various health and social care professions for recognition and status in health and social care provision can result in better interprofessional outcomes. The mobilising of health science students to learn with and about one another in a simulated interprofessional team is explored using the example of the very successful Health Care Team Challenge held each year at the University of Queensland in Australia and at a number of other international sites.

Chapter 12

Thistlethwaite and Nisbet focus on a vital component of interprofessional education and learning for practice: the development of trained interprofessional educators. The attributes required for effective interprofessional teachers and facilitators are considered as is the question of whether they also need to be clinical practitioners. Both sociological and educational learning theories are discussed and a module developed by the authors for health professionals wishing to become involved in interprofessional education is outlined and its contribution analysed.

Chapter 13

Boyce, Borthwick, Moran and Nancarrow address the key issue of workforce reform and the impediments to authentic interprofessional education and practice raised by the jurisdictional, boundary and competitive positions that underpin the existing professions involved in health and social care. As in other chapters analysis of some of the sociology of the professions contributes to our learning. The chapter asks is medical hegemony sustainable in the current climate of workforce shortages and workforce redesign or can a 'new professionalism' implemented via interprofessional education and practice come into being?

Chapter 14

In conclusion, we problematise the very notion of interprofessionalism and situate its emergence as symptomatic of a very particular period of governing health care environments within Canadian, UK and Australian governments over the last two decades. We attempt to theorise this problem and signal the challenges of 'thinking otherwise' about effective health care practice from within a hegemonic discourse of interprofessionalism.

REFERENCES

Barr, H., Koppel, I., Reeves, S., Hammick, M., & Freeth, D. (2005). *Effective interprofessional education: Assumption, argument and evidence.* London: Blackwells.

CAIPE. (1997). *Interprofessional education: a definition.* London Centre for the Advancement of Interprofessional Education.

Casto, M. (1994). Inter-professional work in the USA - education and practice. In Leathard A. (Ed.), *Going inter-professional. Working together for health and welfare* (pp 188-205). London: Brunner-Routledge.

Cotgrove, S., & Duff, A. (1980). Environmentalism, middle class radicalism and politics. *Sociological Review*, 28, 333-351.

Draguns, J.G. (2008). Universal and cultural threads in counselling individuals. In Pedersen P.B., Draguns J.G., Lonner W.J., Trimble J.E. (Eds.), *Counseling Across Cultures* (pp 21-36). Los Angeles: Sage.

Freeth, D., Hammick, M, Reeves, S, Koppel, I., & Barr, H. (2005). Effective Interprofessional Education. *Development, delivery and evaluation.* Oxford: Blackwell.

Hoffman, S.J., Rosenfield, D., Gilbert, J.H.V., & Oandason, I.F. (2008). Student leadership in interprofessional education: benefits, challenges, implications for educators, researchers and policymakers. *Medical Education,* 42, 654-661.

Ivey, S., Brown, K., Teske, Y., & Silverman, D. (1977). A model for teaching about interdisciplinary practice in health care settings. *Journal Allied Health*, 17, 189-195.

Lemieux-Charles, & L., McGuire, W.L. (2006). What do we know about health care team effectiveness? A review of the literature. *Medical Care Research and Review,* 63, 263-300.

Malone, D., Marriott, S., Newton-Howes, G., & Simmonds, S., Tyrer, P. (2007). Community mental health teams (CMHTs) for people with severe mental illnesses and disordered personality. *Cochrane Database of Systematic Reviews,* Issue 2. [Art. No.: CD000270. DOI: 10.1002/14651858.CD000270.pub2].

Meads, G., & Ashcroft, J. (2005). *The Case for Interprofessional Collaboration in Health and Social Care.* Oxford: Blackwells.

Melucci, A. (1988). Social movements and the democratization of everyday life. In J. Keane (Ed.), *Civil Society and the State.* London: Verso.

Mickan, S.M. (2005). Evaluating the effectiveness of health care teams.*Australian Health Review*, 29(2), 211-217.

Pearson, P., & Jones, K. (1994). The primary health care non-team? *British Medical Journal,* 309, 1387-1388.

Piggott, B. (1975). Multi-disciplinary teaching in the community care unit. *Sydney: RPA Magazine (Winter issue).*

Wagner, E.H. (2000). The role of patient care teams in chronic disease management. *British Medical Journal*, 320, 569-572.

World Health Organisation. (1988). *Learning together to work together for health.* Report of a WHO study group on multiprofessional education of health personnel: the team approach. Geneva: WHO.

In: Sociology of Interprofessional Health …
Ed: S. Kitto, J. Chesters et al.

ISBN: 978-1-60876-866-0
© 2011 Nova Science Publishers, Inc.

Chapter 2

USING THE SOCIOLOGICAL IMAGINATION TO EXPLORE THE NATURE OF INTERPROFESSIONAL INTERACTIONS AND RELATIONS

Scott Reeves

ABSTRACT

This chapter employs Wright Mills' (1967) notion of the 'sociological imagination' to provide an insight into how sociology can extend our understanding of the interprofessional interactions and relations within health and social care. It reviews the contributions made by authors such as Freidson (1970), Larson (1977), Abbott (1988) and Witz (1992) who have enhanced our knowledge of the nature of professions in relation to the strategies they have employed to advance their social, economic and political interests. The chapter also draws upon the theories developed by Goffman (1963) into the nature of the presentation of self and Strauss (1978) into the role of negotiation to illuminate the nature of collaborative interactions during the development and delivery of an interprofessional clinical placement for undergraduate students. Finally, the chapter suggests a number of ways which sociological thinking might deepen our thinking about interprofessional relations within the health and social care field.

INTRODUCTION

The interprofessional literature has been expanding at an impressive rate over the past decade. While we have seen an increase in the range of evaluative, discursive, and more recently, theoretical papers being produced, there remains a tendency for authors to focus their analyses of interprofessional activities on individual, team and organisation-based perspectives. Few employ a wider sociological lens. As a result, our understanding of the interprofessional learning and practice rests largely on empirical and (a much smaller number of) theoretical papers, which given inequalities which underpin the health and social care professions, do not explore social phenomenon such as power, status and legitimacy connected to such endeavours. This chapter aims to provide a discussion of the nature of interprofessional interactions between health and social care professions. Specifically, it draws on the notion of the 'sociological imagination' (Wright Mills, 1967) to explore the potential contribution sociology can provide for generating more informed understanding of interprofessional interactions and relations.

The chapter is divided into four main parts. The first part outlines and also critiques the current interprofessional learning and practice literature. The second part draws upon the notion of the sociological imagination to provide some insights into how a sociological lens can extend our understanding of the interprofessional field. The third part provides an in-depth example of how theories developed by Goffman (1963) and Strauss (1978) can help illuminate the nature of collaboration in the development and delivery of an interprofessional clinical placement for undergraduate health care students. The final part of the chapter offers some ways forward in relation to how other sociological theories can be used to expand our understanding of the interprofessional field.

THE CURRENT PICTURE

Even the most cursory glance at the growing amount of research on interprofessional education and practice reveals that the majority of authors focus their work on individual, team or organisation-based descriptions of their varying initiatives. Studies of interprofessional education, for example, tend to concentrate on reporting positive changes to individual learners' attitudes, knowledge, skills, and to a lesser extent their collaborative behaviour such as Barnes, Carpenter and Bailey (2000), Hind et al. (2003), Carpenter, Schneider, Brandon and Wooff (2003) and Mandy, Milton and Mandy (2004). Similarly, studies of interprofessional practice describe how the nature of collaborative relations are promoted or impeded by team and/or organisational based factors such as willingness, team size, team composition and management support (West & Slater, 1996; Williams & Laungani, 1999; West & Markiowicz, 2004). While this increasing body of empirical studies has helped generate some useful insights into the nature of interprofessional relationships, in general it has failed to use theoretical perspectives which could help deepen its analyses.

Encouragingly though, there is an increasing use of theory in the interprofessional literature. In the past few years much attention has been focused towards the use of a range of different social psychological approaches such as contact theory, realistic conflict theory, social identity theory and self-categorisation theory in the work of authors such as Barnes, et al. (2000), Hind et al. (2003), Carpenter, Schneider, Brandon and Wooff (2003) and Mandy, Milton and Mandy (2004). Similarly, Ginsburg and Tregunno (2005) have employed organisational approaches such as institutional theory to examine how organisational context may influence the development of interprofessional education and practice. In addition, the use of systems approaches such as complexity theory has been drawn upon by Cooper, Braye and Geyer to examine the complicated array of issues associated with implementing interprofessional education initiatives. Authors such as Obholzer and Roberts (1994) and Holman and Jackson (2001) have also employed psychodynamic theories such as Bion's work-group mentality theory and Menzies' social defence theory to explore how the individual unconscious processes may affect interprofessional interactions.

Although use of these theories help expand our understanding of the nature of how individuals act, groups function and how organisations may affect interprofessional relations, their explanations overlook the wider social processes such as power, authority and legitimacy which form an important pillar upon which interprofessional relations and interactions rest. An oversight of this (sociological) perspective also means that the current literature can only provide partial accounts of the factors that underpin interprofessional education and practice.

THE SOCIOLOGICAL IMAGINATION

In his seminal text, Wright Mills (1967) maintained that sociology had an important role to play in understanding the lives of individuals and the social influences that affect their lives. He argued that as, "neither the life of an individual nor the history of a society can be understood without understanding both" we need to develop a way of exploring the links between individuals and the societies in which they live and interact together. Wright Mills termed this particular approach to knowledge generated as the *sociological imagination*. He stated that the use of the sociological imagination could help to understand the greater social patterns related to individuals' desires, fears, wants and concerns. A key element to the use of the sociological imagination for Wright Mills was the need to understand the social world by connecting empirical work with underlying theoretical explanations. Without these links between research and theory, Wright Mills argued that such accounts can offer nothing more than *abstracted empiricism*. Theory was therefore very much needed to offer more comprehensive and meaningful sociological accounts.

While Wright Mills' modernist standpoint of using sociology to connect individual (agency-based) and social (structurally-based) factors have lost favour following the rise in popularity of postmodern approaches, their aim of exploring the notion of the sociological imagination is nevertheless still a helpful tool to apply in beginning to think more about the role of social factors and processes and their affect on interprofessional interactions. In this chapter, it is employed to help re-frame our thinking from the predominant individual, team and organization-based perspectives towards thinking more widely about the potential contribution of sociology to the interprofessional field. To do this, two examples are offered. Firstly, the sociological literature on the nature of the professions is outlined to show how the development of health and social care occupations has been based on different professionalisation projects aimed at securing and protecting exclusive areas of knowledge and tightly regulating entry and work practices for the aim of economic, social and political advantages. Secondly, the nature of the interprofessional relationship shared between medicine and nursing is explored through a sociological lens to demonstrate how their respective social statuses and power differentials emerged and continue to operate in contemporary care settings.

THE SOCIOLOGY OF THE PROFESSIONS

While early sociological accounts of the professions tended to stress their (functional) common 'traits' such as universalism, affective neutrality, expertise and autonomy of practice (e.g. Parsons, 1951) these approaches were widely criticised for presenting an over-simplified version of the professions. Larson (1977) for example argued that such trait approaches replicate the outward face that professions like to project and therefore neglect the inward face, and as a result, these "ideal typical constructions do not tell us what a profession is, only what it pretends to be". [1]

Post-trait accounts of professions tend to adopt a more critical stance of professions, one in which the social and economic power of these groups is stressed (Larson, 1977; Abbott, 1988; Witz, 1992). For example, Freidson (1970) argued that occupational groups actively engage in a process of 'closure' to secure exclusive ownership of specific areas of knowledge and expertise in order to effectively secure economic reward and status enhancement. To protect the gains obtained from professionalisation, Freidson (1970) claimed that all groups guard the areas of knowledge and expertise they have acquired primarily through the regulation of entry and the maintenance of professional standards. Tension is therefore likely to arise if it is perceived that a member from another profession is infringing in their area of expertise. Exploring the issue of professional boundary protection, Abbott (1988, p. 2) stated:

"A fundamental fact of professional life [is] interprofessional competition. It is the history of [this competition] that is the real, determining history of professions."

The licensing of a profession's practice and its legal connection with the state was regarded as the most crucial element in the closure process. Without this formal link, granting the right to a monopoly of practice, it was argued that an occupation will not successfully achieve professional closure and its social and economic rewards. As Larkin (1983, p. 98) stated:

"A profession's relationship with the state [...] is fundamental. Occupations that attempt to secure for themselves the two dimensions of professionalism – market control and social mobility generally seek to establish a legal monopoly through licensure by the state."

More recently, however, it has been argued that the effectiveness of professions to maintain and enhance their political gains has been undermined due to the increasing influence of government who have ensured an increased involvement of health services managers to help control escalating health care budgets (e.g. Hunter, 1994; Clark, 2005). As a result, it has been argued that medicine, in particular, has undergone a process of de-professionalisation (Haug, 1993). While medicine's traditional power base, its professional autonomy, has been to some degree eroded by governments, it has still been able to preserve, and in many instances advance, its social and economic gains (Hunter, 1994).

---

[1] Given its complexity, definitions of the terms 'profession' and 'professional' within the sociological literature have long been problematic – see for example the work of Becker (1970) and also MacDonald (1995). Nevertheless this literature provides a broadly consensual view of common features which help define a professional group. Key characteristics include ownership expert knowledge, a degree of control/autonomy over practice, control over a (lengthy) training process and a monopoly of practice, licensed by the state.

In contrast, other professions, such as nursing, have experienced an increase in their status following the implementation of a number of professionalisation strategies such as a move into university-based education, the creation of nurse practitioner roles with a number of medical duties and the delegation of 'low' status nursing duties to nursing aides and health care assistants (e.g. Daykin & Clarke, 2000; Zwarenstein & Reeves, 2002). While these social processes have certainly created some re-alignment of relations between medicine, nursing and the other health and social care professions, the traditional 'health care hierarchy' remains intact with medicine occupying the dominant position in terms of social, economic and political advantage.[2]

THE SOCIOLOGY OF DOCTOR-NURSE RELATIONS

Early descriptions of the interprofessional relationship between medicine and nursing offered a simplistic view of medical-nursing power differentials. In particular, it regarded medicine as having the dominant position due to their autonomy of practice and higher social and economic status. For example, Etzioni (1969, p. 5) argued that the status of nursing was lower in relation to medicine due to "a less specialised body of knowledge [and] less autonomy from supervision or societal control". Similarly, Katz (1969, p. 70) argued that nursing knowledge was regarded as lower status for it "occupies residual place [when compared with] 'scientific' medicine". As a result, Katz went on to state that nurses "rank low in occupational prestige and financial rewards" in comparison to medicine (p. 54). Indeed, this structural imbalance manifested itself in nurse-doctor interactions where the former would generally adopt a submissive approach with the latter:

"The nurse is expected to react with moral passivity [...] Doctors' mistakes are not to be discussed [...] While her own mistakes can be openly and drastically censured" (Katz, 1969, pp. 59-60).

These descriptions of medicine's relation with nursing were challenged, and essentially overturned, by Leonard Stein's (1967) paper entitled the *doctor-nurse game*. Stein's paper offered an alternative (and more nuanced) view of how nurses had more informal influence in their interactions with doctors than previously considered in the literature. The rules of the doctor-nurse game were relatively straightforward. Physicians, responsible for 'curing' patients could be guided by nurses in their decision making, only if this process was undertaken in a covert manner which never openly questioned the physician's dominant position. Subsequent papers by Stein, Watts and Howell (1991) and also more recently by Reeves, Nelson and Zwarenstein (2008) have suggested that although nurses had become

---

[2] A helpful example of this hierarchy can be found in Cott's (1998) study of interprofessional relations in a rehabilitation setting. She found that the different hierarchical positions held by medicine, nursing and occupational therapy generated different perceptions views towards interprofessional teamwork. In particular, she found that the hierarchical structure was alienating for staff in lower positions who did not share the same (positive) views of collaboration as staff who occupied higher positions.

more assertive of their perspective on patient care, the doctor-nurse game is still in evidence across a number of clinical contexts.[3]

While Stein's paper on the doctor-nurse game was not based on empirical evidence, it was in essence an account of medical-nursing interactions based on his own experiences as a physician, the rules of this game resonated widely in health care. For instance, sociological work undertaken by Walby, Greenwell, Mackay and Soothill (1994), Hughes (1988), Svensson (1996), Allen (1997) and Snelgrove and Hughes (2000) have all drawn upon the doctor-nurse game in their own studies. Porter's (1995) work based on ethnographic observations of doctor-nurse interactions in an intensive care setting, provides a useful example. Porter (1995) revealed that nurses used four different types of interprofessional interactions with their medical colleagues:

- Unproblematic subordination (an unquestioning approach to medical requests);
- Informal covert decision making (where nurses refrain from open disagreement but attempt input into medical treatment on a more covert basis. This is an example of the doctor-nurse game);
- Informal overt decision making (open informal involvement of nurses in medical decision);
- Formal overt decision making (where the nursing process is used by nurses to make decisions about care).

Porter concluded that while both the unproblematic subordination and the informal covert decision-making appeared to be used frequently, closer examination revealed that, with the exception of nurse-consultant (senior physician) interactions, nurses were less dependent on these subordinate modes of decision making. Despite organisational encouragement, it was found that formal overt decision making was also infrequently employed. In addition, it was noticed that senior nurses tended to use informal overt strategies to involve themselves in decision-making sequences

While these sociological studies do provide some important insights into how nursing has resisted and undermined traditional forms of medical power by largely informal means,[4] as Porter, and others such as Davies (1995) and Wickes (1998) have maintained, given the gendered nature of medicine and nursing, their patriarchal relationship continues to essentially shape the interprofessional interactions that these professions share.

As indicated above, this literature has uncovered some important sociological processes (economic, political, social) linked to the creation and maintenance of health and social care professions, as well as the interprofessional relationship shared by medicine and nursing. Collectively, these accounts help develop a more informed understanding about the nature of interprofessional interactions. In particular, they offer a broader insight into the possible sources for friction that can (and do) occur between professionals.

---

[3] While Stein is not a sociologist (he is a psychiatrist by training), his account of physician-nurse interactions provides a useful example of using his *sociological imagination* to articulate the nature of this particular (social) phenomenon.

[4] Other (non-health care) accounts of individuals with limited formal power who have resisted others in more influential and authoritative positions can be found in the seminal work of Mechanic (1963) and Lipsky (1980).

USING SOCIOLOGICAL THEORY: AN EXAMPLE

Having provided a general outline of the use of the sociological imagination, this part of the chapter presents an in-depth account of how sociological theory can help provide a more comprehensive understanding of the nature of interprofessional interactions. It presents the findings from an ethnographic study which drew upon two related sociological theories to help understand the nature of interactions in the development and delivery of an interprofessional placement for undergraduate health care students.

The study focused on an interprofessional planning group who worked together to develop a clinical placement designed to offer students from medicine, nursing, occupational therapy and physiotherapy an opportunity to work in a team and provide care to patients in an orthopaedic setting. The planning group aimed to implement the placement within a large teaching hospital which had been providing traditional profession-specific clinical experiences for their students for a number of years. The hospital was located in an inner-city environment, whose local population faced a number of health difficulties in terms of high levels of tuberculosis, diabetes and heart disease, and consequently the hospital encountered a continually heavy demand for its services.

An ethnographic approach was adopted to explore the processes related to the planning group's work planning and implementing this placement. Observations of placement planning meetings were gathered by the adoption of a 'marginal participant' technique – an approach in which the researcher only plays a minimal role in the social action being observed. In this study, apart from greetings and brief informal conversations before and after meetings, the researcher focused on gathering data. A semi-structured observational schedule was used to ensure that anticipated interprofessional interactions could be gathered as well as any unexpected events. Observational data were collected for a period of two years. In this time, a total of 21 (one-to-two hour) planning meetings were observed.

Interview and documentary data were also gathered to provide a comprehensive understanding of the issues related to designing and implementing this placement. Individual semi-structured interviews were collected with the planning group at the start and at the end of the study. The first set of interviews focused on exploring members' expectations of their collaborative planning work, while the second set concentrated on allowing members to reflect upon their collaborative planning experiences. In total, 26 interviews were undertaken, each lasting for approximately one hour. Documentary data, in the form of minutes of meetings, course documents and discussion papers generated by the group were gathered to provide an additional insight into their collaborative planning work.

In their first year of working together, the planning group designed and delivered a four-week pilot version of the placement to assess the feasibility of operating this type of interprofessional unit within an acute care environment. Following a successfully received pilot, the group worked to re-establish, and then embed, the placement into the hospital and their respective university curricula. In the longer term, however, their mutual efforts were unsuccessful due to a range of group-based challenges (some of which are described below), management changes and organisational reforms. Further information on this study can be found elsewhere (Reeves, 2008).

Findings from this study are offered in two sections. The first outlines how front and backstage locations played a significant role in the collaborative work of the planning group and uses Goffman's (1963) theory of self presentation to illuminate the nature of collaborative work in these different settings. The second describes how the planning group used different types of negotiation in their collaborative work and employs Strauss' (1978) negotiated order perspective to understand the uses and limitation of negotiation in an interprofessional planning work.

FRONT AND BACKSTAGE COLLABORATION

Data from the study indicated that while the planning group undertook a series of regular scheduled front stage meetings to advance the placement their work also progressed during their backstage work. In general, backstage work was formally discussed between members in their formal meetings and was therefore *overt* in nature. For example, after agreement, members spent time outside meetings undertaking backstage negotiations with their respective professional regulatory bodies to ensure that students could participate in the placement. In addition, members spent time outside the meetings preparing the ward for the placement and recruiting clinical staff to act as facilitators. Consequently, the planning group viewed overt backstage work as a valuable aspect of this interprofessional project. Indeed, without the use of this type of behind-the-scenes work, it is unlikely that group members could have made as much progress with the placement as they did.

However, in their enthusiasm to implement the placement in a timely manner, a small four-person subgroup consisting mainly of physicians emerged and began to undertake *covert* backstage work. Without informing the rest of the group, subgroup members informally met together to develop a plan centred upon enhancing the pace of the placement's development. As a result of these small informal meetings they arranged formal meetings with senior school and hospital managers designed to elicit their support to ensure success with this project. Despite agreeing that this type of backstage work contributed to the development of the placement its covert nature was nevertheless viewed by other planning group members as problematic. In general, it was felt that this type of backstage work excluded them from making some important decisions on the placement.

Goffman's (1962) theory of self presentation can be used to help illuminate these findings. Based on his fieldwork exploring the nature of social interaction within a small rural community, Goffman found that communication between individuals took the form of linguistic (verbal) and non-linguistic (body language) gestures employed when individuals *present* their selves to others. For Goffman, the presentation process was regarded as a 'performance', which was undertaken in two distinct areas. Public "front region performances" (Goffman, 1963, p. 109) such as meetings between work colleagues or professional-patient consultations; and private "back region performances" (Goffman, 1963, p. 114) such as interactions between friends and family members. Goffman argued that front region performances were formal and restrained in nature. In contrast, back region performances were more informal, allowing the individual to "relax […] and step out of [their front region] character" (Goffman, 1963, p. 115). Goffman therefore regarded the activities that took place in private settings as crucial in supporting the activities that occurred in public settings. Joseph (1990, p. 316) provides a useful summary of this approach:

"There is a back 'region' where the show is prepared and we rehearse our parts; and a 'front region' where the performance is presented to an audience".

As noted above, planning group members' use of overt backstage work in their negotiations with senior managers, professional regulatory body representatives and clinical staff was also considered a valuable aspect of their work in developing this initiative. The study also helped indicate the importance of backstage work in helping prepare more formal front stage gatherings. The subgroup's use of exclusionary backstage work was, however, viewed in a more cautious way; while it assisted the development of the project, it also undermined the group's collaborative relationships. In addition, the study illuminated how backstage work can be divided into two subsets – pre-arranged 'overt' and more exclusionary 'covert' backstage work. While the former can be regarded as inclusive and can contribute to strengthening interprofessional work, the latter is more problematic. As indicated in the study, it can help the development of an interprofessional project, but at the expense of the collaborative relationships.

USES AND LIMITS OF NEGOTIATION

Data from the study indicated that two forms of negotiation were employed in the development and implementation of the placement – outcome-oriented and process-oriented negotiation. Planning group members only employed outcome-oriented negotiation in their collaborative work. This form of negotiation was undertaken to achieve the group's main project outcome – the creation and implementation of the placement. Planning group members employed outcome-oriented negotiation during their formal meetings, to design the placement and agree on its parameters. They also undertook this form of negotiation in their backstage work with:

- Senior managers (to obtain staff and ward space for the placement);
- Representatives from the different professional regulatory bodies (to obtain their agreement for student involvement in the placement);
- Clinical staff (to ensure they would work as facilitators on the ward).

In general, outcome-oriented negotiations helped produce the placement (its objectives and activities) as well as helped prepare the way for its implementation in a clinical setting. This type of negotiation was, however, impeded by three external factors. Firstly, inflexibility between the four school's curricula resulted in inequalities for student assessments (three of the schools could allow their students to be summatively assessed, while the remainder could only allow their students to be assessed in a formative manner). Secondly, a lack of available time, due to workload pressures of planning group members, meant that many members regularly missed meetings and often failed to complete tasks in between meetings. Finally, a busy organisational context, specifically a heavy demand for hospital services and a lack of available clinical space meant that planning group members found it very difficult to implement the placement after its pilot phase.

While the planning group designed a placement in which students from four professional groups regularly spent time engaging in *process-oriented* negotiation (focused on exploring and understanding interprofessional interactions and processes linked to their collaborative work on the placement) they failed to employ this type of negotiation in their own work. The data indicated that the planning group never employed any process-orientated negotiation. Indeed, it appears that in their enthusiasm to progress the placement the group failed to consider the processes of their collaborative work. As a result, a number of difficulties in the way in which they worked together emerged, such as the emergence of the small subgroup who worked in an exclusive fashion and confusion over group leadership as the group did not spend time negotiating project roles and responsibilities. Although the interprofessional literature has found that a focus on both shared team goals and attention to team processes is vital for the successful function of health and social teams (e.g. Øvretveit, 1993; Williams & Laungani, 1999; Onyett, 2003), the explicit role of negotiation in this type of work is generally overlooked.

The negotiated order perspective was developed by Strauss, Schatzman, Ehrlich, Bucher and Sabshin (1963) from their research into the nature of staff relations within psychiatric hospitals. For these authors, previous explanations of social order within organisations tended to stress formal structures and rules, and neglect the influence of micro-level negotiations. For Strauss and his colleagues, negotiation between individuals (through processes such as bargaining, compromising and mediating) essentially creates and shapes organisational rules and structures. Consequently, micro-level negotiation contributes to the development and maintenance of social order that exists within an organisation. Strauss (1978) modified this theory following criticism that it failed to pay sufficient attention to the influence of structural factors (e.g. Day & Day, 1977; Benson, 1977). He subsequently argued that although micro-level negotiation was central to creating and maintaining organisational life, negotiations were also constrained by the existence of structural influences. However, in keeping faithful to his interactionist roots, Strauss continued to argue that while macro influences provided the parameters for relationships, micro level negotiations still played the pivotal role in forming and shaping organisational life.

In relation to Strauss' theory, it is possible to see how the micro-level negotiations undertaken by planning group members played a central role in formulating and shaping the placement as well as helping create a social order within the group. The study indicated that the use of outcome-oriented negotiation contributed to achieving the collective goals of the group in the development of the placement, their neglect of process-oriented negotiation resulted in a number of problems related to the way they worked together. The findings also support the stress Strauss placed on the influence of external structures in constraining the effects of negotiation. Indeed, while planning group negotiations were influential in the development of the placement and the delivery of its pilot; education, professional, organisational and ultimately financial constraints restricted the influence of these negotiations.

REFLECTION ON THESE THEORIES

Although the study indicated that the use of Goffman's and Strauss' theories can help illuminate the nature of the interactions during the development and implementation of this placement, such theories have been criticised in two main areas. Firstly, it has been noted that as interactionism is preoccupied with eliciting a micro-level social perspective, it overlooks the impact of wider social structures on interaction (Silverman, 1993). Secondly, interactionism has been criticised for a preoccupation on only uncovering 'underdog' perspectives and therefore neglecting the influence of 'top dog' accounts and how power operates between the individuals who occupy these two positions (Dingwall, 1980). Mindful of such criticisms, the final part outlines some ways forward for using sociological theory in the interprofessional field.

CONCLUSION

As discussed above, while the current literature has offered some useful accounts of interprofessional education and practice from an individual, team and organisational based perspectives, there is only a limited use of sociology in this field. As this chapter has discussed, the application of a sociological imagination can yield rich insights into the nature of the health and social care professions and the interprofessional interactions and relations they share. In particular, work by authors such as Freidson (1970), Larson (1977), Hughes (1988), Porter (1995) and Allen (1997) has showed how economic, political and social processes played an important role in the creation and maintenance of health and social care professions, as well as shaping the interprofessional relationship shared by medicine and nursing. In addition, the use of interactionist theories such as Goffman (1963) and Strauss (1978) can offer an-depth insight into the role negotiations can play in interprofessional care settings.

While the further use of these approaches will provide some very valuable insights into the nature of interprofessional relations and interactions, due to the inequalities that exist between the health and social care professions, theoretical perspectives which offer a more explicit focus on power are particularly welcome in the interprofessional literature. Indeed, given Turner's (1990) argument that the adoption of 'interdisciplinarity' within the health and social care will entail a re-alignment of traditional professional power bases there is a need to re-examine them to understand how this particular movement may have affected the nature of their interprofessional relations and interactions.

The sociological theories are offered by, for example, Lukes' (1974) in his radical theory of power which examines how the role of ideology plays a critical role in shaping perceptions and preferences to ensure dominance of one group over another. In addition, Giddens' (1984) theory of structuration provides another interesting approach to power, which explores the interplay of societal structures and individuals in the creation and maintenance of both facilitative and conflictual power relations. Foucault's theories of social power, in particular, his work on discourse (Foucault, 1972) and surveillance (Foucault, 1979) provide another way to understand the nature of interprofessional power relations. For Foucault, discourses help to define particular societal cultures – the actual language and the behaviours of individuals who belong to them. Discourses therefore have the ability to provide the overall shape and definition to different cultures and define what becomes accepted as 'truth' and 'fact'. While discourses shape culture and language, Foucault believed that surveillance was required to help maintain the existence of a particular discourse. Surveillance of others (and self-surveillance) was therefore regarded as another dimension of power, crucial in ensuring that individuals remained compliant to a particular discourse.

The application of such theories approaches can provide a useful set of approaches to explore the nature of interprofessional power relations and interactions from some potentially illuminating vantage points. For example, the application of Lukes' work could help examine how the medicine's dominant ideology is enacted in their interprofessional interactions with other professional groups. Similarly, Foucault's theories could be employed help examine the emergence of an interprofessional discourse within health and social care and how it may have affected the power relations. Indeed, the use of such perspectives will help provide a much needed sociological analysis for the interprofessional education and learning literature, which over time, can offer some important contributions to our insights into the nature of this field.

REFERENCES

Abbott, A. (1988). *The System of Professions: An Essay on the Division of Expert Labour.* Chicago: University of Chicago Press.

Allen, D. (1997). The nursing-medical boundary: a negotiated order? *Sociology of Health and Illness,* 19, 498-520.

Barnes, D., Carpenter, J., & Bailey, D. (2000). Partnerships with service users in interprofessional education for community mental health: a case study. *Journal of Interprofessional Care*, 14, 189-200.

Barr, H., Koppel, I., Reeves, S., Hammick, M., & Freeth, D. (2005). *Effective Interprofessional Education: Assumption, Argument and Evidence.* London: Blackwell.

Becker, H. (1970). *Sociological Work.* Chicago: Aldine.

Benson, J. (1977). Organisations: a dialectic view. *Administrative Science Quarterly*, 22, 1-21.

Carpenter, J., Schneider, J., Brandon, T., & Wooff, D. (2003). Working in multidisciplinary community mental health teams: the impact on social workers and health professionals of integrated mental health care. *British Journal of Social Work*, 33, 1081-1103.

Clark, C. (2005). The deprofessionalisation thesis, accountability and professional character. Social Work and Society, 3:2. Available at: *http://www.socwork.net/2005/2/articles/490* (Accessed 7 January 2009).

Cooper, H., Braye, S., & Geyer, R. (2004). Complexity and interprofessional education. *Learning in Health and Social Care,* 3, 179-189.

Davies, C. (1995). *Gender and the Professional Predicament in Nursing.* London: Taylor & Francis.

Day, R., & Day, J. (1977) A review of the current state of negotiated order theory: an appreciation and critique. *The Sociological Quarterly,* 19, 499-501.

Daykin, N., & Clarke, B. (2000). 'They'll still get the bodily care'. Discourses of care and relationships between nurses and health care assistants in the NHS. *Sociology of Health & Illness,* 22, 349-363.

Dingwall, R. (1980). Ethics and Ethnography. *Sociological Review*, 28, 871-891.

Etzioni, A. (1969). *The Semi-Professions and their Organisation: Teachers, Nurses and Social Workers.* New York: Free Press.

Foucault, M. (1972). *The Archaeology of Knowledge.* London: Tavistock.

Foucault, M. (1979). *Discipline and Punish: the Birth of the Prison.* London: Penguin.

Freidson, E. (1970). *Profession of Medicine: A Study of the Sociology of Applied Knowledge.* New York: Harper & Row.

Giddens, A. (1984). *The Constitution of Society.* University of California Press: Berkeley.

Ginsburg, L., & Tregunno, D. (2005). New approaches to interprofessional education and collaborative practice: lessons from the organizational change literature. *Journal of interprofessional Care*, 19, S177-S187.

Goffman, E. (1963). *The Presentation of Self in Everyday Life.* London:Penguin.

Hammick, M., Freeth, D., Koppel, I., Reeves, S., & Barr, H. (2007). A best evidence systematic review of interprofessional education. *Medical Teacher,* 29, 735-751.

Haug, M. (1993). De-professionalisation: an alternative hypothesis for the future. *Sociological Review Monograph,* 20, 195-211.

Hind, M., Norman, I., Cooper, S., Gill, E., Hilton, R., Judd, P., & Newby, S. (2003). Interprofessional perceptions of health care students. *Journal of Interprofessional Care*, 17, 21-34.

Holman, C., & Jackson, S. (2001). A team education project: an evaluation of a collaborative education and practice development in a continuing care unit for older people. *Nurse Education Today,* 21, 97-103.

Hughes, D. (1988). When nurse knows best: some aspects of nurse-doctor interaction in a casualty department. *Sociology of Health and Illness,* 10, 1-22.

Hunter, D. (1994). From Tribalism to corporatism: the managerial challenge to medical dominance. In J. Gabe, D. Kelleher & G. Williams (Eds.), *Challenging Medicine* (pp. 164-172). London: Routledge.

Katz, F. (1969). Nurses. In A Etzioni (Ed.), *The Semi-Professions and their Organisation: Teachers, Nurses and Social Workers.* New York: Free Press.

Larkin, G. (1983). *Occupational Monopoly and Modern Medicine.* London: Tavistock.

Larson, M. (1977). *The Rise of Professionalism: a Sociological Analysis.* London: University College Press.

Lukes, S. (1974). *Power: A Radical View.* London: Macmillan.

MacDonald, K. (1995). *The Sociology of the Professions.* London:Sage.

Mandy, A., Milton, C., & Mandy, P. (2004). Professional stereotyping and interprofessional education. *Learning in Health & Social Care*, 3, 154-170.

Mechanic, D. (1963). The Power to Resist Change Among Low-Ranking Personnel. *Personnel Administration,* 26, 5-11.

Obholzer, A., & Roberts, V. (1994). *The Unconscious at Work: Individual and Organisational Stress in the Human Services.* London: Routledge.

Onyett, S. (2003). *Teamworking in Mental Health.* Palgrave: Basingstoke.

Øvretveit, J. (1993). *Co-ordinating Community Care: Multidisciplinary Teams and Care Management.* Milton Keynes: Open University Press.

Parsons, T. (1951). *The Social System.* New York: Free Press.

Porter, S. (1995). *Nursing's Relationship with Medicine.* Avebury: Avershot.

Reeves, S. (2001). A review of the effects of interprofessional education on staff involved in the care of adults with mental health problems. *Journal of Psychiatric and Mental Health Nursing*, 8, 533-542.

Reeves, S. (2008). *Developing and Delivering Practice-Based Interprofessional Education. Munich:* VDM publications.

Reeves, S., Nelson, S., & Zwarenstein, M. (2008). The doctor-nurse game in the age of interprofessional care: a view from Canada. *Nursing Inquiry,* 15, 1-2.

Silverman, D. (1993). *Interpreting Qualitative Data.* London: Sage.

Snelgrove, S., & Hughes, D. (2000). Interprofessional relations between doctors and nurses: perspectives from South Wales. *Journal of Advanced Nursing,* 31, 661-667.

Stein, L. (1967). The doctor-nurse game. *Archives of General Psychiatry,* 16, 699-703.

Stein, L., Watts, D., & Howell, T. (1990) The doctor-nurse game revisited. *New England Journal of Medicine,* 322, 546-549.

Strauss, A, (1978), *Negotiations: Varieties, Contexts, Processes and Social Order.* London: Jossey-Bass.

Strauss, A., Schatzman, D., Ehrlich, R., Bucher, M., & Sabshin, C. (1963). The hospital and its negotiated order. In E. Freidson (Ed.), *The Hospital in Modern Society* (pp. 147-169). New York: The Free Press.

Svensson, R. (1996). The interplay between doctors and nurses: a negotiated order perspective. *Sociology of Health and Illness,* 18, 379-398.

Turner, B. (1990). The interdisciplinary curriculum: from social medicine to postmodernism *Sociology of Health & Illness,* 12, 1-23.

Walby, S., Greenwell, J., Mackay, L., & Soothill, K. (1994). *Medicine and Nursing: Professions in a Changing Health Service.* London: Sage.

West, M., & Markiowicz, L. (2004). Building Team-based Working: A Practical Guide to Organisational Transformation. *British Psychology* Society/Blackwell: London.

West, M., & Slater, J. (1996). Teamworking in Primary Health Care: A Review of its Effectiveness. *Health Education* Authority: London.

Wickes, D. (1998). *Nurses and Doctors at Work: Rethinking Professional Boundaries.* Milton Keynes: Open University Press.

Williams, G., & Laungani, P. (1999). Analysis of teamwork in an NHS community trust: an empirical study. *Journal of Interprofessional Care,* 13, 19-28.

Witz, A. (1992) *Professions and Patriarchy.* London: Routledge.

Wright Mills, C. (1967). *The Sociological Imagination.* Oxford: Oxford University Press.

Zwarenstein, M., & Reeves, S. (2002). Working together but apart: barriers and routes to nurse-physician collaboration. *The Joint Commission Journal on Quality Improvement,* 28, 242-247.

In: Sociology of Interprofessional Health …
Ed: S. Kitto, J. Chesters et al.

ISBN: 978-1-60876-866-0
© 2011 Nova Science Publishers, Inc.

Chapter 3

THE HISTORY AND SOCIOLOGY OF THE HEALTH PROFESSIONS: DO THEY PROVIDE THE KEY TO NEW MODELS FOR INTERPROFESSIONAL COLLABORATION?

Lesley Bainbridge and Mary Ellen Purkis

ABSTRACT

Examining the historical evolution of Western-based health professions provides insight into their development as sociologically distinct cultures. Development of professional cultures has been constructed by way of securing an exclusive body of knowledge, unique skills, distinct values base, and behaviours rooted in societal sanction, need and approbation. Probing the historical development of professions can help us to determine new models of interprofessional collaboration that honour professional history while embracing emerging practice models.

This paper describes the historical development of medicine, nursing, pharmacy and physical therapy from the perspective of sociological phenomena. It draws on the stereotyping literature to determine how specific uniprofessional barriers to collaboration may inhibit the development of a health care culture of collaboration. It describes development of profession-based epistemology, values and behaviours that may help us to understand how we can preserve professional identities, values and contributions, while embracing an interprofessional approach to collaboration.

The final section of the paper examines the impact of professional histories in the context of interprofessional education. It offers practical strategies for educating health professionals in collaborative practice models that reinforce the mutual interests and shared values of the four professions chosen to illustrate this sociological perspective, while respecting the integrity of each profession's autonomy.

INTRODUCTION

Internationally, interprofessional education (IPE) for the health professions is emerging as a new way to address issues of quality of care, patient safety and health human resource shortages. From some perspectives, it is easy to argue that health care has always been delivered by teams, and not just teams within institutional settings but also within community settings. It is interesting then, in light of this perception, that an emphasis on IPE and practice faces many barriers in both health professional education and health service contexts (Gilbert, 2005; Hall, 2005). As the trend towards interprofessional practice strengthens in the face of deepening human resource shortages and increased attention to patient safety, the tensions between discipline-specific learning and practice and interprofessional learning and practice need to be addressed. Indeed, the foundation from which the resistance emanates needs to be discussed openly. In general it is believed that, in large part at least, resistance derives from the fact that on the one hand we have strong, independent professions steeped in historical relationships and values, while on the other we have an emerging imperative to examine the ways in which professions work together. To a large extent, it is assumed that the way health care professionals are educated will impact, both positively and negatively, their ability to collaborate as qualified health care providers. It is therefore critical that we examine the historical context of professions so that we can understand professional behaviours in order to teach collaboration effectively. By honouring the history and valuing a profession's past, we may be able to move more seamlessly into a new way of doing business in health care.

Practitioners hold onto their professional history very strongly in times of change. It is the historical relationships and values that have seen them through many previous assaults on their credibility. At the same time, they are aware of the need to communicate more effectively with their colleagues in different professions. Many share these perspectives with our practicing colleagues and recognize that as we move toward interprofessional collaborative practice, asking learners and practitioners to embrace shared competencies without also having discussions about responsibility and regulation can be threatening. Inadvertently barriers to interprofessional learning and practice may be reinforced.

This chapter explores the emergence of this interest in interprofessional team practice against the historical backdrop of the sociology of professional work. The questions this chapter seeks to address are – what are the implications of current trends in health human resource planning for IPE and interprofessional practice? What can a critical exploration of the historical premises of professional education and practice offer us as we seek to support educational and practice initiatives pertaining to interprofessional care? What can those historical analyses offer us as we make decisions about educational and practice models that support an interest in enhancing the quality of patient care through interprofessional care?

This chapter briefly reviews the historical development of four health professions: medicine, nursing, physical therapy and pharmacy. It illustrates the political and professional factors that influenced a heavily profession-specific focus in both learning and practice. The characteristics of stereotyping in the health professions are examined to illuminate the fundamental values and beliefs of these four professions that we may need to respect while asking learners and practitioners to work together in different ways.

An overview of the primary drivers and trends emerging in IPE will then be used to articulate the overarching need to honour our professional roots while teaching and requiring interprofessional collaborative practice in the future. Finally, practical strategies for teaching collaborative practice across professions while attending to the fundamental soul of each profession are offered.

HISTORICAL ISSUES

The development of professional cultures has been constructed by way of securing an exclusive body of knowledge, unique skills, distinct values base, and behaviours rooted in societal sanction, need and approbation. Probing the historical development of professions may be able to help us determine new models of interprofessional collaboration that honour professional history while addressing the urgent need to refine practice models in light of emerging human resource challenges. In the learning and practice contexts, the historical professional silos still appear to be the dominant practice model and as we attempt to break down the silos and to move to a model of collaborative practice, the relevance of interprofessional learning and practice needs to be made explicit.

Concerns have been raised for many years now about the ability of modern, western health organisations to sustain their capacity to deliver health care within current delivery models. This concern is most often situated within a discourse of 'shortage.' There are widely held beliefs that advanced health care requires large numbers of highly trained professional workers, and that educational systems and capacity can no longer keep pace with a looming demographic challenge. In addition, many of our most experienced, and often expert, practitioners will be leaving these occupational settings for retirement while a new generation of young, inexperienced, probably less expert, professionals enter this complex organisational context.

A common saying is that 'history is written by the victor'. Therefore reading any history of the health professions is a challenge. Accounts of the progression of any given professional group are often told in contrast to the progression or elimination of another. For instance, many historical accounts arising from medicine are based on a strong assumption that nursing emanated from medicine, being its literal and figurative 'handmaiden' (Tosh, 2007). Others would challenge this interpretation. For instance, Ehrenreich and English (1973) argue in their classic text that nurses emerged through an entirely different line of caregivers, that of lay healers (in many instances treated as witches) and midwives.

Three key factors may influence the real or perceived control that one profession has over others including the attributes used to compare professions, the control a profession has over another profession's role, and a profession's response to boundary infringements (Halpern, 1992). Most often gender, social class or acquisitions of a complex body of knowledge are the sorts of attributes that are studied and used to explain differences between occupational groups. It is only in recent years that the male/female ratio has changed altering the social conceptions of specific professions. More women are now engaged in medical education and more men in nursing and physical therapy, for example. The shift in the gender balance in professions can alter the way in which that profession is practiced. Physical therapy and occupational therapy were viewed as suitable professions for British women from the middle classes whereas nursing was associated with the lower classes in its early days in Britain. Most often it is medicine's knowledge base, scientific perspective and anticipated outcomes that serve as the standard against which other professions are judged. Given this approach, it is not surprising that medicine's dominance is perceived as unassailable.

Halpern's (1992) second factor suggests that one dominant profession can control another "subordinate" profession's scope of practice and regulatory structure, for example. A study of professional associations, certification systems and the development of ethical codes to support claims to professional status was considered (Linker, 2005). Halpern argued that this unilateral professional control is grounded in professional power theory that characterizes occupations as contesting "zero-sum quantities of authority" (p. 995). Organisational strategies to develop and support interprofessional practice must address issues of real and perceived authority between and among professions if the effectiveness of interprofessional learning and collaborative patient care is to be fully realized. Professional races to see who can gain the most authority will be counterproductive.

Halpern (1992) attributes his third factor, a profession's response to boundary infringements, to Abbott's (1988) professional systems model. In this model, jurisdictional disputes are said to be central to the shaping of any given professional group's ultimate scope. Conflicts among professional groups "create or extinguish work domains and when one profession in the system abandons or moves to encroach upon an occupied area" (Halpern, 1992, p. 995), interprofessional conflict results. Regulatory or licensing frameworks provide an example of frameworks that are often developed individually for a range of health professional groups This increases the likelihood of conflict as the professional groups must address the areas of overlapping scope of practice.

There is one additional consideration that, according to Halpern (1992), may help to explain the ways in which professional groups have come to distinguish themselves from one another and that is "the influence of relations between segments within a profession on its boundaries with other, neighbouring occupations" (p. 996). That is, the impact of *intra*-professional relations on *inter*-professional boundaries. Halpern suggested that professions have managed to exclude some occupational categories by simply creating a sub-division of their own work within their own professional domain.

The histories of many of the health professions have intersected intermittently over time. According to a newsletter circulated by the International Society for the History of Pharmacy (ISHP, 2008), the ancient Greek physician, Galen, is claimed by many to be the father of pharmacy (p. 2). Many historical sources acknowledge the synergy between these two disciplines, whether explicitly or implicitly, by referencing the historical use of herbal remedies for illnesses by the ancient physicians. Nursing's history is most often traced to two quite distinct traditions – that of lay healer and that of religious practitioner (Nelson, 2001; Nelson & Gordon, 2004; Boulton, 2007). There is a strong sense of overlap amongst these three professions alone, pharmacy, medicine and nursing, from ancient times through to the mid-eighteenth century when, perhaps drawing on the influence of seventeenth century empiricism, two major sociological processes began to separate these groups of health care providers from one another.

The first division emerged as scientific inquiry came to be seen as a more reliable basis for the formation of knowledge about both the cause and preferred treatment of disease. The second division had a more administrative intent. With a differentiation of knowledge made possible through particular methods (e.g. scientific methods), preferences for one form of knowing (with all its associated professional practices) over another become stronger. At that point, an 'unassuming public' was believed to need protection from those who might continue to practice discredited forms of care. Systems of regulation of formal health professionals began to take shape in the nineteenth century, further inscribing and underlining distinctions between professional and para-professional groups. The outcome of these regulations has, until very recently, been to separate one professional group from another.

The impact of scientific inquiry, regulation and protection of the public has been demonstrated in another profession: physical therapy. Popular histories link the development of physical therapy to Hippocrates by noting his advocacy of massage and hydrotherapy as useful healing practices (Eugene Physical Therapy, 2004). However, more credence is given to a much shorter history. The website of the UK-based Chartered Society of Physiotherapy (2009) specifies 1884 as the inception of physical therapy as a professional practice. Established by four nurses, these early physical therapists began their work under the banner of the Society of Trained Masseuses working primarily with injured soldiers returning from war (Cleather, 1995). The First and Second World Wars intensified the need for practitioners who could focus on the rehabilitation of bodies damaged by violent warfare. Linker (2005) notes that, in the US, by 1935, a code of ethics to guide the proper conduct of physical therapy practice was developed. Linker's analysis of the development of that code provides a glimpse into the unique relationship, at least in the United States, between physical therapists and physicians. Linker's argument is interesting because she demonstrates how, through the development of their own code of ethics, the predominantly female profession of physical therapy "avoided rhetoric construed as feminine and instead, created a 'business-like' creed in which they spoke solely of their relationship with physicians and remained silent on the matter of patient care" (Linker, 2005, p. 320). Commenting on an early version of this code, developed at Reed College Oregon, an early leader in physiotherapy education, Linker notes that physiotherapists:

"Composed a highly state-oriented code of ethics, promising alliance to the U.S. government, not to their patients. Although the notion of the common good is a shared element among the Nightingale Oath, the Occupational Therapy Pledge and the Reed College oath, the definition of 'the good' differs in crucial ways. Whereas physiotherapists dedicated their lives and skills to the betterment of their country, nurses and occupational therapists geared their efforts toward a more universal goal of improved health" (p. 328).

Linker's work exemplifies the very social nature of the distinctions that have emerged historically among the illustrative examples of health professions we have reviewed here. Noting that the strongest antagonism between these two groups of health care professionals (i.e. physicians and physiotherapists) came in the early 1930's when physicians' incomes dropped by nearly 50% in the turbulence of the depression (Linker, 2005, p. 344), this very 'business-like' arrangement that came to characterize the very different relationship with medicine taken by two female dominated professions, nursing and physiotherapy, is understandable.

This necessarily brief historical account of some of the characteristics of the four professions we have chosen as exemplars, physiotherapy, nursing, medicine and pharmacy, illustrates some commonalities of heritage – from the ancient healer – through to our now, much more modern, perhaps all-too-modern, concerns related to interprofessional practice. Historical accounts of the professions of nursing, pharmacy and physiotherapy each detail particular relationships with medicine often describing a period of significant tension. Bulger and Bargato (2000) offer an interesting perspective on the source of these tensions and their ideas can, we believe, offer us a useful frame as we consider new models for health care delivery in the twenty-first century.

Bulger and Bargato (2000) note that "there is within the text of the (Hippocratic) oath the requirement to make a special commitment, a commitment that may almost extend beyond the limits of a profession to the establishment of a priesthood" (p. S7). They go on to ponder how Hippocrates might respond in the contemporary context if he were called back to a meeting of his followers now. Considering the intertwined histories of medicine, nursing, physiotherapy and pharmacy, would not all attend such a meeting as 'followers'? Bulger and Bargato wonder if Hippocrates would limit admission to those only with the M.D. designation. Or would he "examine other practitioners for possible participation in the meeting?" (p. S7). They conclude by acknowledging that "we would be less than candid if we did not point out how much almost every one of these ideas and principles is being challenged within our democratic and entrepreneurial society in ways that seem both constructive and destructive" (Bulger & Bargato, 2000, p. S7).

Through time and in response to structural arrangements of power that have positioned these professions in relation to one another through reference to gender, class, and knowledge practices, we now approach the business of addressing current health care human resource challenges as those where the distinctions amongst these professions are evident and natural. We would argue that these distinctions are, rather, the outcome of effective stereotyping.

STEREOTYPING

Stereotyping can be defined as "… ideas held about members of particular groups, based solely on membership in that group. They are often considered to be negative or prejudicial and may be used to justify certain discriminatory behaviours" (www.wikipedia.org/wiki /Stereotyping). In examining the impact of stereotyping on IPE and practice, we are working from three theses, that:

1. Stereotyping does influence education and practice;
2. It gets in the way of collaboration;
3. In the roots of stereotyping we may find the parts of our professional heritages that we need to preserve in order to move forward with collaborative practice.

It is difficult to know another profession intimately and in the absence of this knowledge we make assumptions based upon what we believe others do in their professional practice. Based often upon the media's representation of health care professionals, misunderstanding is widespread. According to Barnes, Carpenter and Dickinson (2000) "segregation has led to ignorance and misunderstanding which is shown though negative stereotypical attitudes towards other professionals" (p. 568). In Barnes and colleagues' study negative attitudes toward other health professionals during IPE encounters did not change over two years of shared learning. These authors suggest that this may be attributed to strong stereotypes that are reinforced in day-to-day contact, possibly because this represents the real picture, or that the environment is not conducive to deconstructing stereotypical attitudes. Hewstone and

Brown (1986) studied in-group and out-group behaviours and suggest that members of the out-group, or the other professions, have to be seen as typical for change in attitudes to occur. If the students from the out-group are perceived to be self-selected and somehow different than the norm within that profession, change will not happen. Based on social contact theory, Barnes et al. (2000) suggest that two changes to IPE may need to be made to change stereotypical behaviours. One, that students should be given encouragement to talk about differences as well as similarities and two, that they should be encouraged to come to the discussions wearing their home profession so that others can observe them in action and judge them according to their observations not according to the stereotypical image. This approach supports the hypothesis that a strong connection to the home profession, including its historical roots, is essential for strong collaborative practice.

If the perceptions of one group about another group are positive, one can hypothesize that collaboration is more successful. In a UK study, relationships between stereotypes, professional identity and readiness for professional learning were examined (Hind et al., 2003). If students are feeling positive about their own profession as they enter their training, then enabling students across professions to learn together early in their training programs may help to capitalize on these positive perceptions.

Power and status differentials within the health and human service delivery system can affect collaboration. Skevington (1981) studied low and high status groups and found that those in a perceived high status group tried to differentiate themselves from the low status group whereas the low status groups tried to express similarities to the high status group need to follow with a rationale as to why this is useful/important. In a study by Knippenberg and Oers (1984) groups that felt superior tried to articulate differences between their groups and perceived low status groups, often exaggerating their skills in order to retain that sense of superiority need to follow with a rationale as to why this is useful/important.

Carpenter (1995) also discovered that stereotypes are not always negative and can be used, when positive, to enhance collaboration. The author defined different types of stereotyping: those views held by students of their own group (autostereotypes), views held of the other group (heterostereotypes) and how a group felt the other group perceived them (perceived heterostereotypes). In a further study (Carpenter & Hewstone, 1996), overall attitudes toward other groups improved through IPE and the students' ability to work together also improved.

The eternal quest for the right timing of IPE in the health and human services is debated from two schools of thought. A sound professional identity is supported by many who believe that it is not possible to participate fully in collaborative practice if the student is not confident in his or her own skills (Funnell, 1995; Mazur, Beeston & Yerxa, 1979). A lack of willingness to share work and responsibility and inflexibility about roles can create conflict if the student is not confident. The impetus for developing the Readiness for Interprofessional Learning Survey (RIPLS) by Parsell and Bligh (1999) is grounded in the tensions that arise between discipline-specific needs and the need to share in an interprofessional context. Mackay, Scorr and Smith (1995) and Areskog (1995) support earlier introductions to IPE in order to develop positive attitudes towards other professions, including the theory and practice of teamwork.

In the work by Hind et al. (2003), the findings indicated that first year health and human service students are both excited by their chosen profession and willing to share and collaborate. The authors suggest that this may be true because they have had little exposure to their home profession and are still able to see themselves as a part of a greater whole. Future studies aimed at identifying factors that sustain attitude change in support of interprofessional collaboration are needed. In Hind and colleagues' study, a negative relationship between professional identity and readiness for interprofessional learning is well supported but the relationship between stereotypes and readiness for IP learning is not clearly established. A positive relationship between in-group stereotyping and professional identity seems clear. However, out-group stereotyping may lead to a decreased willingness to commit to shared learning and practice. Overall, this study suggests that IP teachers may wish to use the early introduction of IPE as a strategy given the enhanced sense of group belonging evident in first year health and human service students. Hind and colleagues also suggest that discovering predictors of attitude changes toward other professions may help to link students' social and other interactions in the early years of their study to sustainable changes that improve collaboration and therefore patient care.

Although not a study of IPE, Levy's (2000) research reinforces the observation that it is the negative stereotypes that tend to predominate. In situations where collaborative interaction is desired, the negative stereotypes of other professions may be major barriers to learning and practicing in shared models. In Levy's research, the impact of the negative self-stereotype was also studied and, in the older adult, it tends to impair memory performance, self-efficacy, and will to live. While not the same as studying attitudes of students in the health and humans service professions, there may be a link. If students are asked to share learning and practice with students from other health and human service professions without a strong sense of positive professional identity, do they begin to self-stereotype themselves in a negative frame? If they encounter negative stereotypes of their home profession, do they activate self-stereotypes thereby developing diminished professional performance? And, if the negative stereotypes tend to predominate, do they form negative opinions about other professions based on personal experience or experience of others close to them?

Despite a lack of research into stereotypes and health and human service professions, there are some interesting studies. As discussed previously, Carpenter (1995) has demonstrated that negative stereotypes among health professions do exist and Ryan and McKenna (1994) suggest that these negative stereotypes diminish professional performance in areas such as communication. Katz, Titiloy and Balogun (2001) found that physical therapy and occupational therapy students who engaged in IPE were more positive about the other profession. Parker and Chan (1986) used the Health Team Stereotype Questionnaire to examine stereotypes between physical therapy and occupational therapy students and found that each profession viewed itself more positively than the other profession. Davidson and Lucas (1995) suggest that perceptions of other professions change according to the education received, not whether that education was interprofessional leading us to examine how the professional culture that is rooted in history is transferred to students often by way of a hidden curriculum. Indeed, McNair (2005) cites Hafferty (1998) suggesting that "professional stereotypes are reinforced for students through a powerful hidden curriculum, delivered by senior colleagues who can role model negative attitudes and behaviours towards other disciplines" (p. 3). Indeed course instructors and preceptors were observed to have contributed negative attitudes toward other professions following a 2-day intervention at Liverpool University in the UK (Leaviss, 2000).

Conditions for positive attitude change (contact hypothesis) are articulated by Hewstone and Brown (1986). The condition most aligned with stereotyping suggests that members of an out-group must be typical and not exceptions to the stereotype. According to Carpenter (1995) and Parsell, Spalding and Bligh (1998) the sustainability of attitude change is questionable and short term interventions may in fact increase negative stereotyping. Tunstall-Pedoe et al. (2003) suggests that defining what one is and what one is not can be useful. It becomes a problem when generalizations are made based upon individual behaviour. Self-created boundaries then become barriers to collaboration. It is still unclear in the literature whether education can minimize stereotyping.

THE EMERGENCE OF INTERPROFESSIONAL EDUCATION

Over the past several decades, health professional education has evolved from an apprenticeship model based on existing patterns of practice with little or no connection to theory, evidence or best practice to a model that is evidence-informed, grounded in theory, and based on sound clinical decision-making principles. During this educational evolution, as health professions other than medicine and nursing burgeoned in the 20th century, strong disciplinary boundaries began to form, reinforcing the perceived need for discipline-specific curriculum content. Education of health professionals globally has therefore typically occurred in discipline-specific silos. There is now, however, a rapidly emerging trend toward more collaborative models of education and practice as one means of improving quality of patient care.

Over forty years ago, Dr. Jack McCreary and Dr. George Szasz introduced IPE at the University of British Columbia (Szasz, 1969). In 1964, a committee on *Interprofessional Education in the Health Sciences* was created at the university and was mandated to examine IPE based on, "...the assumption that if the health professionals are to work together, they also must learn together" (p. 3). The idea of IPE languished over the following decades, however, finding it difficult to gain traction during a time when professional turf appeared to be critical for the survival of specific health professions. In recent years the concept of IPE, or education that involves two or more health professions, has rapidly re-gained momentum in post-secondary educational institutions, health service organisations and provincial and federal governments. Publications related to IPE or interdisciplinary education can be found in the literature as early as the 1950's (Koch, 1951; Youmans, 1953). Yet the development and uptake of teaching models that cross professional boundaries has been slow to catch on until the past decade. The current and rapidly escalating acceptance of IPE as a critical approach to the training of future health care professionals is predicated on three major health care issues.

PRIMARY DRIVERS

There are currently several catalysts for IPE and collaborative practice. The first and most prominent is patient safety. Two specific reports, the Institute of Medicine's *To Err is Human* (Kohn, Corrigan & Donalson, 2000) and the *Canadian Adverse Events Study* (Baker et al., 2004), suggest strongly that patient safety is at risk if health care providers do not communicate effectively with each other and work collaboratively. In addition, new attention to human factors through dedicated research related to patient safety is proving useful in identifying strategies to improve patient safety in acute care settings, many of these relating to interprofessional communication and teamwork.

The *To Err is Human* report suggests that organisations should, "...establish interdisciplinary team training programs, such as simulation, that incorporate proven methods of team management" (p. 156) as one of three key recommendations for improving patient safety. The report concludes that "excellence might focus on particular types of errors (e.g., medication-related errors), errors in particular settings or clinical specialties (e.g., intensive care), or types of interventions or strategies that might be applied across many areas and settings (e.g., interdisciplinary teams)" (p. 30). Throughout the examples cited in the report, team management, communication, team training and interdisciplinary issues are consistent themes highlighting the imperative to view IPE and collaborative practice, including interdisciplinary communication, as essential to improved patient safety.

The *Canadian Adverse Events Study* defined adverse events (AEs) as "...unintended injuries or complications that are caused by health care management, rather than by the patient's underlying disease, and that lead to death, disability at the time of discharge or prolonged hospital stays" (p. 1). One of four key factors identified in the causality of AEs is described as "...the complexity of care in teaching hospitals means that patients may receive care from several different providers, which may increase the risk of AEs related to miscommunication and coordination of care" (p. 1684). While the recommendations from the study are not as specific as those from the Institute of Medicine, system change is highlighted including attention to communication across professions in the provision of patient care. The importance of interprofessional communication is also highlighted in the context of discharge planning and follow-up care in home and community, an area often neglected in studies of acute care patient safety.

Human factors research is an emerging area of inquiry that is often applied to industrial safety and, more recently, patient safety. Lynch and Cole (2006) suggest that increasing pressures and complexities in the health care system as well as changing roles through advanced practice models, demand attention to improved communication, effective interprofessional teamwork, conflict resolution and leadership. A human factors study of medical errors in intensive care units (Donchin et al., 1995) found that dangerous errors occurred and were closely linked to lack of communication between physicians and nurses. In another human factors study of perinatal units (McFerron, Nunes, Puce & Zuniga, 2005) units with low incidence of medical errors tended to be "...built on a solid foundation of timely communication and collegial teamwork to maintain patient safety as a top priority" (p. 1). Teamwork and collegiality were high priorities and an interesting *Just Culture Statement* was adopted that aimed to "promote open communication within the multidisciplinary ... team and between the many disciplines participating in perinatal care" (p. 6) Other studies in the human factors domain also support patient safety as a critical driver for IPE for collaborative patient care (Streitenberger ,Breen-Reid & Harris, 2006; Molloy & O'Boyle, 2005).

The second major driver of IPE is recruitment and retention of health care professionals. By reducing professional isolation, observing the positive effects of interprofessional teamwork on patient care, and creating opportunities for health care providers to learn from each other, employers are using IPE and collaboration to attract and retain employees. This approach is increasingly used in rural communities where recruitment and retention of health care providers are critical to the overall health of the community. These compelling arguments, along with a belief that improved quality of care is achieved through collaborative practice, have fuelled a large increase in IPE at both pre-licensure or entry-to-practice levels as well as in the context of continuing professional development.

The third trend impacting the uptake of IPE is the changing focus of health human resource planning processes. Typically numbers of specific professionals alone have guided planning for future health care needs rather than integrated or inclusive approaches. As early as 1994, the World Health Organization (WHO) suggested that workforce planning had been fragmented and narrow in scope. In its 2000 report, *Integrating Workforce Planning, Human Resources, And Service Planning*, the WHO suggested that integrated workforce planning should incorporate discussions related to multidisciplinary or multiprofessional approaches to workforce design. With the burgeoning legislation for advanced practitioners such as nurse practitioners, midwives, and physical therapy practitioners, there is a rationale for introducing more integration into planning ways to meet current and future health needs of individuals and communities. These emerging practice trends provide fertile ground for integrated health human resource planning that would only be strengthened by a focus on evidence-informed patient outcomes, IPE and collaborative practice. If we can conceptualize working together differently in collaborative practice patterns and interprofessional teams, health care can be provided more efficiently and effectively. This may be the only way to ensure that the older adults of the next 30 years will have their health care needs met.

IPE is increasingly used to educate health professionals in areas of curriculum and practice that do not require specialized knowledge or skills. Issues such as ethical practice, professionalism, legal aspects of health care, social determinants of health, communication skills, conflict resolution, end-of-life issues, and healthy communities are but a few of the areas of curriculum content that lend themselves well to IPE. Rich dialogue and engagement in learning across professional cultures and approaches can break down professional barriers to communication and collaboration in these key learning areas.

PRACTICAL STRATEGIES FOR TEACHING INTERPROFESSIONAL COLLABORATION

From this very brief review of professional histories and the emerging field of interprofessional collaboration it is clear that the health care providers of tomorrow must be taught differently today. In addition, practitioners of today must be encouraged to learn and practice in a truly interprofessional manner. There are several practical strategies that may help us to achieve the goals of interprofessional collaborative practice while honouring the core of specific professional expertise:

1. In order to focus interprofessional collaboration in both learning and practice environments, we need to provide, in consultation with the client and family, clarity around the goals of care and to identify together the expected outcomes from an interprofessional team approach.
2. The link to regulation as a consolidation of the history and growth of professions may offer us an explicit place to examine interprofessional practice through a better understanding of full scope of practice, including shared competencies.

3. By using professional history as a base, we can provide novice and expert practitioners opportunities to talk about their understanding of themselves as representatives of a professional group, both within and outside that profession.

4. The most effective timing of IPE is still not well understood but it may be that real immersion in collaborative practice models is best undertaken when there is a sense of professional self.

5. We can explicitly honour and trace the history of professions as part of each education program. Both within and among professions, this historical perspective may help to clarify points of professional divergence and convergence over decades of development and growth. By providing the histories and the factors that influenced each profession's development, a new approach to learning "about" each other may assist us to more effectively embrace interprofessional collaboration.

CONCLUSION

The current shortage of health care professionals available to fill vacancies throughout the health care sector as it is experienced in western health care contexts is, of course, a complex phenomenon. What is not in doubt, however, is that such a change in the number and range of personnel available to engage in the highly technical forms of care practiced in health care institutions throughout the west provides an impetus for change that may not previously have existed. This is, of course, the worry and concern of many professionals as they are encouraged to work together to generate new models of practice.

And so it is important that all partners participate together in these changes. The very real danger at this critical point in history is that, under pressure to staff units occupied by sick and vulnerable people, managers will move towards 'generic' workers who can be assigned to work across a range of occupational categories, with no particular professional identity nor affiliation.

In our review of the historical precedents of four distinct health professions (physiotherapy, pharmacy, medicine and nursing), we have argued that there is nothing 'natural' about the current divisions of labour – they all arise from historical contexts that have shaped what we now take to be 'real' and acceptable professional roles. The shape of these professional roles has been influenced by power-related structures that result in hierarchical relations along both gender and class lines, and that pre-figure value systems privileging particular epistemological tradition over others.

Despite this, all health care professionals emerge from historical traditions that share an interest in healing. Each has developed unique, favoured practices to explicate their interest in healing. These favoured practices have been codified in regulations that now frame distinctions between professional groups. Understanding these regulatory frameworks, engaging with them from a critical socio-historical standpoint, would, we believe, greatly assist health science students to both gain a strong sense of identity and affiliation with their chosen professional field – but also make them aware of the historical embeddedness of contemporary health care practice. Learning about the regulatory frameworks that shape the practice of other professional groups may be as important as learning in the same physical location. While there is still debate about whether co-learning opportunities support positive teamwork, there does seem to be reason to support formal and informal learning opportunities for novice practitioners to engage in dialogue with their peers – to be seen as members of the larger group rather than unique expressions of a more specific type. In dialogue, taken-for-granted assumptions about whose knowledge of a patient ought to guide the plan of care can be challenged and compared with other understandings of how healing might be best achieved. These dialogues represent the ultimate in interprofessional practice.

REFERENCES

Abbott, A. (1988). *The System of Professions*. Chicago: University of Chicago Press.

Areskog, N. H. (1995). The Linköping case: A transition from traditional to innovative medical school. *Medical Teacher, 17*(4), 371–377.

Baker, G. R., Norton, P. G., Flintoft, V., Blais, R., Brown, A., Cox, J., et al. (2004). The Canadian adverse events study: The incidence of adverse events among patients in Canada. *Canadian Medical Journal, 170*(11), 1678–1685.

Barnes, D., Carpenter, J., & Dickinson, C. (2000). Interprofessional education for community mental health: Attitudes to community care and professional stereotypes. *Social Work Education, 19*(6), 565–583.

Boulton, J. (2007). Welfare systems and the parish nurse in early modern London, 1650 – 1725. *Family and Community History, 10*, 127-151.

Bulger, R.J., & Barbato, A.L. (2000). On the Hippocratic sources of western medical practice. *The Hastings Center Report, 30*(4), S4-S7.

Carpenter, J. (1995). Doctors and nurses: Stereotypes and stereotype change in interprofessional education. *Journal of Interprofessional Care, 9*, 151–161.

Carpenter, J., & Hewstone, M. (1996). Shared learning for doctors and social workers: evaluation of a programme. *British Journal of Social Work, 26*, 239–257.

Chartered Society of Physiotherapy. (2009). *History*. Available at: *http://www.csp.org.uk/director/aboutcsp/history.cfm* (Accessed April 26, 2009).

Cleather, J. (1995). Head, heart and hands: the story of physiotherapy in Canada. The Canadian Physiotherapy Association: Toronto.

Davidson, L., & Lucas, J. (1995). Multiprofessional education in the undergraduate health professions curriculum: Observations from Adelaide, Linköping and Salford. *Journal of Interprofessional Care, 9*(22), 163–176.

Donchin, Y., Gopher, D., Olin, M.; Badihi, Y., Biesky, M., Sprung, C., Pizov, R., & Cotev, S. (1995). A look into the nature and causes of human errors in the intensive care unit. *Crit Care Med, 23*, 294-300.

Ehrenreich, B., & English, D. (1973). *Witches, midwives and nurses: a history of women healers*. Old Westbury, NY: Feminist Press.

Eugene Physical Therapy (2004). *History of Physical Therapy*. Available at: *http://www.eugenept.com/history.html* (Accessed April 12, 2008).

Funnell, P. (1995). Exploring the value of interprofessional shared learning. In K. Soothill, L. Mackay & C. Webb (Eds.), *Interprofessional relations in health care* (pp. 163–171). London: Edward Arnold.

Gilbert, J. (2005). Interprofessional learning and higher education structural barriers. *Journal of Interprofessional Care,* 19(2), 87-106.

Hafferty, F.W. (1998). Beyond curriculum reform: confronting medicine's hidden curriculum. *Academic Medicine, 73*(4), 403-407.

Hall, P. (2005). Interprofessional teamwork, Professional cultures as barriers. *Journal of Interprofessional Care.* 19(2), 188.

Halpern, S. A. (1992). Dynamics of professional control: Internal coalitions and crossprofessional boundaries. *American Journal of Sociology, 97*, 994-1021.

Hewstone, M., & Brown, R. J. (1986). Contact is not enough: An intergroup perspective on the "contact hypothesis." In M. Hewstone & R.J. Brown (Eds.), *Contact and Conflict in Intergroup Encounters* (pp. 1-44). Oxford: Blackwell.

Hind, M., Norman, I., Cooper, S., Gill, E., Hilton, R., Judd, R., & Jones, S.C. (2003). Interprofessional perceptions of health care students. *Journal of Interprofessional Care, 17* (1), 21-34.

ISHP, (2008). Society Newsletter. Available at: *http://www.govi.de/iggp.htm.* (Accessed: March 4, 2009).

Katz, J. S., Titiloye, V. M., & Balogun, J. A. (2001). Physical and occupational therapy undergraduates' stereotypes of one another. *Perceptual and Motor Skills, 92*, 843–851.

Knippenberg, A., & Oers, H. (1984). Social identity and equity concerns in intergroup perceptions . *British Journal of Social Psychology, 23*, 351–361.

Koch, C.C. (1951). Education in interprofessional relations. *American Journal of Optometry and Archives of the. American Academy of Optomology,* 28(6), 283-289.

Kohn. L.T., Corrigan, J.M., & Donaldson, M.S. (2000). *To Err is Human: Building a Safer Health System.* Commission on Quality of Health Care in America: National Academic Press, Washington DC.

Leaviss, J. (2000). Exploring the perceived effect of an undergraduate multiprofessional educational intervention. *Medical Education, 34*(6), 483-486.

Levy, B.R., Hausdorff, J.M., Hencke, R., & Wei, J.Y. (2000). Reducing Cardiovascular Stress With Positive Self-Stereotypes of Aging. *Journal of Gerontology: Psychological Sciences, 55B* (4), 205–213.

Linker, B. (2005). The business of ethics: gender, medicine and the professional codification of the American Physiotherapy Association 1918-1935. *Journal of the History of Medicine and the Allied Sciences, 60*, 320-354.

Lynch, A., & Cole, E. (2006). Human Factors in Emergency care: The Need for Team Resource Management. *Emergency Nurse, 14*(2), 32-36.

Mackay, L., Scorr, P., & Smith, D. (1995). Restructured and differentiated? Institutional responses to the changing environment of UK higher education. *Higher Education Management*, 7, 193–205.

Mandy, A., Milton, C., & Mandy, P. (2004). Professional stereotyping and interprofessional education. *Learning in Health and Social Care, 3* (3), 154–170.

Mazur, H., Beeston. M., & Yerxa, E. (1979). Clinical interdisciplinary health team care: Art educational experiment. *Journal of Medical Education, 54*, 703–713.

McFerran, S., Nunes, J., Pucci, D., & Zuniga, A. (2004). *Perinatal Patient Safety Project: A Multicenter Approach to Improve Performance Reliability at Kaiser Permanente.* Perinatal Patient Safety Project, Kaiser Permanente, Northern California Region.

McNair, R. (2005). Breaking down the silos: Interprofessional education and interprofessionalism for an effective rural health care workforce. In L. Fitzpatrick, G. Gregory (Eds.), *Proceedings, 8th National Rural Health Conference*. 10-13 March 2005; Alice Springs, Australia. Canberra, ACT: National Rural Health Alliance.

Molloy, G., & O'Boyle, C. (2005). The SHEL model: a useful tool for analyzing and teaching the contribution of Human Factors to medical error. *Academic Medicine, 80*(2), 152-155.

Nelson, S., & Gordon, S. (2004). The rhetoric of rupture: Nursing as a practice with a history? *Nursing Outlook, 52*, 255-261.

Nelson, S. (2001). From salvation to civics: Service to the sick in nursing discourse. *Social Science and Medicine, 53*, 1217-1225.

O'Brien-Palla, L., Birch, S., Baumann, A., & Tomblin, G. (2000). *Integrating Workforce Planning, Human Resources, and Service Planning*. World Health Organization: Geneva.

Parker, H. J., & Chan, F. (1986). Stereotyping: Physical therapists and occupational therapists characterize themselves and each other. *Physical Therapy, 66*, 668–672.

Parsell, G., & Bligh, J. (1999). The development of a questionnaire to assess the readiness of health care students for interprofessional learning (RIPLS). *Medical Education, 33*, 95–100.

Parsell, G., Spalding, R., & Bligh, J. (1998). Shared goals, shared learning: Evaluation of a multiprofessional course for undergraduate students. *Medical Education, 32*, 304–311.

Skevington, S. (1981). Intergroup relations and nursing. *European Journal, 11*(1), 43-59.

Streitenberger, K., Breen-Reid, K., & Harris, C. (2006). Handoffs in care – can we make them safer? *Pediatric Clinics of North America, 53*(6), 1185-1195.

Szaz, G. (1968). *Second Interim Report of the Committee on Interprofessional Education in the Health Sciences*. Health Sciences Centre, University of British Columbia: Vancouver, BC

Tosh, K. (2007). Nineteenth century handmaids or twenty-first century partners? *Journal of Health Organisation and Management, 21*(1), 68-78.

Tunstall-Pedoe, S., Rink, E., & Hilton, S. (2003). Student attitudes to under-graduate interprofessional education. *Journal of Interprofessional Care, 17*(2), 161-172.

Youmans, J.B. (1953). Interdisciplinary collaboration. *Journal of Psychiatric Social Work, 23*(1), 1-8.

In: Sociology of Interprofessional Health …
Ed: S. Kitto, J. Chesters et al.

ISBN: 978-1-60876-866-0
© 2011 Nova Science Publishers, Inc.

Chapter 4

WHAT IS AN INTERPROFESSIONAL HEALTH CARE TEAM ANYWAY?

Julia Coyle, Joy Higgs, Lindy McAllister and Gail Whiteford

ABSTRACT

Developing a better understanding of health care teams (HCTs) and the behaviours that frame HCT practice is aided in this chapter by interrogation of theories relevant to groups, teams and human interaction. This understanding is also informed by research that provides insight into the realities of HCT practice. This chapter discusses teams in health from three aspects: perspectives on why people would choose to work with others rather than in isolation; an examination of social groups and the individual; and findings from research that explored physiotherapists' perspectives and experiences of practising in HCTs. In combination these theories and research findings help illuminate the complexity and fluid nature of HCTs, and the impact that individuals have, in making each team unique.

INTRODUCTION

Teams have become a fundamental component of modern health service delivery. Inspection of health care employment advertisements reveal that current employers require health professionals to be able to work in multidisciplinary teams. Likewise, promotions panels seek out people for senior positions who have proven ability in *multi-* or *interdisciplinary* practice. It is evident that professionals working in the health care context are expected to be able to practise effectively in *health care teams* (HCTs). In this chapter we aim to develop an understanding of health care teams by examining differing perspectives on why people would chose to work with others as opposed to working in isolation. This understanding will be enhanced by exploring findings from research into current practice in HCTs.

Membership of HCTs requires professionals to integrate their client management in an interprofessional context (Leathard, 1994; Wolf, 1999). This integrated approach is thought to be associated with many benefits. Research in the business literature reports several benefits of effective teamwork, including reduced cost to the organisation, improved morale of employees, improved use of people's time and talents, improved decision making and reduced duplication of work (Housel, 2002). Likewise, in the health literature, it is thought that when teams work effectively they result in more efficient work practices through reduction in duplication, improved patient care by preventing gaps in service delivery (Doran et al., 2002; Leathard, 1994; Øvretveit, 1990) and improved patient safety (Smith & Christie, 2004). Perhaps because of this Australian governments advocate the use of teams; for example, the NSW Department of Health (2009) stated in their document *Caring together: the health action plan for NSW*:

> "New doctors, nurses, midwives and allied health staff will be trained to work in teams in the interest of patient safety. Clinical skills will be taught, practised and assessed. They will also learn how the team can work better together, particularly when a patient's condition starts to deteriorate."

Wherever health professionals work they are likely to encounter HCTs, as they are found across the spectrum of health care. HCTs range in scope from acute pain management teams (McDonnell, Nicholl & Read, 2003) to gerontology teams (Williams, Remington & Foulk, 2002), and in location from teams within the hospital system (Lake, Keeling, Weber & Olade, 1999) to those in the community (Johnson, Wistow, Schulz & Hardy, 2003).

The terms 'team' and 'teamwork' indicate quite different phenomena. Manion, Lorimer and Leander (1996) were careful to differentiate between these expressions by defining a team as a "specific structural unit in the organisation" (p. 5), while teamwork was "the way people work together cooperatively and effectively" (p. 5). Unfortunately the common practice of using the terms team and teamwork interchangeably, as occurs in the health literature, causes confusion in this field (Manion et al., 1996) perhaps leaving the impression that all teams cooperate.

The chapter is divided into three sections. The first section explores two differing perspectives on why people would chose to work with others rather than in isolation. Section two examines social groups and the individual. The final section, presents research that explored physiotherapists' perspectives and experiences of practising in HCTs to reveal two factors that influenced their behaviour as a member of a HCT.

WHY WOULD PEOPLE CHOOSE TO WORK WITH OTHERS?

Individuals tend to form groups including small social groups, such as families, volunteer groups and sports teams, or larger, organisational groups such as political parties, education systems and health care systems. In society like-minded individuals form groups that reflect common identities that are expressed through common cultural forms (dress, values, habits) (Jureidini, Kenny & Poole, 2003). Even when individuals strive to be different they may coalesce to form groups of like-minded 'different' individuals, such as when individuals adopt non-conformist practices in a collectivist way (same clothes, likes, dislikes, behaviour) in reaction to their perception of a society (McNair, Brown, Stone & Simms, 2001). Frequently in health care groups of professionals are brought together to form HCTs. By exploring factors that influence the formation of groups in society and individuals' decisions to work with others we may reach a deeper understanding of HCTs and our work within them.

Debate about why individuals form groups or work with others in society can be traced back to the Greek philosophers (Haralambos, van Krieken, Smith & Holborn, 1999). This debate has evolved over the years involving two seemingly diametrically opposed theoretical perspectives, the structuralist perspective and the social action perspective. Structuralist perspectives have been criticised for their deterministic focus on the overall structure of society and how distinct components interact to impact on individuals (Haralambos, et al., 1999). A variety of structuralist viewpoints have evolved as different theorists such as Hobbes, Durkheim and Parsons have developed models relating to how components of society meet a set of basic needs that are common to all societies. From a structuralist perspective the behaviour of HCT members would be determined by the society in which the HCT is set.

Conversely, social action perspectives, driven by theorists such as Mead and Blumer, see society as a product of human behaviour (Haralambos et al., 1999). Social action perspectives are concerned with individuals and their groups and the impact they may have on society. Although social action perspectives herald a significant shift away from the structuralist theories where society enforces its will on the individual, they have been criticised for their reductionist focus. Both perspectives are important to an understanding of health professionals' experience of working in HCTs as they help researchers add new dimensions to understanding individuals, groups and society.

Structuralist perspectives focus on the forces that construct and constrain individuals rather than on the individuals themselves (Jureidini et al., 2003). Parsons (1951) felt that control in society originates from integration between personalities and separate cultures within society. He held that social systems strive for equilibrium, with deviance resulting in dysfunction. In Parson's interpretation, accepted norms of behaviour would sustain equilibrium, with deviance or non-conformity resulting in instability. He contended that the commitment of individuals to the same values provided a common identity which in turn provided a foundation for cooperation and common goals (Parsons, 1951). In HCTs, members may share a common purpose, that is, the provision of health care to a specific group of clients. However, sharing a purpose does not mean that they would also share a commitment to the same values. For example, members of different disciplines can work in different practice models. In addition, the values, rights and obligations that are assigned to individual roles may be influenced by the predomination of genders in specific roles and the unequal distribution of power (e.g. through hierarchical role power). The influence of gender and power in HCTs is important, as it highlights a key criticism of Parsons' Structuralist Systems Theory that by focussing on normative values, in that ascriptive differences such as power, gender and race are ignored (Zajdow, 2003).

Proponents of social action perspectives have differed significantly in their views on the structure of society in that they do not believe that a structured society dictates the way in which people behave (Haralambos et al., 1999). For instance, Mead (1967), (the founder of the theory of symbolic interactionism), argued that society and human consciousness emerged through the social act. That is, the individual, or self, is constructed in interaction with society, and society in turn is constructed in interaction with the individual. Proponents of social action perspectives also acknowledge the importance of the relationship between the individual and the group (Schuler, Aldag & Brief, 1974). Mead (1967) argued that individual acts were components of larger, social acts. Therefore, understanding the behaviour of an individual is dependent upon understanding the behaviour of the whole social group to which they belong. He disagreed with structuralist views that all people are equal, arguing that society was made up of complex organisations of individuals and groups that hold varying degrees of power and status. In addition, he maintained that the freedom of one group often infringed upon the freedom of another as people strongly identified with their own group through hostility to another (Mead, 1967), essentially an 'us' and 'them' mentality. This concept has important implications for HCTs with membership drawn from a multiple professional groups where individuals have a strong identity with their profession.

Consideration of structuralist and social action perspectives is useful in understanding the impact of societal structures such as professional groups and HCTs on societal rules and values. Structuralists tend towards a belief that distinct rules and generalised values form the framework for individuals' behaviour, whilst proponents of a social action perspective argue that although individuals are not controlled by the system they are influenced by processes of norming and standardisation in society. Blumer (1969) shifted strongly away from the structuralist perspective that the system determines human behaviour, maintaining that the meaning each individual derives must be unique to the individual. In addition, he held that as people interact with others in the social world, they constantly re-evaluate their understandings of the meaning of things, modifying their previous constructions. Importantly, Blumer (1969) held that human behaviour could not be explained through set roles, culture, status or drives in the absence of interaction, rather, rules are developed and upheld through the interaction of individuals in a group. A classic example of this complex phenomenon in health care teams is demonstrated through the seating patterns commonly adopted by teams (for instance the dominant or senior person sits in the designated or accepted 'leader's chair', with the 'note taker' or support person alongside). Seating arrangements are seldom random, they speak to individual and group acceptance and reinforcement of societal norms enacted within their particular practice context. Norms such as these are thought to reinforce internal differentiations in society.

Increasing differentiation and specialisation, as has occurred in health, results in rising numbers of discrete entities or roles. How might this influence the roles within HCTs? Structuralists such as Parsons (1951) contended that society predetermines roles with each individual having defined rights and obligations within a group. He also held that the group would have a set of values which all individuals adopt. The difficulty with this for HCTs is that each member would have defined rights and obligations that relate to their professional group, requiring multiple, differing sets of rights and obligations to be integrated within a HCT.

Social action perspectives on roles differ from structuralists in that they believe that roles are not fixed. For social action protagonists roles change during the course of human interaction. Mead (1967) described a process known as '*role-taking*', where people frame their own behaviour by putting themselves in the position of others in order to interpret the intention and meaning of the symbols and actions adopted by other people. Mead's concept of '*role taking*' needs to be understood within the framework of his theories about an individuals' development of a concept of self. He maintained that the self consisted of the *I* and the *me*, where *I* is impulsive and uncontrolled and the *me* is the censor or the social self (Mead, 1967) . The *I* is a person's view of him/herself as a whole and is developed through interpretation of the reactions of others, while the *me* defines the person in a specific social role (Mead, 1967). The *I* wields considerable influence over a person's behaviour (Mead, 1967). For instance, if previous social interactions have led a health worker to see him/herself as being unsure in team situations, this is likely to result in a lack of self-confidence working in the HCT. Mead did not intend for this to be seen as a battle between the *I* and the *me*; once the *I* acts it becomes the *me*, and is the way that people express their uniqueness (Mead, 1967). Mead (1967) believed that people responded practically to environmental demands. That is, through the concept of '*role taking*', knowing and acting were integrated. Mead thought that '*role-taking*' and cooperative action stemmed from an awareness of the expectations of society (Mead, 1967). Societal control is exerted as individuals become aware of the expectations of others and modify their actions in response. In effect, control is exerted through socialisation.

It can be seen that both the structuralist perspective and the social action perspective centralise the importance of socialisation and its contribution to social order. Structuralists contend that individuals cooperate because they have been socialised into believing that it is right to obey the rules of society (Durkheim, 1974; Parsons, 1951). According to Durkheim's (1974) theories, health professionals' behaviour and consciousness would be shaped by socialisation from a range of sources, including HCTs, individuals' childhood, professional groups, work and environment. As with the structuralists, an important facet of the social action perspective is socialisation, that is, how people learn to behave in society (Mead, 1967). Mead linked socialisation to individuals' development of a concept of self. Social action protagonists believe that it is through social dialogue or interaction that society is formed. Blumer (1969) argued that the meanings that people have for objectivess determine the way they act towards those objectivess and that social interaction refines people's interpretation of these objectives. From a structuralist perspective individuals in HCTs would learn how to respond in predetermined patterns. Whereas, from a social actionist perspective individuals' responses would be mediated by their interpretation of social interaction, that is, that there is a fluid nature to the society found within HCTs.

HCTs, INDIVIDUALS AND THEIR AFFILIATIONS

Rather than viewing an organisation such as a hospital as having a distinct unified culture, current thinking sees organisational cultures as fluid and unstable (Chan, 2000). Within organisations there are cliques, cabals and groups; these are subcultures, with clearly articulated cultures of their own (Gagliardi, 1990). Organisational cultures are thought to be simultaneously integrated, differentiated and fragmented (Martin, 1992). Contributing to this cultural melange in the health care sector has been the shift towards a 'knowledge-based' society with increasing specialisation of the workforce (Wilenski, 1964) and the emergence of professional groups. As a result, HCTs in hospitals are made up of representatives from a range of professional groups.

Belonging to any group provides people with comparators and a context through which they may develop an understanding of who they are (Ashforth & Kreiner, 1999). Through collective values and meanings individuals construct their sense of self-worth (Hogg & Terry, 2000). For people to engage in collective action (as may occur in HCTs) they need to strongly identify with that group and its members (Kramer, Hanna, Su & Wei, 2001). In this way, engaging in collective action as a member of a HCT seems to run counter to belonging to a discipline-specific group.

Social identity theory encompasses a body of ideas that combine to form an approach to understanding social identity and intergroup relations. This approach builds upon the pioneering work of Taifel from the 1970s. Taifel (1979) theorised that social behaviour could be viewed on a continuum from interpersonal behaviour to intergroup behaviour. At the extreme of interpersonal behaviour, interactions are determined by the personal relationships between individuals. At the extreme of intergroup behaviour, interactions are determined by individual's membership of social groups. This theory has been used to explain the different ways people react when beliefs about the social structure or their social status challenge their social identity (Turner, 1999).

Social identity theory was further developed by the addition of the self-categorisation theory (Turner & Oakes, 1989) that contended that behaviour along the interpersonal and intergroup continuum could be explained by a distinction between two identities: one personal and one social. Personal identity defines what makes a person unique and individual from other people, including those who are in the group. Social identity defines individuals according to characteristics they share with others in a group. These group characteristics are in contrast to characteristics of other groups, and identify the group as "us" in contrast to "them". For health professionals working in hospital HCTs, social identity would encompass their membership of the HCT as well as their membership of other social groups to which they belong, such as being a physiotherapist, or being a woman or a man, Australasian or Eurasian. Sense of identity with a group is considered to be dependent upon the balance between an individual's personal and social identity (Turner & Oakes, 1989).

Three key principles underpin self-categorisation theory. First, when social identity has greater saliency than personal identity people switch from individual behaviour to collective behaviour (Turner, 1999). That is, the more strongly they identify with a group the more likely they are to adopt the behaviours and norms of the group. Second, when the saliency of social identity is greater than personal identity this leads to self-depersonalisation, where people accentuate attributes that make them similar to the group (Turner & Oakes, 1989). Third, the level of identification a person has with a group varies, being dependent upon the context and the values and expectations of the person (Turner & Oakes, 1989). High levels of identification with a group depend upon the level of similarity people perceive they have with group members, their perception of interdependence with group members, and the degree to which they value membership of the group (Turner, 1999).

When individuals' social identity has greater saliency than their personal identity they transfer from individual behaviour to collective behaviour (Turner, 1999). This process, known as the depersonalisation of self, is the central hypothesis of the self-categorisation theory (Turner & Oakes, 1989). When health professionals self-categorise as a member of a specific hospital group their personal identity has less saliency to them. For instance, self-categorisation as a physiotherapist would require them to perceive that they had similarities with other physiotherapists, that they were interdependent with other physiotherapists and that they valued the physiotherapists as a group. Importantly, once they identified with the physiotherapist group these features would be heightened through self-depersonalisation as they formed a group of "us", in contrast to "them". In identifying with the physiotherapists they would accentuate their similarities and reduce personal attributes that made them different. This process would also increase, perceptually, their difference from other cultural groups such as doctors or porters, through self-stereotypes. The more strongly they identified with the physiotherapist group the more membership of the group would shift from being a label to being a psychological reality.

Self-categorisation is reinforced when the group is central to a person, is valued and is ego-involving (Doosje & Ellemers, 1997). As health professionals are generally educated in relative isolation from other health workers it is likely that they would perceive many similarities with their peers and few similarities with other health professionals. Cumulative professional enculturation during training may result in strong identification with their professional group and perceived interdependence. Of importance, perceived interdependence can cause self-categorisation and lead to psychological group formation even before positive experiences reinforce the perception (Turner, 1999).

Self-categorisation subjectively changes people's relations according to judgements of whether someone is one of 'us' or one of 'them' (Turner, 1999). Perceptions of attraction or dislike, agreement or disagreement, cooperation or conflict would be dependent on perceptions of similarities or differences. Recategorisation results from the need to resolve uncertainty about judgement of whether someone is one of 'us' or 'them'. Recategorisation of one's own membership of a group results in reduced identity and affinity with the original group and strengthened identity with a different group. Just as people perceive themselves as members of different groups in different contexts, they perceive others as different in one context but similar in another (Turner, 1999). Recategorisation of another's membership of the group results in people shifting others out of the 'us' group into a 'them' group. So how does this interplay with known models of HCTs formed from representatives of different professional groups?

Professional groups are the protectors of a body of knowledge and skills that is generally not shared with others (Higgs & Bithell, 2001). In addition, they are said to possess a specific set of attributes that define them: 'altruism, honour and integrity; caring and compassion; respect; responsibility; accountability; excellence and scholarship; and leadership' (Inui, 2003, p. 12). High levels of expertise and autonomy are integral to professional identity (Raelin, 1986). Therefore, it is no surprise that the dominant themes evident in analyses of professionalism are privilege and power, themes that run counter to the idealistic attributes of Inui (2003) listed above. The key resource of professional groups is that they alone are able to perform specific tasks (Freidson, 1993). The degree of uncertainty and complexity that is associated with such tasks perpetuates the need for the professional (Southon & Braithwaite, 1998). High levels of uncertainty and complexity require individual assessment by the professional in order to achieve the outcome desired. As a task becomes less uncertain, it may be handled by standardised procedures even though it may still be complex, and it could therefore be handled by a technician rather than a professional (Southon & Braithwaite, 1998). Thus professionals retain autonomy through ownership of specific knowledge and skills. Power and privilege may be built through protection of that knowledge as others come to depend upon the ability of professionals to handle specific tasks.

Professionalism would seem to progress individualistic rather than cooperative tendencies as professionals seek to protect specific tasks and craft knowledge which may determine the type of team practice. Three key classifications predominate in HCT classification; they use the prefixes, multi-, inter- and trans and describe a continuum of team practice with multi- at one end and trans- at the other. Common descriptors for multi- can be found to involve the inclusion in the team of different professionals who work separately and who either report information or share information. Essentially the prefix multi- denotes the retention of role boundaries by the professions with individuals practising in parallel models of practice. The definitions of inter- exhibit the most confusion in the literature with professionals sharing roles (Sorrells-Jones, 1997; Masterson, 2002) or working separately (Stepans, Thompson & Buchanan, 2002), retaining boundaries (Paul & Petersen, 2001) or merging (Masterson, 2002). It is only when trans- is used that consensus clearly appears with an emphasis on shared roles, role blurring and even role exchange. In HCTs it may be that professionals with high levels of professional identity and protectionism would fall into multidisciplinary models of team practice whilst those who can relinquish control over set tasks may be able to practise in a trans-disciplinary model.

There have been two scholarly departures from these three classifications of HCT. The first is Øvretveit's classification based upon team organisation (1996) using five dimensions. The second is Boon, Verhoef, O'Hara and Finlay's (2004) description of the range of integrated practices found along the pre-existing continuum of team-oriented health care practice.

Øvretveit (1996) described five dimensions based on aspects of team organisation to classify HCTs. These dimensions were: the degree of team integration; resource management; membership; decision making; and leadership. Each dimension was expressed across a continuum that captured the spectrum of teamwork. For instance, the team integration continuum moved from a low level of integration with a 'loose knit association' to a high level of integration with 'collective multidisciplinary policy' and 'decisions made at team meetings' (Øvretveit, 1996). The spectrum of practices that may describe the level of team integration lay in between. When this approach to classification is used to address all five dimensions, it is unlikely that a HCT would fit each element at the same relative point in the range; it may be classified in the high range for integration, the low range for resource management (in that the HCT has no control over its own resources), and middle of the range for leadership. Whilst Øvretveit's (1996) classification system is better placed to capture the uniqueness of a HCT its focus on organisational dimensions limits its scope because for a number of dimensions, such as level of trust or respect, are not addressed.

Boon et al. (2004) define "seven different models of team-oriented health care practice: parallel, consultative, collaborative, coordinated, multidisciplinary, interdisciplinary and integrative" (p. 2) that range across the continuum of health care practices. These models were based upon their understanding of the key components of integrative health care practice: philosophy or values, structure, process, and outcomes. Boon et al. (2004) believed that on one side of the continuum where parallel and consultative practice models reside there is a predominance of the biomedical model of health. As one moves towards the other end of the continuum greater emphasis is placed upon holistic models of client care with the psychosocial determinants gaining emphasis. Structure varies across the continuum with hierarchical models disappearing as the emergence of trust and respect developed in the team. They felt that communication would increase as teams move towards more integrative models because the number of members increases in response to more holistic models of care. Finally, Boon et al. (2004) believed that the 'complexity and diversity of outcomes' (p. 2) would increase as teams move towards more integrative models of care. They believed that the choice of practice model was determined by clients' needs rather than team members' behaviour. For instance, they contended that a client presenting with an acute myocardial infarction was better managed in practice models on the left of the continuum. They believed that their classification system could be used by emerging health practitioners to decide which practice settings best suited their interpersonal and professional needs. In addition, the authors recommended that health care managers should recognise the different structural styles, from hierarchical to integrative, that would need different funding and leadership training. Essentially, there are a range of factors that would seem to play a role in influencing individual professional's decisions to work with others. There are also different ways of viewing HCTs.

RESEARCH EXPLORING INFLUENCES ON PROFESSIONALS' DECISIONS TO WORK WITH OTHERS IN HCTs?

This final section presents findings from doctoral research, (undertaken by the lead author with supervision from the co authors), into Australian physiotherapists' perspectives and experiences of working in HCTs. In this research the differences between teams and teamwork was illuminated by findings which emphasised the importance of trust, security in team membership and the challenge of juggling multiple team memberships.

Given the complexity, dynamism and situated nature of the phenomenon of teamwork, the research was necessarily contextualised and interpretive in orientation using multi-source data collection methods including semi- structured, in-depth interviews and participant observation. Following recruitment, ethics approval and informed consent processes, six physiotherapists agreed to participate in the study which had a duration of 18 months. Gender-neutral pseudonyms were assigned to ensure the anonymity of the participants: Alex, Chris, Jo, Kim, Pat, and Sam.

Data analysis was guided by principles described by scholars of hermeneutic phenomenology (Heidegger, 2005; Gadamer, 1975). Three reflective approaches as described by van Manen (2001) were used in the analysis of the data: the wholistic approach, the selective approach and the detailed approach. These strategies helped to uncover thematic aspects in the data. The process of interpretation continued until a point was reached where further interpretation proved to be redundant, the point of theoretical saturation.

HCT STRUCTURE, THE ENVIRONMENT AND THE IMPACT OF TRUST

It is a common practice in the literature to classify health workers' team membership in a simple model based purely on their clinical affiliation, that is, that they are on the rehabilitation team, or the orthopaedic team. However, in this research the reality for the participants was considerably more complex. Service delivery in the participants' hospitals depended upon the work of multiple intersecting teams formed from a range of different professional groups. Some professional groups formed distinct teams (for example, the hospital physiotherapy team and the orthopaedic and rehabilitation teams); others formed less distinct, loosely connected teams (for example, the acute care team and the sub-acute care team). Participants' concurrent membership of multiple teams can be seen in the excerpt from Chris's interview in which we were discussing meetings.

"We have an inpatient physio meeting, we have an inpatient allied health meeting, and once a month the business unit manager attends that from up on the ward. Then we have patient-based team meetings, including case conferences and the family meetings. Then we have our neuro admin meetings. So lots of meetings and lots of teams within teams, but its good and somehow it works" (Chris I1: 321).

Essentially, the participants' teams could not be seen as separate entities because the different teams were interconnected. As teams often shared responsibilities and frequently shared members, the participants needed to learn to effectively balance and juggle their responsibilities and relationships in order to become empowered practitioners in their HCTs.

It was evident in this research that the physiotherapists engaged concurrently in a range of practice models from separate models of practice as seen in multidisciplinary teams, to integrated practice models as seen in trans-disciplinary teams. Integrated practice models emerged with participants who were able to more fully appreciate the value others added to patient care. The ability to adopt such models has been found to require professionals to blur roles, to accept differences and to have a shared vision of service delivery (Boon et al., 2004). As these requirements needed high levels of trust and respect, integrated practice models occurred only with the participants' most trusted colleagues. Invariably this was with occupational therapists.

"They are all probably different relationships, but the OT [occupational therapist] … we were similar in our frustrations and difficulties at times so we had that common link. The OT and physio goals often overlap and kind of work together. They've been working on doing breakfast group in a standing position and that correlates with my goals of increasing standing balance and standing symmetry. So we often liaise and try and make sure we are on the same track and what we're working on is either complementing or working towards the same thing" (Chris I1: 112).

In spite of the different professional philosophies and approaches to treatment, Chris sensed a commonality with occupational therapists. This feeling was repeated across participants. Contrary to anecdotal evidence that these two professions are often in conflict, in this research it was evident that there was a complementary and synergistic relationship between them.

Youngson (1999) described the complex and seemingly chaotic social construction of their role for practitioners who were dealing with sector changes, practice challenges, uncertainty and confusion. Such complexity mirrors the findings of this research where the participants worked in a complex, fluid environment dealing with multiple layers of change and complexity. However, in contrast to the literature that states that complexity increased professional territorial protection (Jones, 2005), in this research complexity actually fostered closer integration and interdependence, that is, less conflict and less territorial protection. Simplifying and controlling their complex, fluid environment was crucial to participants' capacity to complete their work. To this end, participants solve established links with their most trusted colleagues to form small informal teams. They used these teams to informally bridge professional separation that they confronted within the organisation.

Core teams were small, generally involving no more than three health workers, and had predictable patterns of membership. The participants' preference was to establish stronger relationships with those people who could be trusted to respond in similar ways to the participant and with whom they shared similar values and expectations. In this way, membership of the core team was exclusive, being reserved for people who consistently showed that they were trustworthy. Core teams varied according to the context of their work and the level of trust participants had for workers around them. Core teams reduced the number of people with whom they needed to interact, and provided a safe environment in which there was reciprocal support, respect and reliance. As they worked with these people they recognised and developed greater similarities, which strengthened their affinity with their core team, making it even more valuable. In this way they significantly enhanced participants' practice and were distinctly different from their other teams.

Core teams broadened their perspective. Core teams were problem solving teams. The members of these teams united to develop a stance on a patient's capacity to achieve an outcome or determine timelines for patients to achieve outcomes. Meetings of these teams showed a flat hierarchy with shared decision making. It was evident that team members valued individuals when their input led to modification of team decisions. In addition the combined knowledge of team members was used to develop strategies to work more effectively with powerful health workers like the senior doctors.

It was apparent in this research that the physiotherapists concurrently identified with multiple teams. They also shared an identity with representatives from different professional groups, through the establishment of and participation in their core teams. There is congruence between these findings and a modification to social identity theory known as crossed categorisation (Turner, 1999). Crossed categorisation involves a person identifying with multiple groups simultaneously, and has been found to weaken group boundaries by enhancing a person's perception of similarities rather than differences between groups (Gaertner et al., 1993). As argued in crossed categorisation theory, when the participants in this research shared an identity with representatives from other professional groups it helped to limit conflict between these professional groups. In this research the formation of relationships with their fellow core team members was founded strongly on participants' levels of personal affinity for these people as individuals. Essentially, participants' sense of value for people in their core teams did not extend to the professional groups from which core team members arose.

THE INFLUENCE OF TRUST ON PHSIOTHERAPISTS' DECISIONS TO WORK WITH OTHERS

A feature of participants' behaviour in HCTs was seeking to manage risk within a framework of trust. Fukuyama (1995) defined trust as 'the expectation that arises within a community of regular, honest and cooperative behaviour, based on commonly shared norms on the part of other members of that community' (p. 26). Learning to trust meant that participants had to have sufficient empathy with their colleagues to believe that they were working to capacity, that all were pulling their weight. In turn, participants built trust through being reliable, that is, by not adding to others' workload through failure to do their own. The importance of the reciprocal nature of this element of trust was apparent when Kim described the way that two physiotherapists working in the same unit handled the workload.

"What doesn't get done gets done by someone else. So you just have to trust that everyone within the team is working to what they can. I think that's true. If they can't get it done they can't get it done. I'm not sitting there thinking 'she should have'. It's the same as there being another new patient to see today, and there may be more admissions after lunch, there'll be a limit to what I can do. If I can't get it done I can't get it done. My expectation is that other people will say well, you know, that's as much as could be done" (Kim I2: 135).

Believing that all will work to their full capacity enabled Kim to accept additional work without judging others or thinking badly of them. In return Kim expected others to understand that work left undone reflected time constraints rather than laziness. Inter-reliance helped foster their understanding that they were 'pulling together', supporting each other. Trust relied upon them having empathy with others, being able to put themselves in another's place. Believing that others were working to their capacity meant giving them the benefit of the doubt if work was not done, behaviour that would help prevent conflicts within the team.

Being reliable was not just doing what you said you would do, but doing it within a stated time-frame. Participants expected others to share their sense of urgency about their work, expecting them to handle matters in a timely fashion. However, the importance of good communication was apparent, as people who were responsible for delays were not necessarily deemed unreliable.

"I'm expecting them to give me a response that will tell me when. It doesn't mean that they have to do it straight away, but I expect that they will let me know when, yeah, basically when. Generally if I'm not happy with that then I can negotiate from there, but I don't want to be sitting around waiting. If it is going to be the end of the week, I would just rather know that it is going to be the end of the week, that's fine" (Kim I4: 188).

Participants' appreciation that all were working to their capacity helped them to attribute delays to heavy workloads, time constraints or staff shortages. Being reliable entailed keeping people informed as to when the matter would be handled. They appreciated it when others gave them honest and accurate estimates of the timing of action, as this prevented unanticipated delays. Being let down repeatedly as deadlines came and went frustrated them more than the single disappointment of being informed about a lengthy delay. Perhaps this was because accurate communication of a delay enabled the participants to manage their work. Unpredictable timelines might reduce their sense of control, leading to a feeling of disempowerment. In addition, uncontrollable timelines that delayed the participants' work might result in themselves being deemed unreliable. Regaining control in such situations left the participants with two options: to accept the loss of trust associated with being seen as unreliable, or to blame the team member who put them in that position. Both of these had negative implications for the team.

Choosing to work with more reliable colleagues was associated with additional benefits that helped to build trust and participants' sense of security. When the participants repeatedly sought out a colleague they were selectively increasing their time with that individual, providing opportunities for better understanding of the other's roles. More time also gave participants a chance to get to know the colleague better, which could enhance their relationship. Choosing to work with specific individuals was driven by the need to save time. They chose people who had proved their capacity to enhance their work, or who assisted them to complete their work in the available time. Participants' preference was for people with proven reliability, as can be seen in the following excerpt from Alex's interview.

> I suppose I tend to probably seek out the ones I know well and I know are good. Earlier on I had to talk to somebody. The one I needed wasn't there so I asked another to pass the message on, as I knew she was reliable. If there's a group of nurses and you know one of them well, you know is good, you go for her even though you know she may not be the right one. It's just human nature. (Alex I2: 595).

The act of preferentially seeking out a colleague was a way of showing that the colleague was valued and respected. This could serve to further enhance the relationship and develop a feeling of mutual respect, an important factor in trust. It can be seen in the excerpt from Alex's interview that colleagues who rejected the participants' approach were seen as unreliable. The participants choose not to work with such people. A refusal was seen by the physiotherapists not only as a lack of interest, but also as a mark of disrespect. People who did this ran the risk of being tagged as difficult to get on with and being avoided in future.

CONCLUSION

Developing a better understanding of HCTs and the behaviours that frame HCT practice is aided in this chapter by interrogation of theories relevant to groups, teams and human interaction. This understanding is also informed by research that provides insight into the realities of HCT practice. In combination these theories and research findings help illuminate the complexity and fluid nature of HCTs, and the impact that individuals have, in making each team unique.

REFERENCES

Ashforth, B. E., & Kreiner, G. F. (1999). How can you do it?: Dirty work and the challenge of constructing a positive identity. *Academy of Management Review, 24* (3), 413-434.

Boon, H., Verhoef, M., O'Hara, D., & Findlay, B. (2004). From parallel practice to integrative health care: a conceptual framework. *BMC Health Services Research, 4*(1), 15.

Doosje, B., & Ellemers, N. (1997). Stereotyping under threat: the role of group identification. In R. Spears, P. Oakes, N. Ellemers, & S. Haslam (Eds.), *The social psychology of stereotyping and group life* (pp. 257–272). Oxford: Blackwell.

Doran, I., Baker, G. R., Murray, M., Bohnen, J., Zahn, C., Sidani, S., & Carryer, J. (2002). Achieving clinical improvement: an interdisciplinary intervention. *Health Care Management Review, 27* (4), 42-56.

Durkheim, E. (1974). *Sociology and Philosophy.* New York: The Free Press.

Freidson, E. (1984). The changing nature of professional control. *Annual Reviews of Sociology, 10,* 1-20.

Fukuyama, F. (1995). *Trust: the social virtues and the creation of prosperity.* New York: Free Press.

Gadamer, H.G. (1975). *Truth and method.* New York: Seabury.

Gaertner, S.L., Dovidio, J.F., Anastasio, P.A., Bachman, B.A., & Rust, M.C. (1993). *European Review of Social Psychology,* 1479-1277X, 1-26.

Gagliardi, P. (1990). *Symbols and artifacts: View of the corporate landscape.* Berlin: de Gruyte.

Haralambos, M., van Krieken, R., Smith, P., & Holborn, M. (1999). *Sociology: themes and perspectives, Australian edition.* Melbourne: Longman.

Heidegger, M. (2005). *Being and time.* Oxford: Blackwell publishing

Higgs, J., & Bithell, C. (2001). Professional expertise. In J. Higgs, & A. Titchen (Eds.), *Practice knowledge and expertise in the health professions* (pp. 59-68). Oxford: Butterworth-Heinemann.

Hogg, M. A., & Terry, D. J. (2000). Social identity and self-categorisation processes in organizational contexts. *Academy of Management Review, 25* (1), 121-140.

Housel, D. J. (2002). *Team Dynamics.* Cincinatti USA.: Thomson Learning.

Inui, T.S. (2003). A Flag in the Wind: Educating for Professionalism in Medicine. Association of American Medical Colleges.

Johnson, P., Wistow, G., Schulz, R., & Hardy, B. (2003). Interagency and interprofessional collaboration in community care: the interdependence of structures and values. *Journal of Interprofessional Care, 17*(1), 69-83.

Jones, M. (2005). Cultural power in organisations: the dynamics of interprofessional teams. In G. Whiteford, & V. Wright St Clair (Eds.), *Occupation and practice in Context.* Churchill Livingstone.

Jureidini, R., Kenny, S., & Poole, M. (2003). The search for society. R. Jureidini, & M. Poole (Eds.), *Sociology: Australian connections* (3rd ed., pp. 3-25). Crows Nest NSW: Allen & Unwin.

Kramer, R. M., Hanna, B. A., Su, S., & Wei, J. (2001). Collective identity, collective trust, and social capital: Linking group identification and group cooperation. In M.E. Turner (Ed.), *Groups at work: Theory and research* (pp. 173-196). Mahwah: Lawrence Erlbaum.

Lake, M., Keeling, P., Weber, G. J., & Olade, R. (1999). Collaborative care: a professional practice model. *Journal of Nursing Administration, 29*(9), 51-6.

Leathard, A. (1994). *Going Inter-Professional: Working together for health and welfare.* London: Routledge.

Manion, J., Lorimer, W., & Leander, W. J. (1996). *Team-based health care organisations: Blueprint for success.* Aspen: Gaithersburg, MD.

Martin, J. (1992). *Cultures in Organizations – Three Perspectives.* Oxford: Oxford University Press.

Masterson, A. (2002). Cross boundary working: a macro political analysis of the impact on professional roles. *Journal of Clinical Nursing, 11*, 331-339.

McDonnell, A., Nicholl, J., & Read S.M. (2003). Acute pain teams and the management of postoperative pain: a systematic review and meta-analysis. *Journal of Advanced Nursing, 41*, 261-273.

McNair, R., Brown, R., Stone, N., & Sims, J. (2001). Rural interprofessional education: promoting teamwork in primary health care education and practice. *Australian Journal of Rural Health, 9(Suppl.)*(S19S26), S19-S26.

Mead, G. H. (1967). *Mind, self, and society from the standpoint of a social behaviourist.* Chicago: University of Chicago Press.

New South Wales Department of Health. (2009). *Caring together: the health action plan for NSW*. Sydney: NSW Health Department.

Øvretveit, J. (1990). Making the team work. *Professional Nurse, 5*, 284-288.

Øvretveit, J. (1996). Five ways to describe a multidisciplinary team. *Journal of Interprofessional Care, 10*(2), 163-171.

Parsons T. (1951). *The social system*. London: Routledge & Kegan Paul.

Paul, S., & Petersen, C. Q. (2001). Interprofessional collaboration: issues for practice and research. *Occupational Therapy in Health Care, 15*(3/4), 1-12.

Raelin, J. A. (1986). An Analysis of Professional Deviance within Organizations. *Human Relations, 39*(12), 1103-1129.

Schuler, R. S., Aldag, R. J., & Brief, A. P. (1974). Behaviour and Human Performance. *Journal of Abnormal Social Psychology, 13*, 159-172.

Smith A.R., & Christie C. (2004). Facilitating transdisciplinary teamwork in dietetics education: a case study approach. *Journal of the American Dietetic Association, 104*(6), 959-962.

Sorrells-Jones, J. (1997). The challenge of making it real: interdisciplinary practice in a 'seamless' organisation. *Nursing Administration Quarterly , 21*(2), 20-30.

Southon, G., & Braithwaite, J. (1998). The end of professionalism? *Social Science & Medicine, 46*(1), 23-28.

Stepans, M. B., Thompson, C. L., & Buchanan, M. L. (2002). The role of the nurse on a transdisciplinary early intervention assessment team. *Public Health Nursing, 19*(4), 238-245.

Tajfel, H. (1979). Individuals and groups in social psychology. *British Journal of Social and Clinical Psychology, 18*, 183-190.

Turner, J. C. (1999). Social identity and self categorisation. In N. Elllemers, R. Spears, & B. Doosje (Eds.), *Social Identity: context commitment and content*. Oxford: Blackwell Publishers.

Turner, J., & Oakes, P. (1989). Self-categorisation theory and social influence. In P. B. Paulus (Ed.), *Psychology of group influence* . Hillsdale New Jersey: Lawrence Ehrlbaum.

van Manen, M. (2001). Transdisciplinarity and the new production of knowledge. *Qualitative Health Research, 11* (6), 850-852.

Wilenski, H. L. (1964). The professionalisation of everyone? *American Journal of Sociology, 70*, 137-158.

Williams, B. C., Remington, T., & Foulk, M. (2002). Teaching interdisciplinary geriatrics team care. *Academic Medicine, 77*(9), 935.

Wolf, K. N. (1999). Allied Health professionals and attitudes to teamwork. *Journal of Allied Health, 28*(1), 15-20.

Youngson, R. M. (1999). *Medical blunders: Amazing true stories of mad, bad and dangerous doctors*. New York, NY: New York University Press.

Zajdow, G. (2003). Parsons and structural functionalism. In R. Jureidini, & M. Poole (Eds.), *Sociology: Australian connections* (3rd ed., pp. 83-101). Crows Nest NSW: Allen & Unwin.

In: Sociology of Interprofessional Health …   ISBN: 978-1-60876-866-0
Ed: S. Kitto, J. Chesters et al.   © 2011 Nova Science Publishers, Inc.

Chapter 5

"CONTACT IS NOT ENOUGH": A SOCIAL PSYCHOLOGICAL PERSPECTIVE ON INTERPROFESSIONAL EDUCATION

John Carpenter and Claire Dickinson

ABSTRACT

The focus of this chapter is on interprofessional education (IPE) as an encounter between members of two or more professional or student groups. It considers, from the perspective of social psychology, a key aim of IPE which is to improve interprofessional working by changing attitudes and perceptions. The underlying assumption of many, if not most, programme of IPE is that if the professions are brought together they have the opportunity to learn about each other and dispel the negative stereotypes which are presumed to hamper interprofessional collaboration in practice.

The 'contact hypothesis' proposes a set of necessary conditions for the beneficial outcomes of bringing groups together in order to reduce hostility and promote positive attitude change between their members. These are that the groups should have equal status within the contact situation, they should work on common goals, have the support of authorities (institutional support) and cooperate with each other in joint work which has a successful outcome. Participants should have positive expectations and there should be a focus on both similarities and differences between members of the groups. Finally, participants should perceive members of the other group as typical, so that attitude changes may be generalised. Social Identity Theory offers a number of perspectives on generalisation. The chapter also considers cognitive processes which are thought to underlay attitude change; these include social categorisation, cognitive dissonance, and the role of emotions and insight.

The chapter reviews empirical studies where the researchers have drawn on the contact hypothesis in the design of IPE programmes at both prequalifying and postqualifying levels and which have measured attitude change before and after the educational intervention. These studies provide evidence to argue that educators should pay explicit attention to an intergroup perspective in designing IPE. This would increase the chances of the planned contact having a positive effect or in changing attitudes.

INTRODUCTION

One of the aims of interprofessional education (IPE) is to "...change attitudes and perceptions by countering prejudice and negative stereotypes" (Barr et al., 1999). The underlying assumption is that if the professions are brought together they have the opportunity to learn about each other and dispel the negative stereotypes which are presumed to hamper interprofessional collaboration in practice. As McMichael and Gilloran (1984), the authors of one of the earliest evaluations of IPE pointed out, the study of intergroup behaviour and attitude change has long been the province of social psychology. In this chapter we will review some theoretical perspectives, consider their application to IPE and conclude with some evidence from evaluation studies informed by this approach.

THE CONTACT HYPOTHESIS

Over 50 years ago, while accepting the proposition that the best way to reduce hostility between groups was to bring them together, Allport (1954) nevertheless argued that 'contact is not enough'. In other words, simply putting together a collection of students from different professions would not be enough to produce attitude change, a conclusion which McMichael and Gilloran (1984) quite easily demonstrated. Allport proposed as necessary conditions that the groups should have equal status within the contact situation, they should work on common goals, have the support of authorities (institutional support) and finally that they should cooperate with each other. These conditions, together with others discussed below, are referred to as 'contact variables' in the sense that they are hypothesised to account for the extent to which attitude change may take place.

Allport's 'contact hypothesis' has been tested in a number of laboratory and field studies. For example, it has been applied to intergroup situations with Arabs and Jews in Palestine, Catholics and Protestants in Northern Ireland as well as being used during the desegregation of schools in the United States. A review of the literature by Hewstone and Brown (1986) identified four additional factors: these are firstly that participants in the contact have positive expectations and, secondly, that the joint work is successful. Thirdly, there should be a focus on both similarities and differences between members of the groups. Finally, that the members of the conflicting groups who are brought together perceive each other as typical members of the other group, referred to hereafter as the 'outgroup'. However, Pettigrew (1998) warned that there is a danger of creating an open-ended list of conditions, which is ever expandable and thus eludes falsification. He asserted that many writers mistake 'facilitating' conditions as 'essential' conditions. Further, he warned about the 'causal sequence problem'. The basic tenet of the contact hypothesis is that contact reduces prejudice, however, most prejudiced people are likely to avoid contact with the people they dislike. Thus, those who take part in intergroup encounters will usually be those who are least prejudiced and it is therefore difficult to establish that intergroup contact reduces prejudice.

COGNITIVE PROCESSES AND ATTITUDE CHANGE

A limitation of the contact hypothesis is that it does not specify *how* change will occur. While intergroup attitudes are influenced by many factors, including historical, social and political ones, cognitive processes also play a role. Changes in cognitive processes alone will not necessarily improve intergroup relations but an understanding of these processes can increase our comprehension of the factors involved in IPE. These include social categorisation, cognitive dissonance, the role of emotions and insight.

Social categorisation involves the reduction and organisation of the social world into social categories and is a central cognitive process (Tajfel, 1981). It is vital to our functioning in the social world as it enables us to reduce the complexity of information we have to process. We then use the information to predict and guide our behaviour. While categorisation enables us to deal with large amounts of complex information quickly it has the drawback of sometimes leading us to make simplistic inferences. In particular, the mental shortcuts that are essential to our daily lives sometimes cause us to ignore individuality. Thus we tend to see all members of another group as the same, a process known as stereotyping. Stereotypes are generally seen as negative and considered by many to be something to be overcome. However, in the field of social psychology there is recognition that stereotypes play an important cognitive role and stereotypes can frequently be positive as well as negative.

Hewstone and Brown (1986) have outlined the essential aspects of stereotyping. These are firstly, that other individuals are categorised, usually based on some observable characteristic such as gender, race or perhaps professional uniform. A set of attributes is then ascribed to most, if not all, of the members of that category. Everyone who belongs to that category is then assumed to be similar to each other and different from other groups. Thus outgroups (those groups of which we are not members) are generally seen as homogeneous while the ingroup (groups to which we perceive we belong) is seen as more diverse. Stereotypes generate expectations and, as Cooper and Fazio (1979) demonstrated, we tend to 'see' behaviour that confirms our expectations, even when it is absent. Rothbart, Evans and Fulero (1979) further showed that disconfirming evidence tends to be ignored, but confirming evidence is remembered. As Hewstone and Brown (1986) put it, contact situations can easily become self-fulfilling prophecies. This may explain why contact alone is not enough to change intergroup attitudes.

Our need to categorise and the resulting stereotypes and self-fulfilling prophecies show some of the cognitive processes that may prevent attitude change during intergroup encounters, but what factors actually assist attitude change?

Pettigrew (1998) proposed four interrelated processes that mediate attitude change. The first is that contact improves attitudes between groups by providing opportunities to learn about outgroups. This is in line with the view that ignorance promotes prejudice (Stephan & Stephan, 1984). Not surprisingly, Rothbart and John (1985) showed that positive change only occurred when the outgroup's behaviour was not in line with the traditional stereotype (e.g. that the surgeons taking part in IPE revealed themselves to be caring and not at all arrogant) but also that these outgroup members were seen as being typical (of surgeons in general).

The second process is cognitive dissonance (Festinger, 1957). This posits that individuals seek consistency in their cognitions (what we know about ourselves, our behaviour and our surroundings). If we find ourselves holding two cognitions that are inconsistent we experience a state of psychological discomfort (dissonance). Strategies to reduce dissonance include changing one's attitude, opinion or behaviour. They also include searching for consonant information and avoiding dissonant information. Thus, participants in IPE may be required to interact with other (disliked) professionals in a cooperative task and find themselves achieving this successfully and enjoyably. Because this behaviour is inconsistent with their pre-existing negative attitudes about say, nurses, then they may revise their opinion of nurses. New situations, such as IPE, require adapting to new expectations. If this includes accepting the outgroup (other professionals), then this behaviour has the potential to produce attitude change.

The third cognitive process concerns the role emotions play in intergroup encounters. Anxiety is common in such situations, including IPE, and can spark negative reactions (Carpenter & Hewstone, 1996). Conversely, it may be proposed that positive emotions can be facilitated by the development of friendships between participants.

Finally, intergroup contact may provide insight into how others see us, and this may lead to a reappraisal of how we see ourselves. For example, we may not have thought about our own profession as being particularly knowledgeable, but faced by other professionals who clearly think this, we may revise our opinions. Furthermore, perceptions of one's own group, the 'ingroup' are reshaped in this way; this can lead to a less narrow-minded view of the outgroup ('they obviously value what I have to say. Maybe they are not as ignorant as I first thought.')

Generalisation

Generalisation beyond the immediate contact situation is vital if the impact of intergroup contact is to have lasting consequences. Of course, when applied to IPE it is hoped that positive attitude change about other professionals engendered through the programme will extend to other professionals with whom they work. Thus, if a social worker attends IPE with nurses and then changes her attitude about nurses on the programme we hope that this attitude change will extend to other nurses with whom the social worker deals on a daily basis.

Social Identity Theory

There is however no one accepted view of how best to achieve generalisation. Brown (2000) identified three models, all forms of the contact hypothesis and all based upon Social Identity Theory (Tajfel & Turner, 1986). Tajfel and Turner proposed that we derive our identity from our membership of social groups and further that we prefer to have a positive rather than a negative identity. Therefore, it is argued that we will perceive the ingroup more positively than the outgroups. Support for this theory came from studies that showed that mere categorisation was enough to elicit negative, discriminatory intergroup behaviour. In a classic minimalist experiment, Tajfel, Billing, Bundy and Flement (1971) assigned schoolboys to one of two groups on an entirely arbitrary basis and then asked them to allocate money. The participants consistently awarded more money to ingroup members than the outgroup, even if this was to their own absolute disadvantage. This was despite the fact that the groups were essentially meaningless, having no social or political history or even any future. It appeared that simply being assigned to a group, i.e. categorisation alone, had predictable effects on intergroup behaviour. Once historical, economic, political and legal aspects of intergroup relations are taken into consideration it is not surprising that intergroup bias is such a difficult area to address.

So, what is the best way to deal with the negative consequences of group identification? Three models have been suggested: 'decategorisation', 'common ingroup identity' and the 'salient category' model.

The decategorisation model (Brewer & Miller, 1984) proposed that the distinction between groups should be played down during intergroup encounters. In this way categorisations of ingroup and outgroup become psychologically less important. Brewer and Miller suggested various ways of doing this such as personalising the intergroup situation so participants get to know each other as individuals rather than as members of a group. Thus, IPE participants should get to know each other as 'Sarah' or 'Bill' rather than as an occupational therapist or a social worker.

The 'common ingroup identity' model (Gaertner, Dovidio, Anastasio, Bachman & Rust, 1993) proposed instead the creation of a superordinate group identity so that members of previously competing groups would share membership of a new larger category. For example, instead of nurses and social workers perceiving themselves by their professional group a common categorisation of 'mental health workers' could be emphasised during intergroup contact situations. However, this new identity is unlikely to be accepted unless it was more positively valued that the original professional identity. Thus 'psychological therapists' might be more attractive than 'mental health worker', because it suggests higher status.

Both the decategorisation and common ingroup identity models have been criticised for advocating the dissolution of category boundaries and therefore group identities (Brown, 2000). Brown noted that while such a strategy may be successful in a laboratory setting with ad hoc groups of a transitory nature it is psychologically and physically much more difficult to implement with real life groups. It certainly seems that with political, historical and economic factors that are related to the health and social work professions attempts to dissolve group identities may be strongly resisted.

Hewstone and Brown (1986) alternatively proposed that salience is maintained for the original groups and contact conditions are optimised. This model attempts to maximise the *group* nature of the contact as opposed to the *personal* nature. In this way, contact should promote generalisation across members of the target outgroup. Evidence for this comes from Van Oudenhoven, Groenewoud and Hewstone (1986) who found that positive effects of contact are more likely to generalise to the outgroup as a whole when the group membership of a person is made salient. Brown, Vivian and Hewstone (1999) showed that the likelihood of this increases when the person in the contact situation is viewed as typical of the outgroup as a whole, as opposed to atypical.

Brown and Hewstone argued that it is important to protect the distinctiveness of groups involved in contact for two reasons. Firstly, the salience of group boundaries can promote generalisation across members of the outgroup and secondly, each group should be seen as distinct in terms of the expertise and experience it brings to the contact situation. This should result in '*mutual intergroup differentiation*' in which groups recognise and value each others' strengths and weaknesses. This is in line with what Turner (1981) terms comparative interdependence and suggests that in order to achieve superordinate goals groups must cooperate with each other. Thus, there is a need for the differentiation and coordination of intergroup activities into separate but complementary work-roles.

Hewstone and Brown went on to assert that a mutual recognition of superiorities and inferiorities would be reflected in intergroup stereotypes. They hypothesised that after intergroup contact which emphasised mutual intergroup differentiation, each group would view itself positively and hold positive stereotypes of outgroups. The positive stereotypes of the outgroup would be consistent with those groups' own views of their profession (autostereotypes). In summary, this model argues that after successful intergroup contact each group is seen as it wishes to be seen and desired differences between groups are highlighted.

Hewstone, Rubin and Willis (2002) identified two main problems with the salient category model. First, there is an increased risk of prejudice if the contact reinforces perceptions of intergroup differences and increases intergroup anxiety. Second, as Brown and Gardman (2001) have shown, salient intergroup boundaries may be associated with mutual distrust which undermines the potential for co-operative independence and mutual liking. Hewstone and colleagues therefore suggested integrating an intergroup model of contact with a 'personalisation' model. In other words, they proposed that contact should be both highly intergroup and highly interpersonal. Participants in IPE should therefore be aware of the professional group of all members *and* have the opportunity to engage with outgroup members on a personal level.

SUMMARY: CHANGING ATTITUDES IN IPE

The literature reviewed thus far suggests some conditions for changing attitudes in IPE which is perceived as an intergroup encounter. First, there should institutional support for participation; this should be from the people or organisation that the participants feel to be influential. For prequalification students this may be college tutors; for practicing professionals, it may be their colleagues, managers and/or professional bodies. Secondly, participants should have positive expectations. While it is important that similarities between the groups are emphasised, differences should also be explored. The contact situation should emphasise the equality of participants on the programme even if they have different status outside (e.g. doctors and nurses). The learning atmosphere should be cooperative rather than competitive. Additionally, joint work should be successful if intergroup attitudes are to improve.

For positive attitude change to then be generalised from the outgroup members involved in the contact to all outgroup members, the members involved in the contact situation must be perceived as typical. Thus for example, the nurses on a programme should be seen as representative of nurses whom social workers and occupational therapists encounter in their day to day working if they are to change their attitudes of nurses in general. The contact situation must also allow for both intergroup and interpersonal contact so that participants can relate to outgroup members both as individuals and as representatives of their professions.

SOME EVIDENCE

We shall now review some evaluation studies which provide some evidence of the extent to which these ideas might be relevant in IPE.

The Moray House Study

The first study of IPE explicitly to be informed by an intergroup perspective was reported by McMichael and Gilloran, (1984) (summarised in Carpenter & Hewstone, 1996). Having experienced an 'alarming' degree of negative stereotyping at the end of an integrated lecture and seminar programme for community work, social work and education students, they had concluded that bringing students together was 'not enough'. The new programme was designed to preserve the distinctive social identities of participants which, according to Tajfel's theory, were important in their developing self-esteem. Instead of shared lectures, the students participated in mixed study groups which focused on problem solving and teamwork. In these groups, they were encouraged to take the roles of teachers, social workers and community workers, as appropriate. They then discussed simulated case scenarios from the perspectives of their own professional group. Follow-up semi-structured interviews suggested some positive changes in stereotypes, especially amongst teachers. This, they thought, was based on the acquisition of some new information about the roles and tasks of the other groups (as Pettigrew 1998 suggested) and, more importantly, on rewarding face-to-face contact. Unfortunately, there was also strong negative feedback about the methods of teaching and learning employed and about 'persistent truants'. The latter, McMichael and Gilloran, (1984) suggested, were those whom the staff considered most in need of a challenge to their prejudices – an observation which supports Pettigrew's (1998) 'causal sequence problem'.

The Bristol and St. George's/Kingston Studies

Carpenter and Hewstone reported three empirical investigations of attitude change in IPE for social work, medical and nursing students at Bristol University (Hewstone, Carpenter & Franklin-Stokes, 1994; Carpenter 1995a, b; Carpenter & Hewstone, 1996). The programmes, which were compulsory, were designed in the light of the theoretical framework described above in that every effort was made to incorporate the 'contact variables' identified by Hewstone and Brown (1986) into their design. Thus, in the case of the medical students, the Chair of the relevant department was asked to demonstrate institutional support for the programme by attending and speaking at an introductory session at the beginning of the week. The significance and importance of the programme was stressed in terms of future professional practice and positive expectations were encouraged by depicting it as enjoyable and informative. Each group was given some information about the other's educational background and told that all participants were in the final year of their professional training (implying equal status in the programme).

At the introductory session, participants were asked to sign up for the equivalent of two and a half days of shared learning events. Both full and half-day sessions were on offer. The day events involved practice based exercises working with patients/clients, whereas half-day sessions were usually class-room based, often using video case studies. Topics included: alcohol abuse; psychiatric emergencies; AIDS/HIV; depression in young families; deliberate self-harm; drug abuse; and community based services for people with learning disabilities. Each event was led by a doctor and a social worker or nurse partnership. These facilitators were carefully briefed by the programme co-ordinator so that each understood the educational principles on which the programme was based and a detailed structure for the session could be worked out. In all cases the learning objectives were similarly stated:

- to examine similarities and differences in the attitudes and skills of members of the other profession;
- to acquire a knowledge of their respective roles and duties with respect to the topic under consideration;
- to explore methods of working together co-operatively and effectively in the best interests of their patients/clients.

In order to achieve these, and to set the conditions for positive attitude change, each event was carefully structured to provide opportunities for students to undertake successful joint work in a co-operative atmosphere. The students worked together in pairs, for example planning their approach to a case, and also in groups, for example, explaining and discussing their respective roles. Group membership was emphasized throughout: students were asked to discuss or act 'as a doctor/social worker/nurse'. The group leaders were asked to draw attention to differences as well as similarities and to provide positive feedback on ideas presented by the students.

In these programmes, mutual intergroup differentiation was evident: participants were prepared to acknowledge the superiority of the outgroup on some dimensions. For example, Carpenter (1995b) reported that both medical and nursing students demonstrated strong positive and negative stereotypes: nurses were seen, by themselves and the medical students, as caring, dedicated and good communicators whereas the medics were seen as confident by themselves and the nurses. It is worth noting that these stereotypes were already strong despite neither group having at the time commenced their professional careers. This suggests that stereotypes are formed at a very early stage. Hind, Norman and Cooper (2003) and Hean, Clark, Macleod, Adams and Humphris (2006) investigating health and social work undergraduates, and Mandy, Milton and Mandy (2004), with physiotherapy and podiatry students, similarly found that clear and distinct professional stereotypes were present at an early stage of professional development.

At the end of the Bristol programmes, participants reported statistically significant increases in their self-rated understanding of the knowledge and skills, roles and duties of the other profession. Further, there was encouraging evidence of changes in interprofessional stereotypes, with a reduction in the attribution of negative characteristics to the outgroups and an increase in those characteristics which were valued by the outgroup members. For example, at the end of the programme social work students saw medical students as significantly more caring and less detached, while the medics saw the social workers as less dithering and gave them significantly higher ratings for breadth of life experience. These positive results were associated with students' ratings of the design features of the programme, which supported the relevance of the contact hypothesis to interprofessional education. Nevertheless, Carpenter and Hewstone (1996) pointed out that in almost one in five cases attitudes actually worsened, although in most cases they remained positive rather than negative. This highlights Johnson, Johnson and Maruyama's (1984) observation that physical proximity carries a risk of making things worse as well as the possibility of improving intergroup relations.

At St. George's Medical School and Kingston University in London, Tunstall-Peddoe, Rink and Hilton (2003) adopted a very similar theoretical and measurement approach to the evaluation of a 10-week 'common foundation programme' in the first term for medical, allied health and nursing students. However, results were mixed. Instead of a hoped for reduction in negative stereotypes, the researchers found that at the end of the programme negative stereotypes had actually worsened. For example, doctors were viewed as significantly less caring, less dedicated, more arrogant, and less good communicators and team players than at the start. Similarly, nurses were considered less dedicated, more detached, less hard-working, and not such good communicators. There were statistically significant reductions in the proportions of students giving positive ratings about IPE, such as whether or not it enhanced their own learning. Nevertheless, almost all who responded at the end of the programme still believed that IPE would enhance interprofessional working and lead to better patient care.

The St. George's and Kingston team considered that their programme met some, but not all, of the contact conditions (p. 170). In particular, they believed that the programme had institutional support and they felt that there was a cooperative atmosphere. The students worked together in small groups using problem based learning and undertook joint visits to GP surgeries. The researchers believed that the students were beginning to understand about their similarities and differences. Unfortunately, this study did not collect information about the students' opinions of the extent to which the contact variables were evident; it is the students' perceptions rather than the beliefs of the researchers which are relevant.

In the Bristol studies, there was some evidence that nurses, who were all women, were more inclined to operate on an interpersonal rather than an intergroup model of contact (Carpenter, 1995a). Thus, they were more likely to emphasise similarities than doctors and to see the medics as individuals rather than as typical members of a group. As one nursing student recommended when asked to consider how doctors and nurse might cooperate more effectively:

> "Try to forget stereotypes and see each doctor/nurse as an individual. We don't just communicate with a "doctor" or a "nurse". There is a human being underneath the uniform!" (Carpenter, 1995a).

The Bristol programmes were short (between one day and one week), involved students rather than qualified and experienced professionals, and the outcomes were not followed up into practice. In other words, changes in attitudes may have been insubstantial and transitory. As we have noted, Rothbart and John (1985) considered perceived typicality of the outgroup members to be a necessary component of generalisation. In the Bristol studies, the evidence was mixed. For example, medical students did tend to see the nurses as typical, but only slightly so; this was not surprising however considering that the nurses were on degree programmes and not, at that time, typical of their profession at least educationally.

The Birmingham Study

A later evaluation study at Birmingham University, directed by Carpenter, employed the same contact hypothesis framework and research methods as in the Bristol studies to investigate stereotypes and stereotype change in a much longer (two-year, part time) programme of IPE for experienced community mental health professionals (Barnes, Carpenter & Dickinson, 2000). There was considerable evidence of professional stereotyping. In general, the nurses, occupational therapists, social workers and others (voluntary sector workers, non-professionally aligned workers, psychiatrists and psychologists) on the programme were reasonably positive about each other, giving themselves and each other moderately high ratings for interpersonal skills, professional competence, and life experience. However, psychiatrists and psychologists, who were barely represented on the course, received lower ratings for practical skills and life experience, and were thought to be poor team players. There was some evidence to support the hypothesis of mutual intergroup identification. For example, social workers, nurses and occupational therapists were willing to concede superiority on leadership and academic rigour to the psychiatrists and psychologists, but saw themselves as clearly superior in terms of communication, interpersonal and practical skills.

There was little evidence of change in these stereotypes. Positive stereotypes were not strengthened appreciably, nor were negative stereotypes reduced. Having examined possible reasons, Barnes and colleagues concluded first, that the students tended not to see fellow course members as 'typical' members of the other mental health professions and therefore did not generalise their positive experiences of fellow students to their professions as a whole. In particular, students considered that the main differences between themselves and their colleagues who did not elect to join the programme were their open mindedness and willingness to change. It should also be noted that because there were so few psychiatrists and psychologists on the programme, there was little opportunity for students' negative stereotypes to be disconfirmed. When the same measures of stereotypes were used with a sample of colleagues who were members of their home community mental health teams, but who were not attending the programme, the authors found that, compared to course participants, team colleagues gave significantly more favourable ratings to psychiatrists and psychologists on a number of dimensions. One explanation could be that the contexts in which the ratings were made were different: those on the course might have been thinking about psychiatrists and psychologists in general, whereas their team colleagues might have been thinking about the psychiatrists and psychologists in their teams. This explanation draws on an interpersonal perspective. An alternative, intergroup perspective would suggest that the programme participants were actually an atypical group, whose members also saw themselves as different from those who did not attend the programme. Even at the beginning of the programme, participants scored significantly higher for 'role conflict' than team colleagues. Barnes et al. (2000) also noted that there was evidence of participants negatively stereotyping those who did not come on the programme and how they claimed a positively valued distinctiveness for the programme group. In group interviews, participants suggested that they and their fellow participants were open minded and willing to change, in implied contrast to narrow minded and conservative colleagues who did not come on the course.

Second, there was evidence that students did not perceive the programme as providing the conditions for positive attitude change required by the contact hypothesis. (These perceptions were assessed, as in previous work, by a series of Likert-type scales, see Hewstone et al., 1994). These ratings suggested that many of the conditions had only been met to a moderate extent. In particular, the requirement to explore differences as well as to emphasise similarities was not met. This was confirmed by participant observation of the teaching sessions (Barnes et al., 2000). Another point to consider is that the programme was part-time, with students returning to their workplaces for the rest of the week; here their pre-existing stereotypes might be reinforced.

SOME LESSONS

What do these evaluation studies tell us? We suggest:

1. That professional stereotypes, both positive and negative, are readily elicited from health and social work students and professionals, and also that there is a possibly a general consensus as to what these are.
2. There is some evidence that these stereotypes can be changed, at least in the short term, and with prequalification students. (Although we must caution that these evaluations did not have a control or comparison group.)
3. These changes seem to be associated with the meeting of certain conditions prescribed by Hewstone and Brown's elaboration of the contact hypothesis. However, with Pettigrew's (1998) caution in mind, we cannot say which of these conditions are 'essential' and which are 'facilitative'. These could only be established through a series of experimental studies in which the variables were manipulated.
4. In the relative absence of these conditions, attitude change *may* not take place or be generalised to the workplace. The perceived typicality of course participants seems to be quite important.
5. An appropriate range of students or professionals should be involved in IPE: this is probably the full set of professionals involved in the provision of a service (e.g. all members of a primary care team).

We consider that there is sufficient evidence concerning the relevance of the contact hypothesis to advise educators that they should take account of the contact variables in the design and evaluation of IPE. Thus, we suggest, following Hean and Dickinson (2005, p. 484) that it would be valuable to consider the following:

1. How can you ensure that participants in the programme have equal status? This may be easier to achieve in pre-qualifying IPE, but status also derives from the number of years you have spent at the university and from the specific subject knowledge (expertise) you have attained.
2. Can you develop small group exercises or tasks on practice placement in which participants see common goals and agree on their importance?
3. Is institutional support for the programme obvious to the students? They are likely to be convinced by such factors as the involvement of high status staff, good quality

teaching facilities and prominent place in the curriculum. Formal assessment of learning is also an important indicator.

4. How can positive expectations be engendered? This might involve talking to student representatives, recruiting 'ambassadors' who have previously experienced the programme and preparing good promotional material.

5. Generalisation will be encouraged if participants are asked to take on the role of their professional discipline in IPE workshops. This is not a problem for qualified professionals, but can be difficult for first year students who may not know enough to do this convincingly. Rather than push them into a situation in which they feel uncomfortable and possibly resistant, it may be better to de-emphasise this aspect.

6. An important additional consideration is to ensure, as far as possible, balanced numbers of participants. A solo representative of a profession may feel outnumbered and oppressed by the majority, particularly if this person also feels disadvantaged by gender and ethnicity.

Whether or not the objectives of an IPE programme are explicitly to tackle interprofessional stereotyping and promote attitude change, we believe it is crucial to recognise and plan how to deal with the intergroup aspects of the encounter. Of course these are not the only elements to consider in designing effective IPE; for a recent review of theory, practice and evidence see Carpenter and Dickinson (2008).

CONCLUSION

It is evident that there are many gaps in our understanding of stereotype change through IPE. In addition to knowing more about essential and facilitative contact variables, it would be very helpful to understand how attitude change occurs in IPE encounters. The latter might be explored through hypothesis-testing qualitative research (Silverman, 2000, Ch. 6) into the participants' understanding of the processes involved. Nevertheless, we consider that there is sufficient evidence to argue that the design of IPE programmes should be informed by the theoretical considerations set out in this chapter. Specifically, we consider that educators should pay explicit attention to designing IPE to incorporate those additional variables which boost the chances of the planned contact having a positive effect on attitude change. Contact, in other words, is "not enough".

REFERENCES

Allport, G. W. (1954). *The Nature of Prejudice*. Reading, MA: Addison-Wesley.

Barnes, D., Carpenter, J., & Dickinson, C. (2000). Interprofessional education for community mental health: attitudes to community care and professional stereotypes. *Social Work Education*, 19, 565-583.

Barr, H., Freeth, D., Hammick, M., et al., (1999). *Evaluating Interprofessional Education: A United Kingdom Review for Health and Social Care*. London: BERA/CAIPE.

Brewer, M. B., & Miler, N. (1984). Beyond the contact hypothesis: Theoretical perspectives on desegregation. In N. Miller & M.B. Brewer (Eds.), *Groups in contact: The psychology of desegregation*. Florida: Academic Press.

Brown, R. (2000). Social Identity Theory: Past achievements, current problems and future challenges. *European Journal of Social Psychology*, 30, 745-778.

Brown, R., & Gardman, K. (2001). Social Identity Theory: Past achievements, current problems and future challenges. *European Journal of Social Psychology*, 30, 745-778.

Brown, R., Vivian, J., & Hewstone, M. (1999). Changing attitudes through intergroup contact: the effects of group membership salience. *European Journal of Social Psychology*, 29, 741-764.

Carpenter, J. (1995a). Doctors and nurses: stereotypes and stereotype change in interprofessional education. *Journal of Interprofessional Care*, 9, 151-161.

Carpenter, J. (1995b). Interprofessional education for medical and nursing students: evaluation of a programme. *Medical Education*, 29, 265-275.

Carpenter, J., & Hewstone, M. (1996). Shared learning for doctors and social workers: evaluation of a programme. *British Journal of Social Work*, 26, 239-257.

Carpenter, J., & Dickinson, H. (2008). *Interprofessional Education and Training*. Bristol: Policy Press.

Cooper, J., & Fazio, R. H. (1979). The formation and persistence of attitudes that support intergroup conflict. In W.G. Austin & S. Worchel (Eds.), *The Social Psychology of Intergroup Relations*. Monterey: Brooks/Cole.

Festinger, L. (1957). *A theory of cognitive dissonance*. Evangston, IL: Row, Peterson.

Gaertner, S., Dovidio, J., Anastasio, A., Bachman, B., & Rust, M. (1993). The common ingroup identity model: Recategorisation and the reduction of intergroup bias. In W. Stroebe & M. Hewstone (Eds.), *European Review of Social Psychology*. Chichester: Wiley.

Hean, S., Clark, J., Macleod, J., Adams, K., & Humphris, D. (2006). Will opposites attract? Similarities and differences in students' perceptions of the stereotype profiles of other health and social care professional groups. *Journal of Interprofessional Care*, 20, 162-181.

Hean, S., & Dickinson, C. (2005). The Contact Hypothesis: an exploration of its further potential in interprofessional education. *Journal of Interprofessional Care*, 19, 480-491.

Hewstone, M., & Brown, R. J. (1986). Contact is not enough; an intergroup perspective on the 'contact hypothesis'. In M. Hewstone & R.J. Brown (Eds.), *Contact and Conflict in Intergroup Encounters*. Oxford: Blackwell.

Hewstone, M., Carpenter, J., Franklyn-Stokes, A., et al., (1994). Intergroup contact between professional groups: two evaluation studies. *Journal of Community and Applied Social Psychology*, 4, 347-363.

Hewstone, M., Rubin, M., & Willis, H. (2002). Intergroup Bias. *Annual Review of Psychology*, 53, 575-604.

Hind, M., Norman, I., Cooper, S., Gill, E., Hiton, R. Judd, P., & Jones, S. (2003). Interprofessional perceptions of health care students. *Journal of Interprofessional Care*, 17, 21-34.

Johnson, D. W., Johnson, R. T., & Maruyama, G. (1984). Goal interdependence and interpersonal-personal attraction in heterogeneous classrooms: a meta analysis. In N.

Miller & M.B. Brewer (Eds.), *Groups in Contact: The Psychology of Desegregation* . New York: Academic Press.

McMichael, P., & Gilloran, A. (1983). *Exchanging Views: Courses in Collaboration.* Edinburgh: Moray House College of Education.

Pettigrew, T. F. (1998). Intergroup contact theory. *Annual Review of Psychology*, 49, 65-85.

Rothbart, M., Evans, M., & Fulero, S. (1979). Recall for confirming events: memory process and the maintence of social stereotypes. *Journal of Experiemental Social Psychology*, 15, 343-355.

Rothbart, M., & John, O. P. (1985). Social cognition and behavioural episodes: A cognitive analysis of the effects of intergroup contact. *Journal of Social Issues*, 41, 81-104.

Silverman, D. (2000). *Doing Qualitative Research: A Practical Handbook.* London: Sage.

Stephan, W. G., & Stephan, C. W. (1984). The role of ignorance in intergroup relations. In N. Miller & M.B. Brewer (Eds.), *Groups in Contact* . New York: Academic Press.

Tajfel, H. (1981). *Human Groups and Social Categories.* Cambridge: Cambridge University Press.

Tajfel, H., Billig, M. G., Bundy, R. P., & Flament, C. (1971). Social categorisation and intergroup behaviour. *European journal of Social Psychology*, 1, 149-178.

Tajfel, H., & Turner, J. C. (1986). The social identity theory of intergroup behaviour. In S. Worschel & W. Austin (Eds.), *Psychology of Intergroup Relations*. Chicago: Nelson-Hall.

Tajfel, H. & Turner, J. C. (1986). The social identity theory of intergroup behaviour. In S. Worschel & W. Austin (Eds.), *Psychology of Intergroup Relations*. Chicago: Nelson-Hall.

Turner, J. C. (1981). The experimental social psychology of intergroup behaviour. In J.C. Turner & H. Giles (Eds.), *Intergroup Behaviour*. Oxford: Blackwell.

Van Oudenhouven, J. P., Groenewoud, J. T., & Hewstone, M. (1986). Co-operation, ethnic salience and generalisation of inter-ethnic attitudes. *European Journal of Social Psychology*, 26, 649-662.

In: Sociology of Interprofessional Health …
Ed: S. Kitto, J. Chesters et al.

ISBN: 978-1-60876-866-0
© 2011 Nova Science Publishers, Inc.

Chapter 6

PROFESSIONAL SOCIALISATION AND INTERPROFESSIONAL EDUCATION

Dennis Sharpe and Vernon Curran

ABSTRACT

The development of an identity and pattern of practice in the health care professions has traditionally been based on a process of socialisation into the roles and norms of a particular discipline. Professional socialisation is the acquisition of the knowledge, skills, values, roles, and attitudes associated with the practice of a particular profession. It can be thought of as self-concept, identity formation or the development of a professional world-view.

Different professions have different cultures that have developed unique ways of thinking and acting. These ways of thinking and behaving are founded on prevailing assumptions about appropriate epistemological, behavioural and normative bases of action. The educational experiences of health care students shape their identities, values and norms of practice. Professional values are internalized via education and professional socialisation. In most health professional education programs, the value system is assumed rather than explored, inculcated rather than examined. Students quickly learn that the process of professional acculturation is important to success in their studies.

Interprofessional education (IPE) involves learning with, from and about other health professions to enhance collaboration and the quality of patient care (CAIPE, 2009). Learning to become a member of an interprofessional team is an experiential process and interactive approaches to learning are a recommended approach to facilitating interprofessional learning. Adult learning theory and principles of adult learning have important implications for the design and facilitation of interprofessional learning. Constructivist and collaborative learning theories also have important implications for interprofessional learning methodology. This chapter will discuss the significance of these theories and principles for facilitating interprofessional learning which fosters and promotes collaborative interprofessional socialisation.

INTRODUCTION – THE NEED FOR COLLABORATION

Health care systems have become very complex over the past number of decades, largely because of the rapid progress of medical science and the accompanying emergence of medical and health care specialists from multiple disciplines (Drinka, 1996; Drinka & Clark, 2000; Barr, Koppel & Reeves, 2005). Comprehensive health care today requires the broad spectrum of knowledge that no one practitioner can provide (Fagin, 1992). No one individual can possess all the expertise necessary for the care of patients and families in the highly technical and specialized health care field.

Collaboration has been widely viewed as one of the primary vehicles through which health care organisations can meet the extraordinary challenges they face in today's environment (Liedtka & Whitten, 1998; Barr et al., 2005; Freeth, Hammick & Reeves, 2005). Interprofessional teamwork has been proposed as a method for providing an organized and unified framework for both health care delivery and for the work of health care professionals (Lowe & Herranen, 1981; Barr et al., 2005; Freeth et al., 2005). A health care team is defined by the World Health Organization (WHO) as:

> "A group who share a common health goal and common objectives, determined by community needs, to the achievement of which each member of the team contributes, in accordance with his or her competence and skill and in coordination with the functions of others" (WHO, 1984 cited in Engel, p. 65).

According to Drinka (1996) an interprofessional health care team is a group of health professionals from different disciplines who engage in planned, interdependent collaboration. An effective interprofessional health care team is one with competence, mutual trust, shared goals, defined roles, methods for resolving conflict, active listening, and a free exchange of ideas with clear communication between team members (Drinka, 1996; Freeth et al., 2005). The most important aspect of teamwork is that members must work together in a coordinated manner to address the problem(s) at hand (Tsukuda, 1990; Barr et al., 2005).

Liedtka and Whitten (1998) define collaboration as a process of joint decision making among interdependent parties involving joint ownership of decisions and collective responsibility for outcomes. Teamwork is a special form of interactional interdependence between health care providers, who merge different but complementary skills or viewpoints in the service of patients and in the solution of their health problems (Tsukuda, 1990). A team is a group with a specific task or tasks, the accomplishment of which requires the interdependent and collaborative efforts of its members. According to Tsukuda (1990) this is based on several assumptions:

- The problem is big and/or complex enough to require more than one set of skills or knowledge;
- The amount of relevant knowledge or skills is so great that one person cannot possess them all;
- Assembling a group or team of professionals with more than one set of knowledge or skills will enhance the solution of the problem;
- In the solution of such a problem, the possessors of the relevant skills or knowledge are considered to be equal or equally important;

- All of the involved professionals are working for a common goal for which they are willing to sacrifice some professional scrutiny.

At a practical level, team members may collaborate or relate to a patient and to each other in a variety of ways. They may be involved in shared visits, in which the team members see a patient together, or in alternating or sequential visits, in which each health professional sees a patient independently and meets with other team members at regular intervals. Team members may also refer patients to each other for special diagnostic or therapeutic procedures with the expectation that they will be kept informed and re-involved when necessary (Tsukuda, 1990).

OUTCOMES OF ENHANCED COLLABORATION

Collaboration is believed to enhance the satisfaction that health care providers receive from their work (Liedtka & Whitten, 1998; Barr et al., 2005; Freeth et al., 2005). Other reported outcomes may include improvements in diagnostic turnarounds, decreased nursing turnover, shortened length of stay, reduced cost per case, and increased patient satisfaction (Liedtka & Whitten, 1998). Hill (1998) reports that when team members work in collaboration, the service offered is more comprehensive than one that relies on individual contributions. An interprofessional team harnesses the skills required for the task and combines them in a unique way. This has a number of advantages: an increased range of services; the workload is easier to manage; collegial support; cross-fertilization of ideas; a more holistic approach (Hill, 1998).

According to Makaram (1995) nurses, physicians and other health professionals have identified a range of outcomes from collaborative practice, including:

- Improved understanding of collaboration;
- Enhanced mutual trust and respect;
- Increased job satisfaction among health professionals;
- Working with colleagues who value, foster and are committed to collaboration;
- Increased productivity, increased effectiveness of interventions;
- Optimal patient care.

According to Tsukuda (1990) the advantages of teamwork include a greater access to other health professions and services, availability of a greater range of knowledge, skills and services and a greater efficiency through coordination and integration of services. The advantages to a patient can include availability of a greater range of knowledge, skills and services, better coordination of care and services, greater convenience and more opportunity for preventive and educational interventions.

BARRIERS TO INTERPROFESSIONAL COLLABORATION

Sources of conflict within interprofessional health care teams can be the result of ignorance of the conceptual basis for practice of other professions; poor communication among members of different professions; chauvinistic attitudes; distrust; and lack of confidence in other disciplines (Mariano, 1989; Barr et al., 2005; Freeth et al., 2005). Autonomous and specialized professional training and socialisation also lead many professionals to believe that their profession is 'sovereign'. Few professionals are knowledgeable about the scope of practice, expertise, responsibilities, and competencies of the other professions. Collaboration, that is, a relationship of interdependence, requires the recognition of complementary roles (Makaram, 1995) and a respect for each discipline's scope of knowledge and uniqueness of functions.

Learning about other professions is an important first step in collaboration. Many professionals are remarkably ignorant of the other health professions due to a lack of collaboration during their respective education. In the course of their training, health care students have a tendency to become socialized only into their own professions and may subsequently develop negative biases and naive perceptions of the roles of other health care professions. To practice effectively in an interprofessional manner, however, one must have a clear understanding of other members' contributions, their educational backgrounds, areas of high achievement, and their limitations.

From a clear understanding of others comes the basis for respect which underlies all successful collaborative endeavors. The need to establish the trust and respect of other team members derives from a central feature of collaboration: no individual is responsible for all aspects of the patient's care, and therefore each member must have confidence that other team members are capable of fulfilling their responsibilities.

VALUE DIFFERENCES

Conflict within teams is influenced by the values that team members hold (Hill, 1998). The development of a truly interdisciplinary team requires recognition of the importance of knowledge and value-related dimensions of professional practice. Values in particular are a major source of conflicting and competing communication patterns among health processionals who are educated and trained in very different models and methods of practice (Clark, 1995). Conflict among physicians, nurses and administrators has been linked to the differing values, work styles, and even personality traits seen as characterizing the different professional groups (Liedtka & Whitten, 1998).

PROFESSIONAL SOCIALISATION

According to Clark (1997) the development of an identity and pattern of practice in the health care professions is based on a process of socialisation into the roles and norms of a particular discipline. The educational experiences of health care students shape their identities, values and norms of practice in ways that may either enhance or inhibit effective communication and collaboration.

Professional socialisation is the acquisition of the knowledge, skills, values, roles, and attitudes associated with the practice of a particular profession. The acquisition of unique patterns of language, modes of dress, demeanor, and norms of behaviour are all manifestations of professional socialisation. Clark (1997) views socialisation as a developmental process which is based on a continual interaction between the person being socialized and his/her environment. It can be thought of as self-concept or identity formation and can also be viewed as the development of a unique voice, perspective, or personal and professional world-view.

Different professions have different cultures that have developed unique ways of thinking and acting. These ways of thinking and behaving are founded on prevailing assumptions about appropriate epistemological, behavioural and normative bases of action. It is critical that professionals gain insights into how knowledge is generated, used and shared in professional practice. They must be able to understand equally well the value maps of other professions (Clark, 1995) and be able to appreciate and respect the values represented by interprofessional collaboration. It is essential that professionals learn to recognize and appreciate that each has a different voice - a perspective or way of "being in the clinical world" that is equally valid and valued (Clark, 1997).

Studies have shown that teaching staff and training ward staff do not present learners with a uniform approach to their professional socialisation. Wilson and Startup (1991) conducted a study to observe the influence of teaching staff and ward staff upon nursing students' belief systems. Teaching staff, together with those in authority on a ward, play a fundamental role in shaping the student's existence. The new student nurse does not experience an integrated professional socialisation process. Faculty present the student with conflicting and divergent views and influences. Interactions with faculty, other students, and patients all influence the emergent nature of the practitioner's identity. As the professional enters practice, socialisation does not stop but continues.

PROFESSIONAL VALUE SYSTEMS

Clark (1994) argues that values define and guide the practice of health care professionals. Glen (1999) views values as the preferred events that people seek; an enduring belief that a certain behaviour or a certain condition of life is desirable. A value system is the rank ordering of values in terms of their importance with respect to one another. Values give our personal, professional and collective lives structure, direction and meaning.

Values represent what a person considers to be important in life and serve as standards by which we determine if a particular thing (object, idea, policy for example.) is good or bad, desirable or undesirable, worthy or unworthy, or someplace in between these extremes. Values constitute those ideas, ideals or beliefs by which individuals (or groups) will guide their behaviour. Values are expressed as behaviours or as the verbalized standards of conduct that a person endorses or tries to maintain. Carl Rogers (1969, cited in Glen, 1999) has defined values by distinguishing among three uses of the term:

1. 'Operative values' are employed when one makes a preferred choice for one kind of object over another;
2. 'Conceived values' are the preferences one shows for a symbolized object, ideal, or goal;
3. 'Objective values' are what is objectively preferable, 'whether or not it is in fact sensed or conceived of as desirable.'

The very fact that there are different professions suggests that there are fundamentally different ways of approaching individual problems. Values are influenced through patterns of professional acculturation.

Clark (1994) states the physician is trained to perform diagnoses by narrowing down the range of possibilities until only one problem remains. In this process, 'objective' data such as laboratory reports are extremely important. The basis of physician education can be viewed as an unequal struggle between two different value systems: one more reductionistic and scientific; the other more social-ecological and humanistic. The reductionistic/scientific system is based on a rational solution of medical problems, disinterested concern for patient and society, and dedication to competency in practice and the community of science. For Clark (1997) this orientation discounts the social, behavioural, and personal dimensions of illness. He argues that it relegates familial and social dimensions of practice to the periphery; and dismisses ethical issues as simply 'matters of opinion' not subject to rational discourse. The more humanistic perspective considers the social and behavioural approaches to be as relevant as the biological. This approach emphasizes caring as much as curing, and considers the community as the proper place for medical education.

The value systems of nurses are characterized by a deep concern for human dignity. Nurses develop an identity that is based on understanding patients as people who need to be cared about, rather than simply cared for (Clark, 1997). An integral part of nursing practice is the incorporation of an ethic of caring that places patients at the very centre of what nursing is all 'about.' The lived world, the life story, and the goals of the patient become the experience of caring for and about the patient. Nursing education instills a more holistic approach to the patient, an approach which is less reductionistic and more humanistic in its orientation than the medical model (Clark, 1997).

Social workers are taught the importance of dealing with feelings and relationships. Social work education emphasizes the development of self-awareness and conscious use of the self in transactions with others (Clark, 1997). Social workers are trained to broaden the basis for clinical discussion; to 'rule in' dimensions of problems that may be initially overlooked in assessments (e.g., the psychosocial and economic dimensions of illness). Social workers have traditionally emphasized the rights of their clients to self-determination. Reisch (1995, cited in Netting & Williams, 1996) believes that there are four characteristics of social work which distinguish it from other professions:

1. Its focus on the environment as a critical factor in creating and solving individual and social problems;
2. Its acknowledgment of the importance of history in shaping the lives of people and communities;
3. Its respect for people, their strengths, customs, traditions, and problem-solving capabilities;

4.   Its belief in both the inevitability and the desirability of change.

Values also influence the professional-client/patient service encounter. In traditional medicine, the physician is perceived as very dominant vis-a-vis the patient, who must rely on the doctor's clinical judgment, technical knowledge and skill. Values influence the interactions between members on the interdisciplinary team as well. These value differences can often lead to conflict among team members.

The value of individualism explains the mode of practice based on uniprofessional tenets. Professionals trained in uniprofessional settings assume that their way of framing the problems and solutions for the client are the best. This professional individualism is embodied in the 'cognitive map' of a profession; its overall "paradigmatic and conceptual apparatus," including its basic concepts, observational approaches, problem definitions, and explanatory structures (Clark, 1994). In the process of becoming a team, participants master the cognitive maps of the other members of the group in such a way that they are able to take these alternative views of constructing reality into account when making their own contributions to the interprofessional team (Clark, 1994). Until participants become conversant in the cognitive maps of the other members, so that they are able to modify their own contributions to the team effort in light of these other perspective, they will not be a true interprofessional team.

PROFESSIONAL VALUES AND SOCIALISATION

Most literature (e.g. Drinka & Clark, 2000; D'mour, Ferrad-Videla, Rodriguez & Beaulieu, 2005; Hall, 2005; San Martin-Rodriquez et al., 2005) on interprofessional teams subscribes to three underlying factors:

1.   Team members have a shared understanding of roles, norms, and values within the team;
2.   Team functions in an egalitarian, cooperative, interdependent manner;
3.   The combined effects of shared, cooperative decision-making are of greater benefit to the patient than the individual effects of the disciplines on their own.

There is also literature which suggests that staff have different perceptions of teamwork depending on their professional affiliation (Curran, Sharpe & Forristall, 2007). These different perceptions are believed to exist because each member of the team comes with a different set of values about teamwork based on their professional socialisation, personal experiences and beliefs. Accordingly, effective interprofessional collaboration depends upon establishing an understanding of teamwork that respects differences in values and beliefs.

Cott (1998) conducted a study to examine the relationship between structure and meaning in long-term multidisciplinary teams. According to this author the meaning of teamwork refers to the interpretations or perceptions of individual team members as to the effect of being part of a team for themselves and their work. In the study, Cott (1998) found that if the structure of the team does not reflect the ideology of egalitarian, cooperative teamwork, it can promote alienation from teamwork.

Supporters of a collaborative learning approach emphasize the central importance of community versus individualism (Clark, 1994). In a collaborative learning approach, knowledge is created as a result of collaborative interchange. IPE is intrinsically, a collaborative-experiential learning activity, in which the insights and skills acquired through the process constitute the learning. Over time students acquire different sets of values regarding the team experience. These values relate to the recognition of the power of the team approach, as well as to the interrelationships among the value systems represented by the various professions on the team. Ideally, students come to understand the various value paradigms of the different health professions, the value of their contributions to the interdisciplinary team, and learn to reflect on their own values in light of a team approach to patient care.

PROFESSIONAL VALUES EDUCATION

Education can provide a mechanism for exploring and discussing interprofessional values (Barr et al., 2005; Freeth et al., 2005). It is critical that health professional educators embrace interprofessional approaches to individual and social values. In order to do this, health professional educators need to be clear about their own values and aware of the values of other groups. According to Clark (1994) educators must be more aware of the ways in which academic value systems influence the way students perceive opportunities for collaboration and teamwork. Such value orientations have a significant influence on attitudes towards the dynamics of team functioning and expectations of how team members work with each other and clients. It is important that health professional educators challenge the institutional barriers which inhibit collaborative models of learning.

It is believed that professional values are internalized via education and professional socialisation (e.g. Hall, 2005). In most health professional education programs, the value system is assumed rather than explored, inculcated rather than examined. According to Glen (1999) this may be an effective way to indoctrinate students, but may prove detrimental later in their professions when their values are called into question. Students quickly learn that the process of professional acculturation is important to their doing well in their studies. Teaching and learning experiences often reinforce the solitary nature of learning, with few courses emphasizing the importance of teamwork or working in small groups.

Health care students need to be aware of the meaning of values and the variety of systems within which values are expressed. Glen (1999) believes that professional values education is a necessity. Professional values education can be defined as the systematic effort to help students identify and develop their own professional values. It suggests providing health care students with the abilities, skills or strategies for clarifying values and making value judgements.

Clark (1994) proposes a stepwise, incremental process for collaborative team-based learning which should be introduced into the basic curriculum for each discipline in the health field. Within this model, collaborative interprofessional modules or experiences would be designed to fit students' emerging awareness of their own and other disciplines. This gradual approach is meant to fit with the student's gradual development of their own professional identity. However, such an educational approach must also ensure students are not overcome by their own professional identification, making them inflexible and closed to collaboration.

Glen (1999) proposes a conceptual framework for teaching values to health care students. The elements of the framework are tolerance, compromise and education for dialogue. See Box

Box 1. Glen's (1999) framework for teaching values

Tolerance
This principle is based on the idea of a tolerant society, one involving respect for individuals, their wishes and their freedoms. In such a society there is minimal interference by one person or group with the belief statements or conduct of another. There is a tolerance for persons who have different world-views.

Compromise
This principle is based on an attempt to balance the different considerations against each other, and take whatever course seems to allow due weight to them all.

Education for dialogue
According to Plato (cited in Glen, 1999) only in "the discourse of reason" can fundamental assumptions be uncovered and questioned. Plato's method of rational discourse is based on open, critical dialogue. Dialogue is based on the principle of otherness: otherness of the persons spoken to, other points of view, and other positions. It requires the examination of more than one viewpoint. There must be opportunities for different professionals to bring disciplinary and professional perspective to interprofessional groups.

EDUCATIONAL THEORY

Learning to become a member of an interprofessional team is an experiential process (Clark, 1991) and interactive approaches to learning (Oandasan & Reeves, 2005a; Oandasan & Reeves, 2005b; Parsell, Spalding & Bligh, 1998; Parsell & Bligh, 1999) are a recommended approach to IPE. These approaches should draw upon real-life clinical problems to stimulate interprofessional problem-solving and should incorporate small group, experiential methods of learning. Adult learning theory and principles of adult learning (see Table 1) are important in informing the design and teaching strategies of IPE. Among the key principles are the importance of creating non-threatening learning environments and providing opportunities for learners to develop skills as reflective collaborative practitioners. The use of journals and small group discussion activities are suggested as possible means for fostering the skills of reflective practice.

Table 1. Principles of Adult Learning (Merriam, Cafarella and Baumgartner, 2007)

Principle 1	Adult education requires a climate of respect, that is, an environment which affords students a physical and social climate conducive to learning.
Principle 2	A collaborative mode of learning is central to adult education, that is, the involvement of participants, facilitators, and administrators in the design, implementation, and evaluation of the learning experience.
Principle 3	Adult education fosters critically reflective thinking, that is, learning which involves the examination and questioning of information, values, beliefs and experiences.
Principle 4	Problem posing and problem solving are fundamental aspects of adult education, that is, learning which involves examination of issues and concerns, transforms content into problem situations, and necessitates analysis and development of solutions.
Principle 5	Adult education is best facilitated in a participative environment, that is, a learning climate that encourages and facilitates the active interchange of ideas, content and experience, and the active involvement of each participant.

FACILITATING INTERPROFESSIONAL EDUCATION

There are a number of factors to consider when facilitating IPE, which are considered below.

CONSTRUCTIVIST CURRICULA

Constructivist and collaborative learning theories have important implications for the design of IPE, particularly for those educational strategies which focus upon small group learning strategies. The foundations of constructivism are based, in part, on principles emerging from a number of different theoretical stances. The first is the situated learning paradigm. This approach assumes that most learning is context-dependent, that is what we learn (the meaning that is constructed by the learner) is indexed by the experiences surrounding the learner—which assigns meaning to what is learned. Situated learning and social construction theorists also believe that learning is necessarily a social, dialogical process in which communities of learners socially negotiate the meaning of phenomena. In other words, learning is conversation and is dependant on dialogue with others.

'Meaning making' according to constructivists is the goal of learning processes; it requires, articulation and reflection on what we know. The processes of articulation and reflection involves both internal negotiation and social negotiation. Meaning is the understanding that we derive from these processes; it is a reflective form of knowledge. The application of that meaning in real-world practice is what has been referred to as experiential knowledge.

Constructivists believe that our personal world is constructed in our minds and that these constructions define our personal realities. The mind filters input from the world in the process of making interpretations. The important epistemological assumption of constructivism is that knowledge is a function of how the individual creates meaning from his or her experiences. Each of us conceives of external reality somewhat differently, based upon our unique set of experiences with the world and our beliefs about them.

The constructivist sense of 'active' learning is not listening and then mirroring the correct view of reality, but rather participating in and interacting with the surrounding environment in order to create a personal view of the world. Constructivist educators engage learners through interactive and applied learning activities so that the knowledge they construct is not inert, but rather usable in new and different situations. As a result, it is important to situate learning in the real-world and in authentic learning tasks. Learning that is authentic and situated in the process of solving real-world problems is much richer and better understood.

Constructivist principles in curricula design help educators to create learner-centred, collaborative environments that support reflective and experiential processes. The role of the educator shifts from creating 'prescriptive' learning situations to developing environments that engage learners and require them to construct the knowledge that is most meaningful to them. The key principles which guide the design of those learning environments include:

- *Context:* features of the real world setting in which the task to be learned might naturally be accomplished;
- *Construction:* of knowledge is the result of an active process of articulation and reflection within a context, the knowledge that is created is a product of the mind and results from the individual's experiences with and interpretations of the context;
- *Collaboration:* among learners occurs throughout the learning process—through the process of articulating, learners are able to build new and modify existing knowledge structures; and
- *Conversation:* is entailed by collaboration—conversation is an essential part of the meaning-making process because knowledge, for most of us, is language mediated (Jonassen, Mayers & McAleese, 1993).

Constructivist environments engage learners in knowledge construction, through collaborative activities, that embed learning in a meaningful context, and through reflection on what has been learned, through conversation with other learners.

COLLABORATIVE LEARNING EXPERIENCES

An overarching goal of constructivist learning environments is to encourage manipulation rather than simple acquisition of learning, and to root the learning in concrete experience. Learning in this way frequently involves interaction with other learners. Glaser (1990, cited in Jonassen et al., 1993) argues that cognitive development occurs through the processing of concepts that are originally experienced in social contexts, and that while meaning may be an individual construct, shared understandings result from social negotiations of meaning.

Constructivist processes are considered to be more evident when learners collaborate to produce and share representations of their understandings of the world (Jonassen, et al., 1993). Collaborative learning processes encourage knowledge construction in an environment in which learners share their own understanding in an attempt to negotiate a shared understanding. They become aware of the existence of multiple points of view and in this way, learn from their peers (Jonassen et al., 1993).

Collaborative learning is a way of facilitating the learning process by involving team activities with a problem-solving focus. It encourages both teamwork and networking, and can make learning an immediate, challenging and engaging activity. Social interaction and negotiation of meaning are important to the process, as learners need to learn the communication, collaboration and team building skills necessary for this learning style. Group activities are considered to develop transferable skills, communication and interpersonal skills and to enhance deep learning, leading to improved learning outcomes.

Collaborative learning is best applied to complex problem or case-based scenarios. As context is important, these scenarios need to relate to real world situations so that learners can experience the type of problem-solving task that they will need to deal with in a work environment (Jonassen et al., 1993). Such problems should be structured so that learners need to find more information in order to define the problem, with no single right way to obtain it. The problem must change as new information becomes available. Problems must not have a single correct answer. In this environment, how learners go about the problem-solving task, and incidentally their own learning, is as important as what they learn. Active learning by problem solving is a key aspect of any constructivist environment.

Collaborative learning through small group methods is a key strategy for facilitating IPE. The need for small group interaction in case-based learning (CBL) and problem-based learning (PBL) methods mean they are useful instructional strategies for IPE. The nature and characteristics of small group learning strategies provide optimum processes for IPE experiences. According to Oandasan and Reeves (2005a) several key factors need to be considered in the organisation and design of small group learning: group balance; group mix; and group stability. It is important to ensure that there is an equal mix of learners from each profession in small group learning as it promotes good interprofessional interaction. If the group is skewed in favor of one profession it may inhibit interaction. Group size should also be kept in mind, as large groups can influence interaction. An optimal group size is around 8 to 10 members. The stability of group members is also important as high turnover can impact the quality of the learning experience.

PBL is centred on the use of a clinically-based problem to stimulate small-group discussion and learning among students interspersed with periods of independent, self-directed learning. PBL techniques encourage discussion and critical thinking, and enable the integration of theory with clinical components. The PBL approach helps learners to listen to each other and to collaborate as they work to resolve the problems. Case-based learning is a variation of PBL and both methods, as discussed earlier, are based on principles of cooperative and constructivist learning. Learners must be able to transfer what they have learned to the real-world and the use of cases is useful in establishing a real-world context in which the new learning is to be used. Working with cases exposes students to problematic, real-world situations and challenges them to apply course knowledge to analyze the issues and formulate workable solutions.

Benefits of Collaborative Learning

Learner collaboration not only emphasizes a positive, constructive approach to learning, but it also allows the knowledge and skills of the participants to be shared with their peers and others who have similar interests and concerns. This process is further enriched because the collaborating participants may well bring a whole pattern of experiences and different contextual concerns to the discussion. Collaborative learning has been closely associated with, and draws support from the research of Vygotsky (1978) and his notion of 'zone of proximal development'. Collaboration in learning activities has been described as offering a number of benefits. Most importantly, it supports and encourages the sharing of individual expertise and experience. Also collaboration learning can:

1. Allow for the articulation of an individual viewpoint, and the responding comments from others with differing perspectives, can lead to refinement and deeper understanding, or higher level concept attainment. Articulation is also seen as a process that promotes the development of meta-cognitive skills such as concept refinement and revision;
2. Promote the active construction of knowledge and engagement in the learning process;
3. Lead to a sense of involvement and identification with a group and its product(s): this supports the human/sociological need to operate and interact with others;
4. Ensure learners are active participants;
5. Lead to a generalization of the underlying principles which enable transfer to other contexts and broader application of the knowledge.

EXPERIENTIAL LEARNING

Experiential learning experiences in practice settings in which successful collaborative practices are modeled and learners have the opportunity to observe collaboration in action are also important teaching strategies. Interactive, experientially-based learning in the delivery of IPE also contributes to learner motivation and success (Freeth et al., 2005). Different forms of such processes can be adapted and applied depending on the circumstances and resources available for instruction, but overall, can contribute to the authenticity of the learning experience. A large number of the IPE initiatives reported in the literature are based on experiential clinical learning experiences in which learners are immersed in a collaborative practice setting. The incorporation of teaching methods which involve clinical placement, the use of a simulated clinical environment or going to meet and talk to service users about their health needs are recommended.

SERVICE LEARNING

Another approach for facilitating IPE includes service learning models. Service learning involves the use of contextual learning settings (clinical or community-based settings) which challenge students to work together effectively to address real clinical problems, patient education or health dilemmas within the broader community.

According to Clark (1999) a growing emphasis on prevention and community-based health care services is replacing the more narrowly focused biomedical, acute care model. As a result, health professional educators need to develop new models of education that prepare students for work in community settings emphasizing primary care, cost effectiveness, teamwork and the prevention and management of chronic health problems. Three specific responses to these trends have been the following:

1. To recognize the need to prepare students to work together in interdisciplinary teams;
2. To develop partnerships between academic institutions and the surrounding community;
3. To implement expanded service-learning opportunities which enable students to work toward meeting health needs articulated by members of the community themselves (Clark, 1999).

Service learning is defined as a structured learning experience which combines community service with preparation and reflection (Barr et al., 2005). Students participating in service-learning activities are expected not only to provide direct community service, but also to learn about the context in which the service is provided, and to understand the connection between the service and their academic course work. A central theme of this learning is that it is based on the community's identified needs, issues, and problems. Its success depends on a true partnership in the development and implementation of a program, with equal involvement by students, faculty, administrators and community participants. The following are critical elements of service learning:

- Development in collaboration with the community;
- Enhancement of the standard curriculum by extending learning beyond the classroom;
- Fostering of civic and social responsibility and of caring for others by the student;
- Application of what is learned by students to real-world situations;
- Provision of time for reflection, discussion, and leadership development; and
- Identification and meeting of community needs and assets.

Service learning involves the use of educational methods which combine the preparation of students to work in interdisciplinary teams or collaborative settings with the need for them to experience community-based learning opportunities. Historically, this is quite different from the past, in which health professional education occurred in an academic health science center and institutions in which the disciplines were largely kept separate. Traditionally, the role of the professional has been as 'expert' and the role of the patient has been to follow the professional's recommendation and to be 'compliant'. However, placing the health professional student into the community shifts the power to the individual in his or her social context. In entering the patient's community, the student is forced to broaden his or her scope of understanding of the 'problem.

There is a need to move education from the academic health center into the community through these service learning options. Community-academic partnerships are organisational structures in which the academic center, university or college actively incorporates the surrounding community into its programs. As a result, the issues, concerns, and problems of this community serve to guide the research, teaching, and service agendas of the academic center. The community-academic partnership requires a two-way flow of information. The needs and problems of the community are transmitted to the university where they are incorporated into the research, teaching, and service agendas of the institution. In turn, resources and solutions are redirected outward into the community to address these needs and problems.

Students working in community settings are more likely to discover a broader base of overlap among the different professions they represent. As well, faculty members are more likely to adopt the role of facilitator helping students to see a much broadened basis for health in the real world. For the student, the traditional role of passive participant is transformed by the need for active, reflective learning in settings that can be unpredictable and uncomfortable. According to Clark (1999) learning in the real world is fraught with unexpected problems, unanticipated issues, and unresolved conflicts which may be seen as the learning itself.

CONCLUSION

Effective IPE provides opportunities for health professionals to learn with, from and about each other and thus challenges the more isolated professional socialisation of individual disciplines. Through the facilitation of adult learning in collaborative, experiential and service learning environments the IPE of health professionals can be developed. This facilitation and enhanced collaboration offers a way to build teamwork skills and help develop the values, beliefs and ideals that individuals need to be socialized into interprofessional practice.

REFERENCES

Barr, H., Koppel, I., Reeves, S., Hammick, & M., Freeth, D. (2005). *Effective Interprofessional Education: Argument, Assumption & Evidence*. Oxford, Blackwell Publishing.

Centre for the Advancement of Interprofessional Education. *Defining Interprofessional Education*. Available at: http://www.caipe.org.uk/about-us/defining-ipe/ (Accessed February 18, 2009).

Clark, P. (1991). Toward a conceptual framework for developing interdisciplinary teams in gerontology: Cognitive and ethical dimensions. *Gerontology & Geriatrics Education*, 12(1), 79-96.

Clark, P. (1994). Social, professional and educational values on the interdisciplinary team: Implications for gerontological and geriatric education. *Educational Gerontology*, 20, 35-51.

Clark, P. (1995). Quality of Life, Values, and Teamwork in Geriatric Care: Do We Communicate What we Mean? *The Gerontologist*, 35(3), 402-411.

Clark, P. (1997). Values in health care professional socialisation: Implications for geriatric education in interdisciplinary teamwork. *The Gerontologist*, 37(4), 441-451.

Clark, P. (1999). Service-Learning Education in Community-Academic Partnerships: Implications for Interdisciplinary Geriatric Training in the Health Professions. *Educational Gerontology*, 25, 641-660.

Cott, C. (1998). Structure and meaning in multidisciplinary teamwork. *Sociology of Health & Illness*, 20(6), 848-873.

Curran, V, Sharpe, D., & Forristall, J. (2007). Attitudes of Health Sciences Faculty Towards Interprofessional Teamwork and Education. *Medical Education*, 41, 892-896.

d'Amour, D., Ferrada-Videla, M., San-Martin Rodriguez, L., & Beaulieu, M. (2005). The conceptual basis for interprofessional. *Journal of Interprofessional Care*, 19, (Suppl 1),,116–131.

Drinka, T., & Clark, P. (2000). *Health Care Teamwork: Interdisciplinary Practice and Teaching*. London: Auburn House.

Drinka, T. (1996). Applying Learning from Self-Directed Work Teams in Business to Curriculum Development for Interdisciplinary Geriatric Teams. *Educational Gerontology*, 22, 433-450.

Engel, C. (1997). A functional anatomy of teamwork. In A. Leathard (Ed.), *Going Inter-Professional - Working Together for Health and Welfare* (pp.64-74). London: Routledge.

Fagin, C. (1992). Collaboration between nurses and physicians: No longer a choice. *Academic Medicine, 67(5)*, 295-303.

Freeth, D., Hammick, M., Reeves, S., Koppel, & I., Barr, H. (2005). *Effective Interprofessional Education - Development, Delivery and Evaluation*. Oxford: Blackwell Publishing.

Glen, S. (1999). Educating for interprofessional collaboration: teaching about values. *Nursing Ethics*, 6(3), 202-213.

Hall, P. (2005). Interprofessional teamwork. *Journal of Interprofessional Care*, 19(Supplement 1), 188–196.

Hill, A. (1998). Multiprofessional teamwork in hospital palliative care teams. *International Journal of Palliative Nursing*, 4(5), 214-221.

Jonassen, D., Mayes, T., & McAleese, R. (1993). A manifesto for a constructivist approach to uses of technology in higher education. In T.M. Duffy, J. Lowyck, & D.H. Jonassen (Eds.), *Designing environments for constructivist learning* (pp. 231-247). Berlin: Springer-Verlag.

Liedtka, J.M., & Whitten, E. (1998). Enhancing care delivery through cross-disciplinary collaboration: A case study. *Journal of Healthcare Management*, 43(2), 185-205.

Lowe, J., & Herranen, M. (1981). Understanding teamwork: Another look at the concepts. *Social Work in Health Care*, 7(2), 1-11.

Makaram, S. (1995). Interprofessional cooperation. *Medical Education*, 29 (Supplement 1), 65-69.

Mariano, C. (1989). The case for interdisciplinary collaboration. *Nursing Outlook, 37*(6), 285-288.

Merriam, S. B., Cafarella, R. S., & Baumgartner, L. M. (2007). *Learning in Adulthood: A Comprehensive Guide (3rd Ed.)*. San Francisco, CA: Jossey Bass.

Netting, F. E., & Williams, F.G. (1996). Case manager-physician collaboration: Implications for professional identity, roles and relationships. *Health & Social Work, 21(3)*, 216-224.

Oandasan, I., & Reeves, S. (2005a). Key elements for interprofessional. *Journal of Interprofessional Care*, 19, (Suppl 1)21–38.

Oandasan, I., & Reeves, S. (2005b). Key elements of interprofessional *Journal of Interprofessional Care*, 19(Suppl 1), 39–48.

Parsell, G., & Bligh, J. (1999). Interprofessional learning. *Postgraduate Medical Journal, 74*, 89-95.

Parsell, G., Spalding, R., & Bligh, J. (1998). Shared goals, shared learning: Evaluation of a multiprofessional course for undergraduate students. *Medical Education, 32*, 304-311.

San Martin-Rodriguez, L., Beaulieu, M., D'Amour, D., & Ferrada-Videla, M. (2005). The determinants of successful collaboration. *Journal of Interprofessional Care*, 19, (Suppl 1) :132–147.

Tsukuda, R. (1990). Interdisciplinary collaboration: Teamwork in geriatrics. In C. K. Cassel, D. E. Riesenberg, L. B. Sorensen & J. R. Walsh (Eds.), *Geriatric Medicine* (2nd ed. pp. 668-675). New York: Springer-Verlag.

Vygotsky, L. (1978). *Mind in Society: the development of higher psychological processes*. Cambridge, MA: Harvard University Press.

Wilson, A., & Startup, R. (1991). Nurse socialisation. *Journal of Advanced Nursing, 16*, 1478-1486.

In: Sociology of Interprofessional Health …
Ed: S. Kitto, J. Chesters et al.

ISBN: 978-1-60876-866-0

Chapter 7

CROSSING WORKPLACE BOUNDARIES: "INTERPROFESSIONAL THINKING" IN ACTION

Natalie Radomski and David Beckett

ABSTRACT

How can we come to understand professional practice in the 21st century? This chapter will connect current advances in international research on workplace learning with emerging expectations for improved health care collaboration to show the potential for what we call 'interprofessional thinking' (Winch, 1998; Gherardi, 2001; Beckett & Hager, 2002; Griffiths & Guile, 2003). Linked to our discussion is the idea that it may be possible to open up more attentive and reflexive spaces for thinking about and working with the fluidities and complexities encountered in the 'learning' and 'doing' of professional health care work. In considering these boundary reconfiguration issues we suggest that interprofessional learning goes beyond traditional constructions of health care 'team-work', 'coordination' and 'collaboration'. Instead we consider 'interprofessionality' as a socially situated, relational practice that is perhaps better understood as an emergent property of the embodied connections, negotiated health care decisions and reflective actions among people, processes and things. Interplay and rehearsal of different perspectives, forms of knowledge and professional identities, as well as 'co-ordination' of health care action, may be fruitful areas for exploration. Linking debates about how people learn in the workplace with the current push for professional boundary spanning offers a timely opportunity to re-envisage health interprofessional education into the future.

INTRODUCTION

The very nature of our work means that many of the cases we go to I can't anticipate. A very high percentage of our jobs are non-routine where we have to make creative decisions that are not quite in the prescribed boundaries or protocols of the service. Once we went to a lady who had lost control of her car on a dirt road in the mountains. She was down a steep embankment, the car was resting against a tree and it was going to be very difficult to get her out with the injuries she had. She was also a very large lady. So even though it was a fairly standard sort of job, if you know what I mean, you had all these things to deal with. You make many decisions in conjunction with your partner and you draw on your own and your partner's experiences. We also often have other people who work with us like the police, fire brigade and Emergency Department staff and we use them too. It's a very complex relationship that depends a lot on historical and cultural factors as well as the situation you're in. There's also the nature of the relationship between different people. Because I'm on reserve, I often work with people I don't know, or I may have only worked with them once or twice. If I've worked with someone before, then the decisions become easier and you know whether or not you can trust them. But it's harder when you don't really know what they'll do or not do…(Jenny, Ambulance Officer)

Much has been written in the health education literature in recent times advocating interprofessional teamwork as a rational and effective approach to the coordination and provision of high quality, patient-centred health care (Cashman, Reidy, Cody & Lemay, 2004; Zwarenstein et al., 2007). By creating opportunities for the health professions to learn with, from and about each other (CAIPE, 2008), it is assumed that they will come to "understand each other better, valuing what each [brings] to collaborative practice whilst setting aside negative stereotypes" (Barr, 2005, p. 10).

Yet in the brief anecdote above, our ambulance officer shares a different kind of story that is richer than collaboration. Jenny reminds us that the challenges that arise in the 'doing' of real world clinical practice are messy, and more problematic (Montgomery, 2006). Although health care encounters are 'imagined', 'rehearsed' and 'planned for' (i.e. a fairly standard sort of job; a particular kind of injury; a particular kind of care protocol, a particular team combination), the complexities and interactions that arise in the situation at hand, cannot be fully known, coordinated or structured in advance (Schon, 1986; Wilson, Holt & Greenhalgh, 2001). In this light, collaboration emerges downstream, if at all, from the messiness of daily practices. Why do we start 'upstream', that is, so early on, in the analysis of practice?

We start there because of the vivid nature of those initial experiences of practice. Jenny and her health care colleagues are inevitably caught up in the 'here and now', we might say: It is not merely the *particular* times and sites of practices, which make planning difficult (Beckett & Hager, 2002), but also the *immediate* nature of such practices. In the 'here and now', problem boundaries change, creative decisions are needed and the possibilities for collaborative practice are re-negotiated in the midst of the action. As Mulcahy (2005) puts it, there is "a fluidity and mobility which characterises these worlds" (p. 1). The car has two doors rather than four, there are new people on the team, the woman's injuries are more serious than first thought and extra help may be needed to provide safe care. How do health care professionals think in action? One important ingredient here is that they think, increasingly, as parts of whole systems, or networks, or teams. That is, they think, and act, *socially*, but they do so in particular contexts of pressing immediacy.

Accordingly, by drawing on recent advances in research on workplace learning, this chapter investigates interprofessional learning and health care collaboration as a socially-situated, relational practice. In contrast to educational interventions designed to encourage students from different professions to learn together during their pre or post-registration studies (Barr et al., 2005), we explore a more informal, practice-based approach to understanding aspects of interprofessional thinking and collective action. Linked to our discussion is the idea that it may be possible to open up more reflexive spaces for thinking about and working with the dilemmas and complexities encountered in the 'doing' of real health care work (Romm, 1998). Creating opportunities for the health professions to learn together during their clinical training, whilst a potentially valuable experience, may not be sufficient preparation for the contingencies of daily clinical practices. What is needed, we suggest, is recognition of new, fluid and dynamic ways of working that go beyond current models of the 'stable' health care team (Fraser & Greenhalgh, 2001; Engestrom, 2004). As Lingard, Espin, Evans and Hawryluck (2004) explain, relying on "the traditional ideal of 'team' may, in fact, constrain us from recognising and promoting the functional mechanisms of group effort in the health care domain" (p. 407).

Our further claim is that interprofessional education (IPE) should build on the fluidities of clinical work by embracing the dynamic and decisional nature of knowledge and learning in particular sites of practice. We argue, therefore, in this chapter, that IPE that may be better understood as an emergent property of the embodied connections, negotiated health care decisions and reflective actions among people, processes and things (Gherardi, 2000; Beckett & Hager, 2002; Griffiths & Guile, 2004).

WHAT IS IPE?

IPE is usually defined as "occasions when two or more professions learn from and about each other to improve collaboration and the quality of care" (Barr, 2005, p. 6). Another definition has it that: "interprofessional practice is the collaborative, interdependent use of shared expertise directed toward a unified purpose of delivering optimal patient care" (The Centre for Interprofessional Education and Research website, 2008). We support the relational quality of these definitions: 'learning from and about each other' and the 'interdependent use of shared expertise' imply a sociality which is fundamental to practice, and to learning amongst practices. By this we mean that the location of the practices and the decisional moments and justifications these generate, is found, not in the individual health professional, nor in the connections such individuals have with one other. On the contrary, and more radically, we claim that implicit in these definitions is the location of IPE *within the relationships which constitute such practices.* We expand on this claim in what follows.

WHERE HAS IPE COME FROM?

It was fun to meet other people. You see the medical students at the hospital, but don't actually get to interact with them. (Student nurse)
I thought pharmacists only knew about drugs but they do know a bit about the conditions of a patient. I didn't realise that nurses knew so much about the conditions of a patient too and didn't realise that their role is for patient advocacy. (Medical student)

Interprofessional health education is generally promoted as a 'front-end' intervention designed to encourage interactive learning and sharing of perspectives among two or more professions. Linked to several major health and educational reform movements over the past thirty years, IPE was conceptualized as a means of overcoming ignorance, stereotyping and prejudice amongst health and social care professions (Barr, 2005).

Related to this social and cultural change agenda, IPE has been seen by its advocates as a mechanism for improving interprofessional teamwork and collaboration (Lavin et al., 2001; Braithwaite, 2005; Zwarenstein et al., 2007). By fostering new interprofessional competencies, the aim is to capitalize on the cognitive and practical contributions of different health professions and improve the quality of health care for patients and clients. IPE has also been viewed as a potential lever which operates to enhance the status and role of some of the 'newer' health professions and specialisations who have sought to establish a place in the health care field in recent times (McCallin, 2001). As Duckett (2005) points out:

> The health workforce is now characterised by a large number of separate professions, each with a different course preparation, a different emphasis in practice and, to some extent, a different ideological foundation in terms of the way in which the profession interacts with other professions and with patients and consumers…To some extent, this specialisation has led to increased quality of care as individual professionals have been able to develop in-depth knowledge and skills across a narrower range of areas. However by the late 1990s there was recognition that this increasing specialisation may have a downside in increased coordination costs, leading to inefficiency and problems of continuity of care. (p. 202).

IPE, it is argued, offers both a 'vision' and a practical approach to working together to achieve common health care goals, without duplication or angst, in a coordinated, coherent and cost effective way (Hall & Weaver, 2001; Kavanagh & Cowan, 2004; CAIPE, 2008).

This aim has been supported even further by the move to implement flexible, patient-centred models of health service to provide better continuity of care for people with chronic and complex health problems (Levin et al., 2001; McCallin, 2001; Duckett, 2005). For Mennin and Petroni-Mennin (2006), the shift towards collaborative, community-based health care is a much needed change that has enabled health professionals to:

- interact with people within their socio-environmental contexts in a more holistic way;
- work across the full spectrum of health care; and,
- reconsider traditional professional and disciplinary boundaries, "where biology rules to the exclusion of most of the other social, political, economic and psychological factors that play important roles in the determination of health" (p. 90).

For Stark, Stronach and Warne (2002) however, this vision of interprofessional coordination, harmony and collaboration is a utopian vision, an idealised smoothing mechanism that "jostles against the more chaotic and messy reality" (p. 412) of real world practice. In contrast to the many abstracted 'good news' representations assigned to IPE in the literature, the authors argue for a richer, more complex and contradictory understanding of interprofessional practice and team working that is:

contextual and, further, helps individuals to understand professional discourse; how individuals talk with and about other professionals and how they justify their practice. This offers a way of *reading* groups which does not over-simplify them into good teams and bad characteristics. (Ibid, authors' italics).

Reflecting on approaches to inter-agency collaboration in the child protection field, Hallett, (quoted in Tucci, 1995), raises a similar concern. For Hallett, putting too much emphasis on 'co-ordination' as the framework for working together, may act as a kind of 'conservatising phenomenon' that has the potential to further "institutionalize and entrench established ways of looking at the problem" (pp. 35-36). For Hallett, a significant limitation of the health care coordination metaphor is that it is:

> ... invested with a capacity to solve problems that, of itself, it cannot solve. I am not hostile to coordination, but I do not think coordinated services *[and roles]*, in themselves would necessarily generate the skills or interventive resources that we need to offer an effective protective response to children at risk. (p.36, our italics).

We concur with these views and would argue, in particular, for closer attention to the decisional character of practitioners' justificatory practices.

So, for us, an important issue in advancing the capacity to solve problems, by looking closely at groups which 'co-ordinate' their practices, is to explore how groups in particular health care contexts make what we will call, following Montgomery (2006) and Beckett and Hager (2002), 'practical judgments'.

Exploring approaches to interprofessional practice that reposition individualistic constructions of professional knowledge and 'disciplinarity' may also be fruitful areas for investigation. It is to these two themes that the discussion now turns.

A SOCIAL LEARNING PERSPECTIVE ON INTERPROFESSIONAL PRACTICE

Traditional theories of learning tend to assume that learning is primarily an individual attribute, constructed through a cognitive process involving the transmission, acquisition, storage and application of a "body of data, facts and practical wisdom" (Gherardi & Nicolini, 2000, p. 330). Central to this 'standard paradigm' view of learning is the assumption that "coming to know and understand something, involves arriving "at a *state of mind* as evidenced in accounts of what is cognitively the case" (Beckett, 2006, p. 4, author's italics; see also Beckett & Hager, 2002). When considered from this standpoint, individual practitioners are understood to 'possess' the necessary disciplinary knowledge and professional expertise 'in their heads and bodies' which they then transfer to the situation at hand (Hager & Halliday, 2006). Hall and Weaver's (2001) description of health care team working illustrates this traditional view well:

> Each member of the team contributes his/her knowledge and skill set to augment and support the others' contributions. Each member's assessment must take into account the others contributions to allow for holistic management of the patient's

complex health problems. Team members preserve specialized functions while maintaining continuous lines of communication with each other, placing themselves somewhere along the continuum of interactions and responsibilities. (p. 868).

This conception of health care team working, whilst hinting at the potential for collective learning and interdependent action, is still largely in keeping with traditional characterisations of learning which, according to Hager and Halliday (2006), fail to recognise the possibility of collective learning by teams and workplaces "that may not be reducible to learning by individuals" (p. 143). As Lingard et al. (2006) put it, there is a continuing belief and expectation in health care practice:

> ...that the work of one profession is fundamentally independent from that of other professions. This belief reflects a sense of professional autonomy, [and] a failure to appreciate fully how one profession's competent performance is dependent on the others. (p.480).

Traditional professional formation, for medical practitioners, for example, has been in silos, within which, not surprisingly, the solo, or individualistic, nature of specialised practices has been embedded.

While we certainly recognise the need for sophisticated individual level disciplinary and technical knowledge in health care practice (Beckett & Gough, 2004), we argue for a holistic, contextualised approach to clinical thinking and collaborative practice that calls on both the social and the cognitive dimensions of learning. As Beckett and Gough (2004) explain, taking this socially situated view of learning seriously:

> ...contrasts with traditional classroom learning activities, which...assume an individualistic learner and knowledge that is often presented atomistically, in abstract propositions, and out of context. In the past this epistemology has marked the professional formation of medical practitioners as much as it has many other professionals. (p. 197).

By contrast, an emphasis on the sociality of practice has come from many places. Lave and Wenger's (1991) social practice perspective, for example, is helpful in reconsidering the relationship between learning and "the social situation in which it occurs" (p. 35). For Lave and Wenger, learning:

> is not merely situated in practice– as if were some independently reifiable process that just happened to be located somewhere; [i.e. a particular workplace setting or in an individual's head], learning is an integral part of generative social practice in the lived-in-world. (p.35, our italics).

In exploring a relational, social perspective, we therefore seek to open a more complex clinical learning landscape that recognises the *socially negotiated* character of meaning (Lave & Wenger 2001; Billett 2003) and the role that particular mediating artefacts (such as other people, technologies, languages, mnemonic techniques, domain specific tools) have in contributing to the construction of knowledge and the realisation of purposeful and intelligent action (Gherardi & Nicolini, 2000; Griffiths & Guile, 2003).

This more emergent, particularistic and interdependent view recognises that learning and knowledge generation occurs through engaged action (practice) in the world and is "a function of the activity, context and culture in which it occurs" (Beckett & Gough, 2004, p. 197). Knowing and learning can therefore be seen to extend beyond the individual and beyond traditional disciplinary boundaries (Usher, Bryant & Johnston, 1997). As Gherardi (2003), again helpfully explains,

> [t]he idea is that the relations which constitute the social are continuous. They do not halt at the ontological barriers that separate nature and culture, actor and structure, organisation and environment: the dynamics of interaction prescind from these categories, forming a seamless web. Consequently, knowing is a collective accomplishment which depends on a range of spatially and temporally distributed local practices lying outside the control of any organisation [or individual] and within a network of relationships. *Learning thus becomes an epistemic relation with the world*, and it takes place as much in people's minds as in the social relations among them, in the oral, written and "visual" texts which convey ideas and knowledge from one context to another. Knowledge is in its turn both social and material. It is always unstable and precarious, located in time and space. (p. 352, our italics).

The idea that learning forms an inseparable part of practice stands as a challenging counterpoint to traditional individualistic conceptions of disciplinarity, professionality, learning and human cognition. We argue that to practise is to learn, because the sociality of practising inevitably generates understandings of the world. It is in this sense that learning "becomes an epistemic relation with the world" (as Gherardi puts it).

There is some support for this view, already. Writing from a social work perspective, Bronstein (2003) argues that interprofessional practice is a challenging and potentially problematic way of working, that calls on collaborative action 'in' and 'through' a complex terrain of inter-professional and intra-professional relationships and competing professional accountabilities. Interestingly, Bronstein (2003) defines interdisciplinary collaboration as an "interpersonal process that facilitates the achievement of goals that cannot be reached when *individual professionals act on their own*" (p. 299, author's italics). Although not identified explicitly as 'learning' by Bronstein, the emphasis appears to have shifted beyond the individual to explore how cognitive processes and practices are co-constructed and distributed (however problematically), across and among a number of professionals and resources for a particular activity.

In her ethnographic study of the informal, 'backstage' communication processes enacted by an interdisciplinary geriatric oncology team, Ellingson (2003), notes that although "increased specialisation contributes to the need for collaboration among experts from different specialities" (p. 94), there is little research that investigates the work of professional teams in action. Ellingson proposes the concept of 'embedded teamwork' as a way of recognising the fragmentation and organic nature of interprofessional interactions that emerge in the flow of clinical practice. She calls for development of more holistic models of team working that recognise "the dynamism and multiple sites of communication in the everyday enactment of teamwork" (p. 109). In the cancer clinic setting, interactions among the health team were understood to occur:

...opportunistically rather than on a schedule; emerged in response to team members desires to improve patient care and assessment as they went about providing it, not by a preset agenda; were dyadic and triadic rather than including the entire team; and developed within the process of accomplishing comprehensive geriatric assessments in an outpatient clinic, with all the noise, crowding and simultaneous activities of that space. (Ibid).

We can see that IPE under this newer relational and decisional model requires close attention to particular contexts of health care practice, to the emergent character of the interpersonal relationships of those who share that context, and its issues and problems, and who also share an openness to the complexity of the diagnoses and judgements which are ultimately the shared responsibility of all. The 'here and now' is our daily professional challenge – as significant for ambulatory care as it is for acute care. The decisional nature of such caring is central to all manifestations of it. Practical situations, on a daily basis, require holistic practices, and, we claim, holistic learning - and the skills at the heart of that learning - should be where IPE goes.

We now explore what a more holistic approach to understanding interprofessional health practice look like.

WHERE MIGHT IPE GO?

Based on the forgoing, we argue for 'interprofessional thinking', by which we mean a new conception of the *decisional* quality of practices. Rather than continue to expect that the metaphors of 'coordination' and 'collaboration' will mark out a 'team' from merely a group of solo practitioners, instead, we locate the decisionality of teams in the relationality of the team itself. Clinical decisions are, we argue, emergent characteristics of interprofessional thinking. These decisions constitute 'interprofessionality'.

Such 'interprofessional thinking', however, does not occur in minds alone. Our whole claim is as much ontological, as it is epistemological. We claim that there is a new place for IPE, and it is to be found in purposeful practice at work, which requires an analysis of the "actions we find ourselves undertaking" (Beckett & Hager, 2002, p. 41). These actions "constitute the intentional embodiment of decisions and judgements we make at work" (Ibid). IPE requires thinking, but such thinking is to be found in professionals' workplace actions, and our claim is that these actions are, at once, fundamentally decisional, and fundamentally social.

To put it slightly differently, all such actions require 'practical judgement', that is, decisions about what to do next to bring about the most efficacious result - the "practical, or appropriate, contextually sensitive solution to whatever is the issue or problem" (Ibid). In this emphasis on the decisional and the social, via what Aristotle called practical reasoning or wisdom (*phronesis*), we are embedding interprofessionality in the contingent world of action. This should come as no surprise to those who work in health-related practices. After all, practice is an embodied phenomenon, as is health and illness. What is significant is the intertwining of practice with learning, here, for a new conception of IPE. By participating in social practices such as work, individuals and groups "engage in an ongoing process of knowledge construction and refinement" (Billett, 2004, p. 110).

In the following case vignette we offer a practical example of how this new conception of interprofessionality - as a form of 'interprofessional thinking in action' could be seen to arise in the clinical workplace. The setting for this case is an Australian General Practice Medical Centre.

CASE EXAMPLE ONE: INTERPROFESSIONAL THINKING IN ACTION

Kate [Dietician]
…John is an electrician in his mid fifties with Type One diabetes and has been a regular patient at our Medical Centre for approximately three years. From my perspective as a Dietician, when he came to see me a few weeks ago he seemed to be having a lot of trouble managing his blood sugars. He was testing his blood sugars multiple times a day and was in a bit of a stressful cycle where his blood sugars would make him anxious and depending on the reading, he might, or might not have a snack. And that would influence the next blood sugars. I really wanted to keep his preferences in mind because he was really happy with the more flexible style of administering insulin 'as you eat.' But I didn't think that approach was mixing well with his blood sugars and personality. I thought it was actually creating more stress than necessary. John also has regular appointments with Liz our Diabetes Educator here in the Centre, so I spoke with her about what approach to take from here. We were actually thinking that simplifying his insulin program might help. I really needed to gain Liz's support and make sure I put across my views clearly about how I felt things were going.

And from Liz [Diabetes Educator]
…It was Kate our Dietician who prompted it. Initially it was the old corridor chat I suppose. She just called me aside and asked me to read John's case notes, which I did. Then we both looked at the notes together and agreed it really wasn't working for him. And we had to find out what would work. I think he was getting too involved in the process, making it far too complicated and it was leading to blood glucose levels that were all over the shop. For this particular diabetes management program the patient is supposed to be able to judge the amount of insulin they need for their carbohydrate load and then compensate if they get things wrong. So if they're low or high they've got strategies in place. Even though it wasn't working for John and he was anxious about it, he liked the program and its flexibility - so we then had to change his way of thinking.
I was seeing John anyway in the next couple of weeks so it was really planning with Kate [Dietician] to call her in on the consult as well as Graham [John's GP]. We have linked appointments with our GP's so we arranged to call Graham in on the discussion as well. What I did was explain to John directly that I felt that in talking to Kate that this management program wasn't working…and how did he feel about that situation? It sort of evolved from there. I suppose it developed from us talking together away from the patient, then me reading John's case notes and working out some strategies in my mind. And when John was sitting there I outlined my feelings about the situation and asked him what his feelings were. Then I called Kate into the situation. Graham (GP) came into the consult as well at that point - as our GP link. I needed to work out how much carbohydrate he'd be roughly eating for his insulin and Kate needed to give him a rough indication of what carbohydrate to eat at each meal. Graham sort of summarised and overviewed things with us. That we were all on the right track and let's see how we go.
But it required the three of us to try and make the situation better - I suppose, easier for John.

As highlighted in the case example above, our 'interprofessionality' requires the public, socially-located articulation of justifications (decisions), which reveal clinical understandings and the potential for 'forward-looking' action. To engage in reason-giving for actions invites other community members (including patients) to join in - that is to articulate warranted ways to go on (Beckett & Hager, 2002). This is the sociality of practice fleshed out, if you like, in the dynamics of shared responsibility for clinical outcomes. This is not a 'collaboration' metaphor, but something much richer: we advocate interprofessionality where the doing, thinking and learning are found in what the team and, in some cases, the patient or client undergo. Their practical judgements *constitute* such interprofessionality, and such judgements display new understandings of clinical problems. In this way, practices and learning are co-extensive. To practice interprofessionally is to learn relationally.

THE DYNAMICS OF ATTENTIVENESS

IPE, under this conception, needs to give attention to attention. This curious claim deserves to be developed. What health practitioners pay attention to, (or not) - how their interactions engender new forms of attentiveness - cultivates, we claim, new ways of seeing, acting, and knowing (Romm, 1998). As shown in Case One above, Kate's initial attentiveness to John's anxieties about his diabetes management regime generated new insights and clinical interactions among the health care team.

The co-extensive nature of practices and learning gives us an encouragement to provoke, in IPE, a sensitivity to:

- different clinical perspectives, from the dynamics of 'paying attention';
- what's holistically insightful in clinical situations;
- different perceptions of explicit turning points in clinical care processes;
- ambiguities and inconsistencies in daily practices;
- ways in which health care practices are interconnected (rather than focussing on discrete roles);
- opportunities for group-level reflection and communal self-correction.

For us, IPE as interprofessionality therefore requires close attention to the daily dynamics of health care decision making. For Lingard et al. (2004), this involves:

Knowing about perceptions of ownership, valued commodities and the rules of trade [which] allow team members to shape outcomes and persuade people to anticipate reactions and deflect obstructions…Efforts to improve teamwork must reflect such authentic, everyday 'rules of the game' if they are to affect how work gets done on health care teams in complex settings such as ICU. (p. 407).

Ambulance Officer Jenny, introduced at the beginning of our chapter, also highlights the importance of understanding 'the rules of the game' in order to achieve 'the best' health care outcome for patients when she says:

There are ways of working together without scoring points off each other. And that means I try to approach situations in a less confrontational and more collegial way. So sometimes if I think someone needs a cervical collar on, I'll say, "I'll get the collars for you, shall I?" And so they can say, "Yes that's a good idea". Or if I think perhaps they should have a splint on, or some medication or something else, I'll get it ready and say, "This is here - if you need it". That may sound manipulative, but I don't mean it that way. It's about getting the best outcome for the patient by creating different positions and options for working together.

What is clear from the clinical practice accounts above is that cultivation of new perspectives among the health professions requires an openness to recognising "that any situation provides at least in principle, an opportunity for alternative courses of action" (Griffith & Guile, 2003, p. 61). Engendering commitment towards a shared exploration of underlying relations of power, tacit rules of engagement and the daily negotiations that shape how and why things get done 'as they do', in clinical settings is also central to activation of new 'group-level' understandings (Bleakley, Hobbs, Boyden & Walsh, 2004; Lingard et al., 2006). As Stark et al. (2002) explain:

> students *[and health professionals]* need help to deconstruct group interactions, which does not just reduce them to good or bad team members or effective and ineffective teams, but which helps them to see the dynamics - even contradictory and confusing practices - that might reveal potential weak spots, mutual inconsistencies and, more importantly, the realities in relation to the theory and practice of multi-professional team working. (p. 416 italics added).

Our focus on the public, socially-located articulation of justifications fits well with Stark et al's, call to help practitioners 'deconstruct' and reveal professional action in meaningful ways. How then might this occur in the flow of everyday practice?

For work process theorists such as Griffith and Guile (2003), and Billett (2004), it is the opportunities for participation in work practices, as well as the guidance provided in the work environment (e.g.: by more experienced colleagues; mentors, technologies and tools), which is pivotal to learning in, and through, work. This includes opportunities to: "use context specific language to clarify understandings and resolve problems" (Griffith & Guile, 2003, p.58); opportunities to appropriate and use the cultural resources available in the work environment; and, "opportunities to listen and observe" (Billet, 2004, p. 114). Lingard et al's (2006) analysis of a preoperative interprofessional briefing intervention offers a useful example of the kind of group-level communicative 'spaces' that can be created to encourage interprofessional participation and public articulation of clinical thinking. The aim of team briefings were to "prompt brief but comprehensive review of relevant patient and procedural information" (Ibid, p. 473) among surgery, anesthesia and nursing team members. The team sessions were structured by a preoperative checklist tool. Outcomes from the research suggest this initiative:

> …show[s] promise as a vehicle of team learning and accommodation, as it provide[s]a window onto the professional practice of other team members, fostering understanding and empathy regarding roles, responsibilities and the perspectives of other professions. For instance the opportunity to hear the surgeon's operative plan can offer the nurse new insight into the surgeon's thinking and help the two to synchronize their individual expectations and actions. (Ibid, p. 480).

For our purposes in this chapter, it appears that the interprofessional briefing sessions were not just forums for the public articulation of individual 'know how', but instead opened a more generative, 'forward looking' space for sharing professional insights, questioning intentions, 'rehearsing' clinical plans and identifying emerging patient care risks amongst the team. For us, this example links *'knowing how'* to do something with *'knowing why'*, for a richer, more particularistic, conception of interprofessional thinking in action (Beckett, 2004).

Lingard et al's (2006) model of interprofessional communication highlights the potential for purposeful, group-level reflection and collective learning that is embedded in the flow of daily clinical work (See Bleakley, Hobbs, Boyden & Walsh, 2004 for further examples). It can also be argued that Lingard et al's team briefing intervention goes some way towards helping health professionals with different practice orientations to 'read' particular clinical situations in more nuanced and multi-layered ways, as advocated by Stark et al. (2002). This in turn, raises the possibility of creating new opportunities for communal self-correction and improvement as inconsistencies and 'tensions' in clinical justifications are revealed, and ways of proceeding are 'worked through' (Beckett, 2004). As Lingard et al. (2006), describe it:

> The crux of the model is an elaboration of the causal pathway between concrete communication activities, intermediary processes such as enhanced knowledge and purposeful action, and the quality and safety of collaborative care processes. (p. 481).

Following Griffiths and Guile (2003), we suggest that health professionals (as adult learners), need to be offered opportunities to experience and model new social practices to facilitate questioning of 'taken for granted' understandings and ways of working. For Bronstein (2003), fostering this communal change process may require introduction of new "collaborative acts, programs and structures that can achieve more than could be achieved by the same professionals acting independently" (p.300).

How then might these 'new kinds of collaborative acts' be encouraged in the workplace? In Case Example Two, below, 'Alice' describes some of the organisational-level structures and processes that enabled John's diabetes management issues *(as introduced in Case Example One)*, to be reviewed and 'worked on' from a shared, systems level perspective. Alice is the Allied Health Team Leader and Clinical Coordinator within the Medical Centre.

CAPITALISING ON THE FLUIDITIES OF CLINICAL PRACTICE

Our earlier claim that IPE should build on the fluidities of clinical practice suggests that reliance on 'formalised' team-working structures and work processes *alone*, may constrain opportunities to capitalize on interprofessional thinking 'between' and among different professions and communities of practice (Brown & Duguid, 1991; Engestrom, 2004). As shown in Case Example Two above, attention to process, and collaborative practices, are key features of productive learning. This focus on process should not be confused with the allocation or coordination of team tasks, roles or responsibilities, but rather speaks to a new discourse that values learning through active participation, interaction, reflection and informed action (see also Bleakley et al., 2004).

Following Fraser and Greenhalgh (2001) we argue for further recognition of the "imaginative dimension of professional capability [that] is best developed through non-linear methods - those in which learners embrace a situation in all its holistic complexity" (p. 801). If practice and learning are co-extensive, as we have argued, then, in workplaces what is needed are opportunities for interprofessional mentoring, informal networking through co-location of work groups, role shadowing, significant event audit discussions, shared case discussions, rotational attachments in different service settings, 360- degree appraisals and project-based work groups.

CASE EXAMPLE TWO: CREATING OPPORTUNITIES FOR SHARED PARTICIPATION IN HEALTH PRACTICES

How we do things around here

Alice: We've set up our clinic systems so we can make referrals from our General Practitioners (GP's) to our Allied Health staff - like Kate [Dietician] and Liz [Diabetes Educator]. They're two key health care providers that people need to work with to either avoid chronic disease, or manage it once they have got it. We're all under the one roof and so it's easy for our patients to move between their various appointments. We've also set up our systems so that our staff can work together via linked appointments. Patients are booked in with Kate and Liz for however long and when the patient comes in for the consult they'll phone the person's GP and say, 'we've just brought so and so in and we'll be ready to link in with you in the next 20 minutes', or whenever. That gives the GP's enough time to manage their patient schedules. They can come into Kate and Liz's sessions to discuss things together and with the patient, but still keep their own consults on time. This way we can embrace the patient and their needs so that everybody is working from the same page.

At this Medical Centre, if anyone sees a patient or client and they have any questions or uncertainty, there's always somebody else they can go to, to say, 'can I check this out with you?' So it can be as informal as that. It might be another doctor coming through to the Treatment Room and just asking the doctor or nurses in there what they think about something. Sometimes it's just sitting down and chatting to people in the tearoom about how they might develop their ideas and projects.

We'll obviously email each other using the published case notes if we've got some major concerns with a patient. If someone's door is open you can always just pop in and say, 'look I've got some concerns'. So it can be informal - but then you go on to have another look at your patient's notes and get your thought processes in place.

We also have regular clinical meetings about particular issues and it's open for anybody to say what angle <u>they</u> see it from. So everybody participates in that. If any of the senior doctors, usually it's the senior doctors, think that there's something to be learnt for the Nursing or Allied Health staff they'll say, 'look this might be of interest, or might be new to you'. So that's going on all the time here.

We have whole of staff general meetings twice a year and regular whole of clinic professional development sessions. We try to ensure there's flow and that people aren't forgotten.

As part of our Allied Health team meetings we have a regular space now for any debriefing or workshopping of tricky situations. It's not meant to be a spot where you talk about an individual patient but it's a space to talk about some tricky things - like people who aren't ready to change, or people who might just come in, cross their arms and say, 'Well what are you going to do? How are you going to change me?

At the cultural level, sharing is just an expected part of the norm here.

CONCLUSION

Landscapes can be deceptive. Sometimes a landscape seems to be less a setting for the life of its inhabitants than a curtain behind which their struggles, achievements and accidents take place. For those who, with the inhabitants, are behind the curtain, landmarks are no longer only geographic but also biographical and personal (Berger & Mohr, 1967).

This chapter has argued that interprofessional thinking should be studied situationally - in all of its richness and complexity. Our concern is to recognise and build on the immediacy and fluidity of health care practices as they emerge in the 'here and now'. We have tried to show that what distinguishes 'interprofessionality' from a team of solo practitioners is their *relationality* and a commitment to re-considering and possibly reshaping initial understandings through encounters with different perspectives and ways of knowing. When considered from this standpoint, interprofessional endeavours aim to generate new 'spaces' for clarifying clinical care actions, exploring emerging inconsistencies and addressing problems as they arise in everyday practice.

For us, interprofessional learning in, and through work, begins with the articulation of reasons for one's practical judgements, as Jenny displayed in our introductory anecdote. This is no simple task in health care cultures where the power and social positioning of the health professions still depends to a large extent on 'possessing' and retaining unique forms of 'stable' disciplinary knowledge and individual level expertise (Eraut, 1994). Building on Romm's (1998) conception of interdisciplinarity as reflexivity, we suggest that as health professionals, managers, educators, learners and researchers, it certainly is part of our brief to at least consider "the possible relevance of working the space between the disciplines" (p. 74). As Gibbons et al. (1994) also point out:

> [t]he capacity to cooperate with experts from other fields, to come to see the world and its problems in a complementary way and to empathise with different presuppositions, involves the capacity to assume multiple cognitive and social identities. (p.149).

Embracing the dynamic nature of knowledge and professional action in particular sites of practice requires expanded definitions and descriptions of what counts as 'teamwork', what counts as 'learning', and what counts as 'interprofessionality'. For us, this must include the 'opportunistic' interactions and holistic interprofessional thinking that arises as part of daily clinical practice - no matter how problematic or emergent these decisional moments may be. There is much we can learn from, and amongst, the relationality of participatory workplace practices. We claim there is a form of Aristotelian 'practical wisdom' apparent in this learning, and that this wisdom is already all around us.

By contrast, the pervading view in much of the IPE literature is that genuinely interdependent approaches to interprofessional learning and practice are still 'ideals' whose time is yet to come. More context sensitive accounts of practice-based interprofessionality and embodied team work (such as Ellingson, 2003; Bleakley, et al., 2004; Lingard et al., 2006), are urgently needed to push current conceptions of IPE into new territory. If IPE experiences in pre and post-registration training are to be the "test bed for interprofessional practice" (CAIPE, 2008), then we must look to the real world to learn from the contingencies, sociality and diversity of everyday clinical practices. As Stark et al., (2002) have already noted:

> students *[and health practitioners]* need to be offered insights into the broken stories, the separate logics, unintended outcomes and competitive interactions, as well as the more idealistic notions of effective team-working for quality health care" (p. 412, our italics).

As challenging as this may be, helping learners to 'read' clinical situations in different ways through collective reflection and articulation of clinical judgements may be the best preparation we can offer them for the messy realities of 'interprofessionality' in real-world clinical work.

REFERENCES

Barr, H. (2005). *Interprofessional education: Today, yesterday and tomorrow. Occasional paper one,* Revised Ed. Higher Education Academy, Health Sciences and Practice Centre. Available at: *http://www.health* (Accessed March 20 2010).

Barr, H. Koppel, I., Reeves, S., Hammick, M., & Freeth, D. (2005). *Effective interprofessional education: Argument, assumption and evidence.* Oxford, UK: Blackwell.

Beckett, D. (2004). Embodied competence and generic skill: The emergence of inferential understanding, *Educational Philosophy and Theory,* 36(5), 497-508.

Beckett, D. (2006). A useful theory of agency at work: *Proceedings of the 10th Biennial Conference of the International Network of Philosophers of Education.* University of Malta, Aug 3-6 2006.

Beckett, D., & Gough, J. (2004). Perceptions of professional identity: A story from paediatrics. *Studies in Continuing Education,* 26(2), 195-208.

Beckett, D. & Hager, P. (2002*). Life, work and learning: Practice in postmodernity.* London: Routledge.

Berger, J., & Mohr, J. (1967). *A fortunate man: The story of a country doctor.* London: Penguin.

Billett, S. (2003). Vocational curriculum and pedagogy: An activity theory perspective. *European Educational Research Journal,* 2(1), 6-21.

Billett, S. (2004). Learning through Work: Workplace participatory practices. In H. Rainbird, A. Fuller, & A. Munroe (Eds.), *Workplace Learning in Context* (pp.109-125). London: Routledge.

Bleakley, A., Hobbs, A., Boyden, J. & Walsh, L. (2004). Safety in operating theatres: Improving teamwork through team resource management. *Journal of Workplace Learning, 16(1/2), 83-91.*

Braithwaite, J., & Travaglia, J. (2005). *The ACT Health inter-professional learning and clinical education project: background discussion paper #2. Interprofessional practice.* Canberra: Braithwaite Assoc. & the ACT Health Department.

Bronstein, L. (2003). A model for interdisciplinary collaboration. *Social Work,* 48(3), 297-306.

Brown, J., & Duguid, P. (1991). Organisational learning and communities-of-practice: Towards a unified view of working, learning and innovation. *Organization Science,* 2(1), 40-57.

Cashman, S., Reidy, P., Cody, K., & Lemay, C. (2004). Developing and measuring progress toward collaborative, integrated, interdisciplinary health care teams. *Journal of Interprofessional Care,* 18(2), 183-196.

Center for Interprofessional Education and Research (CAIPE) website. (2008). Defining IPE. Available at: *http://www.caipe.org.uk/about-us/defining-ipe/* (Accessed March 28, 2008).

Duckett, S. (2005). Health workforce design for the 21st century. *Australian Health Review, 29 (2), 201-210.*

Ellingson, L. (2003). Interdisciplinary health care teamwork in the clinic backstage. *Journal of Applied Communication Research*, 31(2), 93-117.

Engestrom, Y. (2004). The new generation of expertise. In H. Rainbird, A. Fuller & A. Munroe (Eds.), *Workplace Learning in Context* (pp.145-165). London: Routledge.

Eraut, M. (1994). *Developing Professional Knowledge and Competence.* London: Routledge Falmer.

Fraser, S., & Greenhalgh, T. (2001). Complexity science: Coping with complexity: educating for capability. *British Medical Journal,* 323, 799-803.

Gherardi, S. (2000). Practice-based theorising on learning and knowing in organisations. *Organisation*, 7(2), 211-223.

Gherardi, S. (2001). From organisational learning to practice-based knowing. *Human Relations, 54(1),131-139.*

Gherardi, S. (2003). Knowing as desiring: Mythic knowledge and the knowledge of communities of practitioners. *Journal of Workplace Learning,* 15(7/8), 352-358.

Gherardi, S., & Nicolini, D. (2000). To transfer is to transform: The circulation of safety knowledge. *Organisation,* 7(2), 329-248.

Gibbons, M., Limoges, C., Nowotny, H., Schwartzman, S., Scott, P., & Trow, M. (1994). *The new production of knowledge: The dynamics or science and research in contemporary societies.* London: Sage.

Griffiths, T., & Guile, D. (2003). A connective model of learning: the implications for work process knowledge. *European Educational Research Journal,* 2(1), 56-73.

Griffiths, T., & Guile, D. (2004). *Learning through work experience for the knowledge economy: Issues for educational research and policy.* Luxembourg: Office for Official Publications of the European Communities.

Hager, P.. & Halliday, J. (2006). *Recovering informal learning: Wisdom, judgement and community.* Dordrecht, The Netherlands: Springer.

Hall, P., & Weaver, L., (2001). Interdisciplinary education and teamwork: A long and winding road. *Medical Education,* 25, 867-875.

Kavanagh, S., & Cowan, J. (2004). Reducing risk in health care teams: An overview. *Clinical Governance: An International Journal,* 9(3), 200-204.

Lave, J., & Wenger, E. (1991). *Situated learning: Legitimate peripheral participation.* Cambridge: Cambridge University Press.

Lavin, M., Ruebling, R., Banks, L., Block, M., Counte, G., Furman, P., Miller, C., Reese, V., Viehmann, V., & Holt, J. (2001). Interdisciplinary health professional education: A Historical Review. *Advances in Health Sciences Education,* 6, 25-46.

Lingard, L., Espin, S., Evans, C., & Hawryluck, L. (2004). The rules of the game: Interprofessional collaboration on the intensive care unit team. *Critical Care,* 8, 403-408.

Lingard, L., Whyte, S., Espin, S., Baker, G., Orser, B., & Doran, D. (2006). Towards safer interprofessional communication: Constructing a model of 'utility' from preoperative team briefings. *Journal of Interprofessional Care,* 20(5), 471-483.

McCallin, A. (2001). Interdisciplinary practice - a matter of teamwork: An integrated literature review. *Journal of Clinical Nursing, 10,* 410-428.

Mennin, S., & Petroni-Mennin, R. (2006). Community-based medical education. *The Clinical Teacher,* 3, 90-96.

Montgomery, K. (2006). *How doctors think: Clinical judgement and the practice of medicine.* New York, NY: Oxford.

Mulcahy, D. (2005). Between work and learning: On pedagogic practice and interstitial space: *Proceedings of the Fourth International Conference on Researching Work and Learning: Challenges for integrating work and learning* pp.1-10. Available at: *http://138.25.75.64/RWL4/RWL4Papers/6789.doc* (Accessed March 10, 2008).

Romm, N. (1998). Interdisciplinary practice as reflexivity. *Systemic Practice and Action Research,* 11 (1), 63-77.

Schon, D. (1986). *Educating the reflective practitioner.* San Francisco, CA: Jossey Bass.

Stark, S., Stronach, I., & Warne, T. (2002). Teamwork in mental health: rhetoric and reality. *Journal of Psychiatric and Mental Health Nursing,* 9, 411-418.

Tucci, J. (1995). The value of co-ordination in child protection: An interview with Christine Hallett. *Children Australia,* 20 (1),35-37.

Usher, R., Bryant, I., & Johnston, R., (1997). *Adult education and the postmodern challenge: Learning beyond the limits.* London: Routledge.

Wilson, T., Holt, T., & Greenhalgh, T. (2001). Complexity science: Complexity and clinical care. *British Medical Journal,* 323, 685-688.

Winch, C. (1998). *The philosophy of learning.* London: Routledge.

Zwarenstein, M, Reeves, S., Barr, H., Hammick, M., Koppel, M., & Atkins, J. (2007). *Interprofessional education: Effects on professional practice and health care outcomes (Review),* The Cochrane Library Collaboration: John Wiley.

In: Sociology of Interprofessional Health …
Ed: S. Kitto, J. Chesters et al.

ISBN: 978-1-60876-866-0
© 2011 Nova Science Publishers, Inc.

Chapter 8

BEYOND PROFESSIONAL CONFLICT: CULTURAL AND STRUCTURAL BARRIERS TO INTERPROFESSIONAL HEALTH CARE TEAMS

Janice Chesters and Mollie Burley

ABSTRACT

Improving health care in Australia via the operation of interprofessional health care teams is proving to be a 'wicked' problem. The difficulty in forming effective interprofessional health care teams is often attributed to the characteristics and practices of the health care professions, especially the medical profession. This concern with conflict between health and social care professions is supported by a significant literature. In this chapter we briefly outline this literature and move on to suggest other reasons why health care teams seem unable to flourish. We consider the elements required for team formation and find they generally include the key requirement for shared goals to drive team performance. This led us to examine a smaller literature, including the Garling Special Commission of Inquiry into Acute Care Services in New South Wales (NSW) Public Hospitals in 2008 that questions the health care sector's practical commitment to high standards of safety and the centrality of patient needs. Safety and delivering patient–centered care are clearly two of the most powerful potential shared goals that might motivate health care teams. However, if these key goals exist only or mainly at the level of rhetoric it may help explain why effective interprofessional health care teams have proved difficult to establish. This chapter begins to examine the links between a lack of shared health care goals and the wicked problem of delivering effective interprofessional team based health care.

INTRODUCTION

This chapter takes a sociological approach to understanding the wicked problems associated with delivering safer more patient-centered health care by enhancing the performance of interprofessional health care teams. There is an extensive literature associated with delivering health care in interprofessional teams. The majority of this literature is focussed on outlining the barriers to interprofessional team practice and suggesting micro, meso or macro level interventions to overcome these barriers. One of the main barriers identified is the nature of the health and social care professions. For example, there is claimed to be a lack of respect between the health care professions, professional stereotyping is said to be common and destructive, and the dominance of the medical profession is claimed to impede interprofessional teamwork (Cashman, Reidy, Cody & Lemay, 2004; Xyrichis & Lowton, 2008; Mickan & Rodger, 2005; Molyneux, 2001; Sargeant, Loney & Murphy, 2008; Jackson, 2008; Reina, 2007; Cook, Gerrish & Clarke, 2001; Dieleman et al., 2004; McCallin, 2001; Pullon, 2008).

Health care professionals in Australia are not generally trained to work in teams and are said to feel more secure working within their own discipline or profession and report feeling more stressed when required to work together across disciplines (Mickan & Rodger, 2000; McKeon, Oswaks & Cunningham, 2006; Lessard, Morin & Sylvain, 2008; Millward & Jeffries, 2001; Sargeant et al., 2008).

These well documented barriers to interprofessional health care team practice are an important topic and are closely associated with our concerns and discussion here but they are not our focus in this chapter. Rather we ask why health care teams cannot find shared goals that help them overcome professional differences and conflicts.

The characteristics required for team formation is both a professional field of study and the stuff of office, lounge room and bar discussions. All teams are said to require shared goals, training, leadership and resources. Many teams also appear to robustly survive power differentials, frequent and regular changes in membership, ownership and some teams even accommodate different professionals working side by side. Interprofessional health care teams seem on the face of it to be the same as other teams and display similar characteristics including the need for shared goals. The most likely goals on offer would include the provision of safe, effective and patient-centered care. Yet is this the case? There is a small body of literature that questions the health care sector's commitment to the reality and practice of safe, effective, patient-centered care. In this chapter we discuss some of this literature and briefly examine a number of health care cultural practices that do cast doubt on the existence of a shared commitment to high levels of safety and to patient-centeredness. Given the strength of safety and patient focused 'talk' or rhetoric we find it perplexing that many obvious quality and risk minimisation systems seem to be overlooked by the health and social care sector. While patients' needs are said to be central, practitioner and administrative convenience and well being often seem to dominate practice. These cultural and systemic factors are not just the preserve of any one discipline. Therefore, unless the health care team is different to other teams, the potential lack of obvious shared goals may be acting as a barrier to interprofessional team formation and effectiveness that is upstream of any conflict between health professionals.

Team based health care is promoted both as the way care is delivered 'now' and as the way health care should be delivered in the future. There is evidence to suggest that in many areas of health and social care, interprofessional health care teams could be central to providing better, safer more patient-centered care. However, real shared goals and some other key components of team formation such as training, training to performance ratios, ongoing fitness to 'perform' testing and simulation hurdles, may need to be put in place before effective health care teams will be able to form and work effectively.

BACKGROUND

Sociologists tend to search for and identify what is problematic about a field or issue. They do this by delineating, either explicitly or implicitly, the nature of the problems they find. This disciplinary habit of problematising issues is a key part of the way sociologists approach their craft. But problems are not all of a piece, some are more readily understandable and have easily identifiable solutions, while other problems are deeply complex and often seem too hard to solve. Even more problems can be masked by layers of other problems and only become visible when solutions to prior problems fail to work as expected or deliver unexpected negative consequences. Complex or difficult problems tend to be repeatedly raised and their importance to a field reiterated again and again without any effective solution being found.

In the early 1970s, urban planners Rittel and Webber (1973) provided a useful if brief taxonomy of problems contrasting 'tame' problems and 'wicked' problems. Wicked problems they argued can barely be defined and may never be solved once and for all. Some players in a field may claim that no problem exists, or not be able to agree on what the problem is, let alone how to solve it. Rittel and Webber (1973) suggest that the best solutions to wicked problems are partial and can be judged only in terms of whether they make things a bit better or a bit worse. Yet judgements on whether situations have been made better or worse may differ depending on the perspectives of different stakeholders. For example, the Special Commission of Inquiry into Acute Care Services in New South Wales (NSW) Public Hospitals (Garling, 2008) calls for a "new culture ... to take root which sees the patient's needs as the paramount central concern of the system and not the convenience of the clinicians and administrators" (p. 3) and finds that "a new model of teamwork will be required to replace the old individual and independent 'silos' of professional care" (p. 4). Yet many health professionals would claim that these 'new cultures' are already in place or may even argue that they are not the answer or even that there is no problem to solve in NSW. Perspectives on the lack of a problem or on the nature of the problem relating to acute care in NSW may also differ on gender, cultural background, class, status and age lines. Patients and providers may also see things differently. Because of these different perspectives the solutions suggested by Garling may be very difficult to implement, as further problems "deeply embedded in the structure" of the field and its individual settings or contexts may be revealed (Periyakoil, 2007, p. 658). The problem of how to get interprofessional teams to deliver safer patient-centered health care seems to fit the definition of a wicked problem.

Interprofessional health care team collaboration is regularly represented as an important solution to wicked health care problems. Interprofessional teams are represented as a key component of 'modern' safer health care as the 'system' struggles to cope with the complex, technical, specialised and uncertain health care environments (Bragg, 1999; Jackson, 2008; McKeon et al., 2006; Mickan & Rodger, 2000; Millward & Jeffries, 2001). The bulk of health problems in affluent nations like the United Kingdom are said to have shifted from acute infectious conditions to complex and chronic conditions often associated with ageing. This change in service demand is represented as occurring in an environment of knowledge expansion or explosion and the requirement for health care services to be safer, risk averse, patient-centered and delivered in an increased number of community based sites and places (Baldwin, Royer & Edinberg, 2007). These elements are said to mean that no one health care professional can safely provide the patient care required (Mickan & Rodger, 2000; Xyrichis & Lowton, 2008). Interprofessional teamwork is therefore recommended as the way forward, it is said to be an essential component of health care and is suggested as a solution to health care problems associated with patient safety, professional-patient trust and the complexity and centrality of health care (McKeon et al., 2006; Xyrichis & Lowton, 2008).

The 'interprofessional health care team' is widely researched and studied with the majority of researchers recording the difficulties of producing effective team work in practice (Hudson, 2007). Factors considered vital for successful health care teams are reported to include: geographical proximity of team members; appropriate team structure; correct size and composition of the team; organisational support; effective communication; trust between team members and between team members and their organisations; confidence in a professional role; respect; knowledge and acceptance of other professions and professionals (Cashman et al., 2004; Xyrichis & Leyton, 2008; Mickan & Rodger, 2005; Molyneux, 2001; Sargeant et al., 2008; Jackson, 2008; Reina, 2007; Cook et al., 2001; Dieleman et al., 2004; McCallin, 2001; Pullon, 2008).In their definition of the interprofessional health care team Xyrichis and Ream (2007, p. 237) include some additional key team parameters; they contend that the health care team is a:

> "... dynamic process involving two or more health care professionals with complementary backgrounds and skills, sharing common health goals and exercising concerted physical and mental effort in assessing, planning, or evaluating patient care ... accomplished through interdependent collaboration, open communication and shared decision-making, [that] generates value-added patient, organisational and staff outcomes".

The staff 'outcomes' that result from effective health care team work are said to include job satisfaction; recognition of individual contribution and motivation; and improved mental health for health professionals. Patient 'outcomes' are said to be improved quality of care and satisfaction with services. Organisational 'outcomes' might include a satisfied and committed workforce, cost control, and improved workforce retention and reduced workforce turnover (Xyrichis & Lowton, 2008; Mickan & Rodger, 2005; Molyneux, 2001; Sargeant et al., 2008; Jackson, 2008; Xyrichis & Ream, 2007).

Interprofessional health care teams are reported as not effective in practice mainly because health professionals have limited understanding of each other's roles. Professional education is said to be siloed and graduates often do not value each other's perspectives; do not have intuitive knowledge about how to work effectively in health care teams; and frequently lack the appreciation that teamwork actually requires sustained time and effort to develop, implement and sustain (Lessard et al., 2008; Millward & Jeffries, 2001; Sargeant et al., 2008). Teams are also said to fail because they include people of different levels of power and status. Physicians are reported as usually taking a dominant role within the team. Team members from other disciplines are reported as being overly influenced by the medical subculture and specialised medical expertise (Mickan & Rodger, 2000: McKeon, 2006). The constantly changing membership of health care teams is also thought to threaten the stability of teams (Delva, Jamieson & Lemieux, 2008; Limeaux-Charles & McGuire, 2006). Health care teams are sometimes represented as different and unique sorts of teams, very different from the other types of teams that we are familiar with (Mickan & Rodger, 2000).

Garling's (2008) proposed solutions of a new culture of patient-centered care and interprofessional practice certainly challenges the health sectors view of itself. Furthermore The National Health and Hospitals Reform Commission (2008), challenges the sector's commitment to safety and quality improvement; saying that while there was a pervasive understanding within Australian health care that quality and safety of health care was important:

"...there are too many barriers and frustrations to achieve more than marginal, piecemeal improvement. Is it the safety of care provided which is paramount or is it more about caring enough to continuously improve the quality of care we provide? How do we do this when many staff feel there are too few staff, too little time and too many patients to manage safely with personalised care" (p. 343).

Garling's perspective and the questions raised by the National Health and Hospitals Reform Commission are supported by researchers from the sub fields of patient, client or consumer rights and health care safety and ethics (Øvretveit, 1997; Gaba, 2000; Musson & Helmreich, 2004; Cruess & Cruess, 2004; Leape, 1994; cited in Quick, 2006; Klein, 1998, Coulter & Fitzpatrick, 2000; Kleinman, 1988; Greenhalgh, 2001). Garling's recommendations would seem set to fail because of the well documented conflict among professionals. But are these so called professional power struggles and differences masking a more fundamental problem? Both reports hint at an upstream problem and both identify problems of culture and meaning that may affect all of the health professions. Perhaps it is these problems that results in a lack of shared goals to drive interprofessional team performance. Perhaps interprofessional health care teams are just like other teams and require strong shared goals to bring them together effectively.

TEAMS IN THEORY AND PRACTICE

Sociologists, and a wide range of other disciplines, formally study the performances and practice of sporting, musical or theatrical teams or the team work associated with particular industries such as airlines. However, from our own experiences from a stadium seat, the sports pages of the local newspaper, the bar or lounge room or even from an airline seat indicates that most teams can manage their power and status differentials, members having different professional backgrounds and roles, changing team membership and even geographical distance. For example, most professional sporting teams include a small number of very highly paid stars who have much more influence than other team members. In addition, many teams work with quite authoritative coaches or conductors who exercise strong direction of the individual performances of the team. Most teams also appear to deal reasonably effectively with personnel change via rosters or selection processes associated with fitness or performance levels and plan and train to accommodate the integration of replacement members. Some teams comprise members from different and competing disciplines or professional backgrounds.

One component that supports team practice is access to appropriate resources for team-building and team training (Xyrichis & Lowton, 2008). A number of teams have established training to performance ratios. These are calculations, some simple and some very detailed, that establish the individual, group and full team training needed to enable a high level of performance. To be successful, teams need to develop trust in each other and in the systems that construct and support the team's existence. For example, organisations that set rules for safer flying and require compliance from air crew must be trusted by the team just as umpires must be relied on to be well trained and generally committed to fair play and equity for all players. Trust between team members is important to team formation. Trust, like team work, thrives on shared values, and a sense of cultural acceptance and understanding. Trust can be built on honesty and explicit and open discussion, for example the airline industry regularly draws attention to how relatively safe flying is (Giddens, 1994 in Quick, 2006). But trust can also be sustained by closing down, concealing risks or minimising discussions of risk, for example in the health industry a reliance on professional reputation such as 'trust me I'm a doctor, or a nurse or a health professional' is sometimes used to conceal risks (Giddens, 1994 in Quick, 2006). Trust in both the open and closed sense can be developed through building understanding of and respect for team roles (Williams, 2006). But a culture of closed trust once broken can cause a significant erosion of trust (Quick, 2006).

Teams of all kinds require shared goals. These goals can be as simple as aiming to win a premiership or sporting contest, transporting passengers safely or performing a piece of music at a very high level. Or they can be to deliver safer patient orientated health care. Mickan (2005) cites evidence that shared objectives were an important predictor of health care team effectiveness. On the other hand Shaw et al. (2005) found that a lack of clear team goals made it difficult for the team to function. As Mickan (2005, p. 212) notes:

> "The clearer the team's objectives, the higher the level of participation in the team, the greater the emphasis on quality and the higher the support for innovation, the more effective the team was reported to be by its members and external raters".

While Mickan does not list any team objectives, the whole tone of the paper is concerned with more and improved 'quality patient care' and more attention to the wellbeing of the health care team. Quality patient care clearly encompasses safe and patient orientated or centered care. Yet, as we have seen, Garling (2008) concluded that patient needs were not the 'central concern of the system' and that teamwork was not occurring. Patient-centered care and safer care are or should be synonymous. As Oakley (2000, p. 3) argues the health and social care team should "develop the most reliable and democratic ways of knowing, both in order to bridge the gap between ourselves and others and to ensure that those who intervene in other people's lives do so with the most benefit and the least harm". But is teamwork in health care a safety conscious and patient-centered domain? As Øvretveit (1997, p. 9) states, "we have all joined a team, only to discover it was not the type of team which we imagined".

The health care field is rhetorically and theoretically committed to risk aversion and to ensuring safe practice and safe working environments. However the health care field arguably doesn't respond practically to risk in the way that other safety conscious domains such as aviation do (Gaba, 2000; Musson & Helmreich, 2004). Many health care practitioners do not have regular health and competence checks, do not have simulation hurdles to pass or have to log team training. Health professionals can be physically or emotionally unwell, affected by drugs or alcohol, colour blind, hard of hearing, aged over the community accepted retirement age, not speak or understand the local language or culture/s well, work long hours without appropriate rest periods and, perhaps most significantly, undertake new procedures or procedures that are beyond their demonstrated and tested competence.

Health registration bodies in Australia seem reluctant to bench or de-list health care team members who are ill, emotionally unstable, affected by drugs or alcohol, are of advanced years, receive public complaints, have problems with practitioner-patient/client and practitioner–peer communication or find it difficult to take directions. A recurring criticism of the medical profession is that it has favoured the individual member's interests over that of public safety. A number of well publicised examples of adverse patient outcomes being 'ignored' or 'explained away' are said to have increased community distrust of the profession's commitment to safety and risk minimisation (Cruess & Cruess, 2004).

Expectations about safety and competence are becoming more important to health care. For example, the European Union has introduced Working Time Directives that restrict the working times of doctors and doctors in training. But adherence to these directives does not seem to be widely implemented or policed in Australia. Truck drivers, fire fighters, airline pilots, musicians and sports men and women have regular drug tests, fitness tests, compulsory rest breaks and performance tests. Yet calculations based on data collected on a large US study of medical errors and adverse events indicated that if the airlines recorded as many fatalities as the US hospital sector "this would equate to three jumbo jet crashes every two days" (Leape cited in Quick, 2006, p. 26). Community assessment of risk is perhaps biased towards concern about multiple deaths or horrific injuries in a single incident rather than widespread adverse events occurring in ones and twos across many different sites (Quick, 2006). Despite this risk assessment bias, litigation in certain health sectors, such as obstetrics and gynaecology, is increasing. However, it is the individual practitioner, usually medical practitioners, rather than the team, who is sued. There is a perception that responsibility for 'team' based care is not shared by the team but is sheeted home to the medical profession.

If safety and risk mitigation is observed more at the rhetorical than at the practical level of health care practice, and responsibility for adverse events is vested in one kind of practitioner only, then a shared view of safer health care is unlikely to form and provide an effective driver of interprofessional health care team practice. Evidence that health care teams provide safer care is unlikely to provide what Plsek and Wilson (2001) following Goldstein (1994) call 'natural attractor patterns' or shared goals or objectives that motivate health care practitioners to change the way they work and practice in interprofessional health care teams. It seems more likely that medical practitioners, who expect to be held responsible for poor outcomes, will adopt practices and checks that have them personally overseeing or signing off on treatment. Alternatively, they are likely to retain allegiance to traditional referrals to other professionals for discreet treatment rather than the embracing of interprofessional health care team practice. Klein (1998) contends that while inquiries and coronial inquests focus on the individual doctor, reducing or avoiding the possibility of individual blame and responsibility will remain the focus of at least the medical players in the team. If collective or team based practice escapes scrutiny and evaluation, it is likely to remain an unacceptable risk for medical practitioners.

If asked, the majority of airline passengers would probably be confident that the pilot or co-pilot had simulated and practiced flying in a particular plane and approaching a particular airport before doing so with passengers aboard. Few passengers would board a plane or use an airline that flouted air traffic regulations and pilot licensing requirements. Good airlines enforce safety briefings and safety requirements on every flight. Indeed, passengers in certain rows of seats are asked to assist the crew in the event of difficulties and are briefed separately about their role and asked if they are able and willing to assist. By contrast, most health care practitioners and teams aren't required to pass simulation hurdles that establish their safety within very particular contexts. Much of their pre-licensure training and examinations assess generic, context-free knowledge and practice. Students and new graduates are often expected to gain contextual and experiential knowledge with 'real' patients. Experienced health care professionals may undertake procedures that they have not ever done or not done for some time, on patients, without the benefits of simulation testing using standardised patients or simulation facilities (Gaba, 2004). In relation to severe failures of safe care, Klein (1998, pp. 1740-1742) discusses the notion of 'learning curve deaths' that occur as practitioners learn procedures that are either new to a field or merely new to a particular practitioner. When learning curves are combined with a system committed to individual rather than systemic responsibility a cover up appears almost inevitable. The trust that would be essential to interprofessional team training and practice, tested via simulation hurdles and team training, would be unlikely to develop.

Sports teams and the aviation industry crews have simulation hurdles to pass and their communication and leadership skills in training environments are assessed. They regularly reflect and review what they do by watching or listening to tapes, video or recordings of performances. Health care teams rarely do this and often don't carefully collect and review the statistics associated with their practice. Sports commentators have the statistics of all players on hand to discuss and mull over during lulls in the play. Sports statisticians record every element of games that rarely involve life or death. The health care team is often involved in life or death activities but have few statisticians on hand and few commentators to scrutinise performance.

Sporting teams, musical teams and the flight deck team in civil or military aviation all practice and train as individuals, as small groups (the violins, the forward line or the air line cabin stewards) and then they practice as an entire team. They are coached again as individuals, as small groups and as whole teams. Sports team's video record games, collect detailed statistics, measure as many performance related parameters as possible and then review and reflect on what they have learned. Ironically, sports physicians, psychologists, physiotherapists, scientists and other health and wellbeing specialists, contribute to reviewing and remediating any sports-related problem they detect. On the other hand, health care professionals rarely train post-licensure and if there are requirements for continuing professional development it is generally an individual exercise. There are some individual coaches in health care but little or no small group or team coaching. There are few health team doctors, psychologists and other support professionals on hand to help the team train well for excellent performance, as Baldwin (2007, p. 39) notes:

> "It is ironic, indeed, to realise that a football team spends 40 hours per week practicing teamwork for those two hours on Sunday afternoon when their teamwork really counts. Teams in [health care] organisations seldom spend two hours per year practicing, when their ability to function as a team counts 40 hours per week."

Sports teams have a carefully worked out individual and team training to performance ratio. That is, they have calculated how much and what kind of training is needed to produce and sustain a certain rate, level or quality of performance both as individual performers and as teams. These training to performance ratios are often finely calibrated and must be as accurate as possible to sustain excellent performance. In health care teams, there is some individual training for a continuation of the right to practice, but few if any individual training to performance ratios and almost no ongoing team ratios beyond specialist civilian retrieval and disaster response teams and within military health care teams. The development of training to performance ratios for health care teams would seem to be an essential ingredient for team formation and safe, effective patient-centered performance. However, in the context of current Australian health care delivery, the resources to enable this to occur seem unlikely to be provided. Overcoming this key barrier to effective interprofessional team formation and excellence of outcome seems one of the most wicked health problems.

PATIENTS ON THE TEAM

Patient-centered care or a commitment to patient outcomes and wellbeing are a central rhetoric of health care. But is patient-centered care just rhetoric or is it the defining element in actual practice? Alford (1975) argued that professional and institutional interests generally prevailed over patient's interests and needs. Garling (2008) argued that this was still the case in NSW. Providing health care in acute circumstances, the main task of health care providers in the past, perhaps demanded less in the way of patient involvement. The patient is often too ill to question or make choices about treatment and care (Coulter & Fitzpatrick, 2000). Patients can either be accepted into treatment or their entry to treatment or actual treatment can be legitimately delayed or rejected outright. Diagnosis can be incorrect, appropriate services may be a long distance away or rationed in some way that denies care. Patients without family, supporters or money, or disadvantaged in other ways, may not gain access to the best care or indeed to any care. Alternatively, care may be provided by poorly trained staff or delayed while more appropriate staff are contacted or become available. Acute care is guided by protocols, guidelines, routines and treatment as usual regimes. This care is rarely individualised for the patient as the pressure on clinician's time under current hospital practices would not allow it (Coulter & Fitzpatrick, 2000).

As the percentage of health care time devoted to chronic conditions increases, the rate of patient involvement is said to be set to rise. In advanced economies, as education levels increase and health related information is more readily available, patients are reported to be interested and motivated to become involved in their chronic health care management. However, this opportunity and interest in involvement intersects with some aspects of the way that health care is delivered. While chronic disease management is a larger part of the health care work load – 53% of general practice work in Australia in 2007/08 – the nature of health care practice may not have changed to accommodate this. Health care professionals are arguably still delivering care that is more suited to acute and serious conditions. Kleinman (1988) and Greenhalgh (2001) among others have argued that biomedicine is a hazard to the chronically ill as many of the symptoms and patient responses to the condition are related to social, cultural and other contextual issues that may lead to poorer health outcomes for certain groups or types of patients. The wicked problems associated with chronic health conditions make it difficult for both health professionals and patients. Patient-centered practice and moves toward integrating the patient into the interprofessional team is laudable but may not be acceptable as a shared goal for health care teams. A patient's inability to contribute effectively to the technical aspects of care is often taken as an indication that they have no useful contribution to make. However, there are many other elements involved in health care that patients can not only contribute to but lead the way in.

Garling's (2008) criticism of a lack of patient-centered care is an important landmark in Australian health care. However, this report's very direct contrast between the goal of patient-centered care and the practice of "addressing the convenience of the clinicians and administrators" (p. 3), contrasts with the more traditional approach taken by the National Health and Hospitals Reform Commission (2008) report. This document calls for the community to take more care about their own health and encourages more choice regarding aged care, but is not explicitly concerned with supporting patient involvement in interprofessional health care teams or in explicitly ensuring patient-centered care is delivered. This is despite comments that during the National consultations leading up to the National Health and Hospitals Reform Commission (2008) report community groups across Australia frequently called for "access to holistic patient-centered care with consumers as partners" (p. 83).

MOVING FORWARD

Hall and Weaver (2001) note the vast amount of literature on interdisciplinary or interprofessional team education and practice, yet conclude that there are still many more questions to be answered. One of their questions is pertinent to this chapter:

> "What is the best way of teaching nebulous but vital concepts, such as the necessity of sharing the burden of care, understanding equality in responsibilities and reciprocity, sharing a common goal, and trusting team members?" (Hall & Weaver, 2001, p. 873).

This question perhaps goes to the heart of the matter of interprofessional health and social care team formation and performance. Expressed in this way it seems to provide support for the wicked nature of the problems surrounding the health care team. Yet thousands if not millions of all sorts of other teams manage to achieve this outcome more or less successfully every day right across the world. If the health care team thought of itself as having more rather than less in common with other types of teams, especially those that work in an environment where safer practice is a practical as well as a rhetorical commitment, perhaps the wicked problem could be gradually and incrementally improved.

Wicked problems can rarely be solved completely, but complex, non-linear interventions gradually applied can help. Rosenhead (1996) suggests dealing with wicked problems by:

- Employing multiple alternative perspectives rather than single solutions;
- Group interaction and iteration;
- Ownership of the problem formulation through transparency;
- Facilitating visual representation for the systematic group exploration of a solution space;

- Focusing on the relationships between discrete alternatives rather than continuous variables;
- Concentrating on possibility rather than probability (pp. 117-131).

Plsek and Greenhalgh (2001) recommend adopting reflective practitioner techniques and the plan, do, study, act cycle associated with quality improvement cycles; while Lemieux-Charles and McGuire (2006) suggested Continuous Quality Improvement (CQI) and Chronic Care Models to help overcome these wicked problems.

CONCLUSION

In this chapter we wanted to start to delineate a problem we associated with interprofessional health care team formation and practice and to help provide a more adequate theoretical and practical basis to move forward. Better interprofessional health and social care team work will only come about via complex, non linear, partial solutions and interventions. These interventions will gradually increase 'what works' and reduce what doesn't work. The success of these interventions must be judged against the need for safety and patient-centered care. Patients, clients or consumers must become part of the team and their needs must be central. Interprofessional health care team education and practice improvement will be enhanced by policy and education models that focus on teaching values in an environment of strong clinical governance, the creative use of evidence, simulation and modelling, the provision of support, coaching and mentoring and the development of training to performance ratios for health care students and all health care professionals.

This better practice will need to take account of the need for knowledge transfer, reflexivity, exploration and innovation. Practice improvement may be enhanced by education models that focus on case based learning, grand rounds, audits and clinical case discussion, increased creative use of realistic simulation and modelling, role play, small group learning and teambuilding exercises that focus on individual, group, team and sector performance. We have concluded that health care teams need to see themselves as more like other teams, especially teams in the aviation industry and in professional sports and music, that try to maximise individual and system safety in dangerous and unsafe environments. But patients, clients and consumers of health and social care will also require education, training and support for their role as key members of the interprofessional health care teams. Because just being together or in contact is not enough.

REFERENCES

Alford, R. (1975). *Health Care Politics*. Chicago: University of Chicago Press.

Baldwin, D.C., Royer, J.A., & Edinberg, M.A. (2007). Maintenance of health care teams: Internal and external dimensions. *Journal of Interprofessional Care*, 21, (S1), 38-51.

Bleakley, A. (2006). Broadening conceptions of learning in medical education: The message from teamworking. *Medical Education*, 40, 150-157.

Bragg, T. (1999). Turn around an ineffective team. *IIE Solutions*, 31, 49-51.

Cashman, S., Reidy, P, Cody, K., & Lemay, C. (2004). Developing and measuring progress toward collaborative, integrated, interdisciplinary health care teams. *Journal of Interprofessional Care.* 18,183-196.

Cook, G., Gerrish, K., & Clarke, C. (2001). Decision-making in teams: issues arising from two UK evaluations, *Journal of Interprofessional Care.* 15, 141-151.

Coulter, A., & Fitzpatrick, R. (2000). The Patient's Perspective Regarding Appropriate Health Care. In G.L. Albrecht, R. Fitzpatrick, & S.C. Scrimshaw (Eds.), *Handbook of Social Studies in Health and Medicine.* London: Sage Publications.

Cruess, S. R., & Cruess, R. L. (2004). Professionalism for Medicine: Opportunities and Obligations. *The IOWA Orthopaedic Journal*, 24, 9-15.

Delva, D., Jamieson, M., & Lemieux, M. (2008). Team effectiveness in academic primary health care teams. *Journal of Interprofessional Care*, 22(6), 598-611.

Dieleman, S., Farris, K, Feeny, D., Johnson, J., Tsuyuki, R., & Brilliant, S. (2004). Primary health care teams: team members' perceptions of the collaborative process. *Journal of Interprofessional Care*, 18(1), 75-78.

Fraser, S.W., & Greenhalgh, T. (2001). Complexity science: Coping with complexity: educating for capability, *British Medical Journal.* 323, 799-803 (6 October).

Gaba, D.M. (2000). Structural and Organisational issues in patient safety: A comparison of health care to other high-hazard industries. *California Management Review*, 43, 83-102.

Gaba, D.M. (2004). The future vision of simulation in health care. Qual Saf Health Care, 13(Suppl 1), i2-i10.Garling, P. (2008). *Final Report of the Special Commission of Inquiry Acute Care Services in NSW Public Hospitals Overview,* State of NSW.

Greenhalgh, S. (2001). *Under the Medical Gaze.* Berkeley: University of California Press.

Hall, P., & Weaver, L. (2001). Interdisciplinary education and teamwork: a long and winding road. *Medical Education*, 35, 867-875.

Hudson, B. (2007). Pessimism and optimism in inter-professional working: The Sedgefield Integrated Team. *Journal of Interprofessional Care*, 21(1), 3-15.

Jackson, D. (2008). Collegial trust: crucial to safe and harmonious workplaces. *Journal of Clinical Nursing*, 17(12), 1541-1542.

Klein, R. (1998). Competence, professional self regulation, and the public interest. *British Medical Journal,* 316,1740-1742.

Kleinman, A. (1988). *The Illness Narratives: Suffering, Healing and the Human Condition.* New York: Basic Books.

Lessard, L., Morin, D., & Sylvain, H. (2008). Understanding teams and teamwork. *The Canadian Nurse*, 104(3), 12-13.

Lewicki, R., & Tomlinson, E. (2003). Trust and Trust Building. Available at: *http://beyondintractability.org/essay/trust* (Accessed 16 June 2008).

Limeaux-Charles, L., & McGuire, W. (2006). What do we know about health care team effectiveness? A review of the literature. *Medical Care Research Review*, 63, 263-300. Available at: *http://www.informaworld,com/smpp/section?content-a905567075&fulltext=713240928* (Accessed 05/01/2009).

McCallin, A. (2001). Interdisciplinary practice – a matter of teamwork: an integrated literature review. *Journal of Clinical Nursing*, 10, 419-428.

McKeon, L., Oswaks, J., & Cunningham, P. (2006). Complexity Science, High Reliability Organisations, and Implications for Team Training in Healthcare. *Clinical Nurse Specialist,* 20(6), 298-304.

Mickan, S. (2005). Evaluating the effectiveness of health care teams. *Australian Health Review,* 29 (2), 211-217.

Mickan, S., & Rodger, S. (2000). The organisational context for teamwork: Comparing health care and business literature. *Australian Health Review*, 23(1), 179-192.

Mickan, S., & Rodger, S. (2005). Effective Health Care Teams: A model of six characteristics developed from shared perceptions. *Journal of Interprofessional Care*, 19(4), 358-370.

Millward, L., & Jeffries, N. (2001). The team survey: a tool for health care team development. *Journal of Advanced Nursing*, 35(2), 276-287.

Molyneux, J. (2001). Interprofessional teamworking: what makes teams work well? *Journal of Interprofessional Care*, 15(1), 29-35.

Musson, D.M., & Helmreich, R.L. (2004). Team Training and Resource Management in Health Care: Current Issues and Future Directions. *Harvard Health Policy Review*, 5(1), 25-35.

National Health and Hospitals Reform Commission. *A Healthier Future For All Australians-Interim Report December 2008*. Commonwealth of Australia Canberra, 2009.

Nielson, B. (2004). The role of trust in collaborative relationships: A multi-dimensional approach. *Management*, 7(3), 239-256.

Oakley, A. (2000). *Experiments in Knowing Gender and Method in the Social Sciences*. New York: The New Press.

Øvretveit, J. (1997). How to describe interprofessional working. In J. Øvretveit, P. Mathias & T. Thompson (Eds.), *Interprofessional working for health and social care* (pp. 9-33). Houndsmills: Macmillan Press.

Paget, M.A. (1988). *The Unity of Mistakes*: A *Phenomenological Interpretation of Medical Work*. Philadelphia, PA: Temple University Press.

Periyakoil, V.S. (2007). Taming Wicked Problems in Modern Health Care Systems. *Journal of Palliative Medicine*, 10 (3), 658-659.

Plsek, P.E., & Greenhalgh, T. (2001). Complexity Science The challenge of complexity in health care. *British Medical Journal*, 323, 625-628.

Plsek, P.E., & Wilson, T. (2001). Complexity Science Complexity, leadership and management in healthcare organizations. *British Medical Journal*, 323, 746-749.

Pullon S. (2008). Competence, respect and trust: Key features of successful interprofessional nurse-doctor relationships. *Journal of Interprofessional Care*, 22(2), 133-147.

Quick, O. (2006). Outing Medical Errors: Questions of Trust and Responsibility. *Medical Law Review*, 14, 22-43.

Reina, M., Reina, D., & Rushton, C. (2007). Trust: The Foundation for Team Collaboration and Healthy Work Environments. *AACN Advanced Critical Care*, 18(1), 103-108.

Rittel, H., & Webber, M. (1973). Dilemmas in a General Theory of Planning. *Policy Sciences*, 4, 155-169.

Rosenhead, J. (1996). What's the problem? An introduction to problem structuring methods. *Interfaces*, 26(6), 117-131.

Rousseau, D., Sitkin, S., Burt, R., & Camerer, C. (1998). Not so different after all: A cross-discipline view of trust. *Academy of Management Review*, 23(3), 393-404.

Sargeant, J., Loney, & Murphy, G. (2008). Effective Interprofessional Teams: "Contact is not enough" to Build a Team. *Journal of Continuing Education in the Health Professions,* 28(4), 228-234.

Sullivan, E., Francis, K., & Hegney, D. (2008). Small rural health services in Victoria: how does nursing-medical division of labour affect access to emergency care. *Journal of Clinical Nursing*, 17, 1543-1552.

Williams, L. (2006). The Fair Factor in Matters of Trust. *Nursing Administration Quarterly*, January 9, 30-37.

World Health Organisation, (1978). *Primary Health Care. Health for All Series, No. 1.*,Geneva. Alma Ata.

Xyrichis, A., & Ream, E. (2007). Teamwork: a concept analysis. *Journal of Advanced Nursing*, 61(2), 232-241.

Xyrichis, A., & Lowton, K. (2008). What fosters or prevents interprofessional teamworking in primary and community care? A literature review. *International Journal of Nursing Studies, 45,* 140-153.

In: Sociology of Interprofessional Health …
Ed: S. Kitto, J. Chesters et al.

ISBN: 978-1-60876-866-0
© 2011 Nova Science Publishers, Inc.

Chapter 9

INTERPROFESSIONAL EDUCATION – WHAT WORKS, WHAT DOESN'T WORK AND SOME OF THE BARRIERS AND FACILITATORS TO SUCCESSFUL IPE

Lynda d'Avray and Peter McCrorie

ABSTRACT

IPE will be examined critically from a practical point of view in an attempt to address the question - *what works?* The success or failure of IPE appears to depend on several issues: its purpose, the model adopted, the needs of participants, how they are assessed, the attitude of facilitators and the active involvement of staff. Simply sitting students from different professions side by side in a lecture theatre is unlikely to be enough and may be counterproductive. More interactive IPE – working together in small interprofessional groups to discuss a health care scenario of common interest, learning shared skills together, or working side-by-side in a shared clinical placement – can provide more effective approaches. IPE seems to thrive when it mirrors real life and involves students working together in mixed teams. In this chapter, a few successful approaches and some of the potential pitfalls will be explored. Barriers discussed include practical problems, professional cultures, facilitation and institutional organisation.

INTRODUCTION

This chapter will attempt to analyse interprofessional education (IPE) with a view to understanding some of the facilitators and barriers to its implementation and to providing suggestions for best practice. The focus will be on pre, rather than post-qualification and on education and learning, rather than working. Although post-qualification IPE and interprofessional working pose challenges and opportunities that may be similar to those at the pre-qualification level, many are quite different. The work focus, especially around a particular client group, makes IPE easier to implement, especially where collaborative services are an on-going feature, such as in community mental health, cancer and coronary heart disease, intermediate care, joint health and social care and so on. Learning together and team building for practitioners can be built into working life, providing credit in continuing professional development. This is very different from pre-qualification IPE.

IPE and spontaneous collaboration between the health and social care professions goes back several decades but since 1997, wide ranging policies to establish the implementation of IPE have contributed to its proliferation in the UK and other countries (Barr, 2007). Relations between staff within health care delivery, particularly between doctors and nurses, and their respective relations with members of the allied health professions have long been a concern (Menzies, 1970). But the rift between health and social care and the danger to patients when communication between these two services does not work effectively has attracted attention and reform (UK Audit Commission, 2006).

The impetus for IPE has also grown in response to other factors: the increasing numbers of different professions (Gyamarti, 1986) and specialists involved in the course of an episode of care; more aged individuals proportional to the rest of the population, many with multiple needs; more complex medical and other treatments; the complicated interface between the primary and acute care environments; and the increasing weight given to the patient's experience as an indicator of quality.

There is a good case for IPE (Meads, Ashcroft, Barr, Scott & Wild, 2005) in today's health and social care delivery context. Collaboration between service providers is essential and unavoidable and it makes sense to prepare future health workers for this. IPE has the potential to support: a shift from profession-focused to user-focused care; demands for more individualised and flexible care packages; increasing demands for optimal skill mix in the interests of efficiency and cost-effectiveness; changing roles in health care occupations such as nurse consultancy and liaison roles, new practitioner grades and new jobs like physician assistant. Furthermore, research by Fay, Borrill, Amir and West (2006) indicates that both the professions and patients benefit from improved team working, and that team working is associated with increased job satisfaction, staff retention and improvements in morbidity and mortality.

However, there is a confusing array of expectations from IPE, many modes of delivery and several potential barriers to implementation. It is important when planning IPE to consider its purpose, the needs of the learners, the attitudes of the teachers/facilitators and the professional and educational cultures that prevail. To understand how these factors influence the delivery of relevant and robust IPE, it is also helpful to consult the underpinning social and learning theory, as well as the current IPE literature.

PURPOSE

Clear and explicit aims and learning outcomes are essential for successful implementation of an IPE programme. Students and staff may be reluctant to embrace it if the perception is that IPE has a hidden agenda, perhaps to advantage one group over another or to blur professional roles in pursuit of workforce flexibility, role substitution and the switching of careers (Vyt, 2009). IPE may be seen as a challenge to the identity of individual professions or as a step towards the creation of a generic health and social care workforce that may provide cheaper but not necessarily better care.

So to avoid IPE being perceived as a negative influence it is important to stress that its purpose is to improve collaborative practice. This is usually articulated through learning objectives that include demonstrating the ability to work together, thereby reducing gaps and overlaps in service, interprofessional communication, a positive attitude towards those from another profession and a shared patient focus.

Multiple and muddled purposes may also be confusing and ambiguous for the universities that are developing IPE (Finch, 2000). Is IPE supposed to provide the same learning content to students who are studying the various professions? This may have the advantage of conferring economies of scale and providing basic common knowledge that they all need for future practice. Or is IPE for students, with their unique and common sets of knowledge and skill, to learn how to combine their abilities through positive interaction? The following modes of IPE delivery fall broadly into one or both of these categories and IPE is commonly defined as "Occasions when two or more professions learn with, from and about each other in order to improve collaborative care" (CAIPE, 1997), aiming at improving interprofessional understanding, collaboration and patient care.

MODES OF IPE AND UNDERPINNING THEORIES

Acquaintance with theories of learning may be helpful in understanding and evaluating IPE designs and making decisions about selecting an appropriate design and mode of delivery. But despite the potential for social and learning theories to bear on IPE design and implementation, they are rarely explicitly cited and those upon which each institution bases its preferred variety of IPE are not always made clear.

The range of delivery formats for IPE concurs with the learning styles approach (Kolb, 1984), which suggests that individuals perceive and process information in very different ways. IPE appears in various forms in the early, middle and final years of professional study; in the university and in practice; in the hospital and the community; in the classroom and the skills centre. It sometimes includes many professions, sometimes a few.

Many learning styles are utilised, from lectures and other forms of common learning that enable students to share essential education, to problem-based learning and early application to practice that encourage interactive learning. Adult learning styles in IPE encourage functioning as team members, good communication, adaptability to change, and continuous life-long learning (Barr, 2002). Encouraging self-direction, critical analysis and reflection in IPE has potential to foster deep and permanent knowledge.

A few examples from common learning, problem based learning and practice-based learning have been selected for discussion.

Common Learning

A single health and social care education programme that straddles all the professions in the first part of the curricula is unusual because of the prohibitively large numbers of students, and the unequal numbers specified by governments for each profession. Despite the difficulties, this model is to be adopted in 2009 in AUT in Auckland, New Zealand, although it will not include medical students who are based at another university.

Common foundation or common learning, whereby certain parts of the first year are shared, has so far been a popular form of IPE. Curricula are manipulated to enable students from across the professions to meet and learn together. Several sites may be included, sometimes with students from more than one university (for example in the UK in South London and in Southampton). Some universities include all or almost all health profession students (King's College London, UK); others are more selective (St. George's, University of London, UK).

Early in professional training, IPE tends to be designed around topics that are common to all and independent of the experience or abilities of any of the students, such as skills or professionalism relating to real patient care. All health care professionals need to communicate with their patients so IPE sessions around basic communication skills, such as listening and empathising provide opportunities for interprofessional rather than just multiprofessional learning. Interaction between students from various professions adds value to common learning and may include a mixture of small group exercises and role-play, graduating to simulated patients if funding is available. Recording students' role plays on video or DVD can be extremely useful, although challenging, since they can observe and learn from their non-verbal as well as verbal communication (Thistlethwaite & Ridgway, 2006).

The basic sciences are also sometimes included in common learning IPE. Even though teaching these subjects to students from different professions may not necessarily have any direct influence on the quality of patient care, it is possible to see that there is value in students at least meeting and getting used to each other (Stephan & Stephan, 1984). Other skills, such as basic life support and patient examination are sometimes taught multiprofessionally and activities such as measuring blood pressure, pulse and breathing rate while exercising can be fun and good for building team spirit. All students can benefit from common learning around information technology, numeracy, self-directed learning, teamwork skills, decision-making, patient safety etc.

A common or interprofessional foundation at the beginning of health training that incorporates some of the above, if it is well-received, may encourage participation in later IPE experiences, which is important if initial gain is not to be lost in the process of becoming socialised into a particular profession (Pekuconis, Doyle & Bliss, 2008). Students can be strongly influenced by role models and not all faculty consistently model interprofessional behaviours. Following common learning in the classroom with interprofessional learning in the practice environment may counter pressures or tendencies to revert to stereotypical behaviour and is discussed below.

Despite the potential for learning through common learning, the numbers of students, cost and teaching resources present real problems. In addition, Barr (2002) argues that IPE based exclusively on common learning might fail to promote positive attitudes between students and fail to foster perceptions that improve working relationships. Despite the contact it permits, studies show that simply placing students together in large mixed classes can be unproductive (Parsell & Bligh, 1998). They may ignore each other, resent sharing their education with other professional groups or feel that their learning is being diluted (Horsburgh, Lamdin & Williamson, 2001).

Problem-Based, Case-Based and Workshop Learning

Constructivism is a philosophy applied to learning that says humans construct knowledge and understanding of the world by reflecting on experiences (Bruner, 1966). Rather than providing given answers, problem-based learning (PBL) (Bergdahl, Eintrei, Fyrenius, Hultman & Theodorsson, 2005) and case-based learning (CBL), with scenarios written and delivered by mixed professional teams (McCrorie, 2001), provide opportunities for reflecting on and solving problems. Contact through workshops, small group exercises and debates can also promote various forms of interaction for interprofessional learning (Dickinson & Carpenter, 2005).

Discovering principles for themselves and constructing knowledge by working on solving realistic problems can help students connect facts and foster new, more informed understanding of collaboration. Open-ended questions are useful for encouraging dialogue between the students (Dewey, 1938; Vygotsky, 1978) and encouraging them to actively build new concepts based upon current and past knowledge and to analyse, interpret, and predict.

Learning style theorists emphasise intuition, feeling, sensing, and imagination, in addition to the traditional skills of analysis, reason, and sequential problem solving. They argue for teaching methods that connect learning styles, using various combinations of experience, reflection, conceptualisation and experimentation (Kolb, 1984). Barr (2002) argues that interprofessional learning processes allow for double reflection or co-reflection, whereby the learner can also see him or herself in the eyes of someone from another profession.

In PBL, students are presented with a patient scenario requiring a range of professional input from which they learn, through self directed learning and discussion, the basic sciences, clinical reasoning, sociological perspective, professional roles etc., which are relevant to the case and which naturally arise from it. Students acquire their knowledge through the PBL process with minimal input from formal lectures (Dahle, Brynhildsen, Behrbohm, Fallsberg, Rundquist & Hammar, 2002). CBL is also based on a patient scenario, but more scaffolding is provided, mostly in the form of lectures, with the danger that some students may come to rely on lecture notes rather than engage with the self directed learning related to the case (McCrorie, 2001).

Learning through the more self-directed PBL is possibly more suited to IPE than the CBL or shorter case format, although both are used, for example at St George's, University of London, UK (McCrorie, 2001) and in Linköping, Sweden (Dahle et al., 2002). A potential pitfall though, with both PBL and CBL, is for them to be designed mainly around the needs of one professional group, with limited reference to the other health and social care professions. This can be avoided if they are written and delivered by a mixed professional team.

The study of law and ethics, sociology, psychology and critical thinking provide further opportunities for learning professional behaviours and attitude. The workshop and/or debating format, where students are facilitated in mixed groups, may be helpful for encouraging interaction between them around, for instance, ethical dilemmas or points of view.

Interprofessional Learning in Practice

IPE developments that resemble real life are said to encourage professional development and understanding about the role of each profession. Authentic and customised learning that mirrors real service delivery is important for positive experiences (Hammick, Freeth, Koppel, Reeves & Barr, 2007). Learning about the work of other professions and learning to work together is good preparation for future employment (Freeth, 2007).

Learners and practitioners belong to 'communities of practice' (Wenger, 1998) and operate in 'situated learning' (Lave & Wenger, 1991). These theories seek to understand both the structure of communities and how learning occurs within them. Learning is seen as a social phenomenon and knowledge is integrated into the shared values, beliefs, languages, and ways of doing things. According to this theory, humans learn by doing as their learning is entwined with community membership and members both belong to and adjust their status according to learning: their identity within the group changes. Thus the community can create powerful learning environments allowing students to engage in real action and its consequences.

Learning together in practice can facilitate the development of self-efficacy through the observation of successful interprofessional role-modelling and the positive consequences of such behaviour (Bandura, 1986). Reflection and reflective practice both on action and in action (Schön, 1987) may encourage adult learners to set aside pre-conceived tendencies such as automatic stereotyping. Understanding from these theories may be implicit in interprofessional practice placements or interprofessional training wards (Wahlström, Sandén & Hammar, 1997; Fallsberg & Wijma, 1999; Fallsberg & Hammar, 2000; Ponzer et al., 2004; Reeves, Freeth, McCrorie & Perry, 2002) and lead to a better understanding about the way health care is actually delivered (Freeth et al., 2001). Mixed student teams working together in practice is not new. Interprofessional work in the USA in the 1960s involved inter-disciplinary groups of students delivering health care to people in underserved Native American communities (Baldwin, 2007).

The 'interprofessional training' or 'student ward', first created at Linköping in Sweden (Wahlström et al., 1997; Fallsberg & Wijma, 1999; Fallsberg & Hammar, 2000) and then implemented at the Karolinska Institute in Stockholm (Ponzer et al., 2004) was introduced to the UK in 1996 at the Royal London Hospital (Reeves et al., 2002). It was followed in 2004 by Queen Mary's Hospital in Roehampton, South West London with students from the London Universities of Brunel, Kingston and St. George's (Mackenzie et al., 2007).

The original Swedish 'student ward' was sited in a specially created orthopaedic ward, which became a training unit when the students attended. In between, it reverted to an ordinary ward. The same arrangement has been adopted in SW London, where six times a year the normal unit becomes a student-led ward taking about 30 final year students at a time from nursing, medicine, physiotherapy and occupational therapy. They are divided into three teams that work day shifts (late, early, then followed by a day off) looking after 14 elderly patients, who are rehabilitating from surgery, stroke and other problems, under close supervision. Each student team hands over the care of patients to the oncoming team at the change of shift. They are given responsibility for the personal care of patients and contribute to the functioning of the ward. Reflective time with a facilitator is set aside at the end of the day for discussing team related issues. There is also clinical tuition from specialists within the individual professions. Each three-week block ends with a series of team presentations, based on an aspect of the experience. Learning outcomes are based on interprofessional and professional behaviours and attitudes.

The advantage of the learning is that it is practice-based involving real patients. Students work together in teams, learning from each other and about each other as they perform their daily work. Attending to patients over a whole shift enables them to practice real communication, it teaches them the importance of accurate handovers and helps them to learn how staff on the ward operate and interact interprofessionally. Students learn how to write patient notes – one unexpected outcome was for the ward to break with the tradition of keeping separate professional records. Medical students begin to engage in the therapeutic relationship with patients; they learn how to provide basic nursing care and to appreciate the nursing students and their work. Nursing students learn aspects of medical care and gain confidence through leading the student teams and presenting cases on the ward-round. Positive evaluation from students, staff and patients has led to its extension to the hospice setting and further clinical sites.

Other examples can be found of practice-based IPE. In South East London in the UK students 'process map' a patient's journey (d'Avray, Cooper & Hutchinson, 2004; d'Avray, Coster & Hall 2005; d'Avray, Coster & Wade, 2006). Mixed groups of students first hypothesise a health care pathway and then visit a hospital ward to interview patients about their actual experience of the episode of care. Perspectives are compared and students consider what could be improved from the patient's point of view. After discussion and reflection, their suggestions for improving the service are fed back to hospital management. In Leicester, also in the UK, mixed groups of learners visit patients at home who volunteer to act as key partners in the IPE programme (Anderson & Lennox, 2004). They interview patients and service providers in order to understand the strengths and weaknesses of the service and how medical and social care issues impact on the patients. The patient's priorities are again compared with those of the service and fed back to service managers.

Each mode of IPE delivery will have advantages and disadvantages for satisfying different aims, and these will need to be carefully considered by a university or service delivery unit before making its selection. But purpose is not the only issue. There are other important factors that can impact on successful implementation and the quality of the learning.

POTENTIAL BARRIERS TO IPE

Different Learning Needs

Problems have long been associated with the socialisation process during professional programmes (McMichael & Gilloran, 1984) and evidence that students can both enter *and leave* professional education with preconceived prejudices about the other professions is a concern. However, although education may be part of the problem, there is potential through IPE for it to become part of the solution (Barr, 2007).

When introducing IPE into the curriculum, through teaching health and social care students together, it is important to construct situations that suit the learners' needs. For pre-qualification students these may vary according to several factors: the job they are being trained to do; their current level of education; and their social background, such as age, gender, ethnicity, culture and belief systems.

Interprofessional groups of students will usually comprise a mix of abilities, interests, cultures and expectations. Therefore because they may have many different learning needs, finding a common level for learning is sometimes difficult. For instance, too basic a level of anatomy may frustrate medical and physiotherapy students, while some nursing students may find it overly detailed (Mitchell, McCrorie & Sedgwick, 2004). It is important to avoid setting students up for difficulty or to fail (Freeth, 2007), which could happen if students taught together have different prior knowledge about a subject and/or need to understand it at a different level for their profession. Although difference may not necessarily be related to capability or intelligence, but to perceived value or usefulness, it can nevertheless reinforce negative stereotypes.

In addition, students will have been exposed to different prior-learning experiences. Some are used to lectures, handouts and seminars, others to problem-based learning, workshops and reflective discussion, and yet others to role-play, simulation or computer games. Presenting IPE through a standard lecture format to hundreds of students of mixed ability and mixed interests may not therefore be successful. If lectures are to be delivered to mixed groups, then care must be taken to be inclusive, taking into account the needs of all the students.

In terms of whether to deliver IPE in the first, middle or final years, it was previously thought that students needed to identify themselves with their chosen profession before they were ready for IPE. Subsequent research has shown, not only that student identification with their own profession is well formed from the beginning of health education, but also that their readiness and willingness to engage with interprofessional learning is also stronger at this point (Coster et al., 2008). Students have been shown to have positive attitudes towards other professions early in their health education and it is therefore advantageous to introduce IPE early (Hind et al., 2003).

Gender, Ethnicity and Class

The social differences in ethnicity, gender and class persist in maintaining status differences between the professions that can be underplayed when designing IPE. Gender is undoubtedly an issue in the evolution of the professions, especially in medicine and nursing. The power relations between doctors and nurses in the health services appear to reflect the respective roles of men and women in society, which despite legislation remains unequal. For example, in the UK, the Equal Pay Act (1970) was designed to give women the same pay as men for doing the same work, and the Sex Discrimination Act (1975) was intended to end gender discrimination in employment, education and other spheres. But this did not extend to the home where many women retained the main responsibility for domestic work and childcare. According to Pateman (1988) women's subordination in the home can prevent them from gaining equality at work because of the way their domestic responsibilities limit their careers.

The UK NHS and social service workforce is made up of large numbers of people from ethnic minorities, and like women, they form a greater proportion of the workforce lower down the pay scale. Despite legislation, the Race Relations Act (1965) and the Race Relations Amendment Act (2000), there is considerable evidence that racial discrimination and ethnic disadvantage remain widespread in the UK and that members of ethnic minorities are rarely found in positions of power and influence (Kenny & Field, 2003).

Similarly with class: nurses and doctors remain in different categories on the UK Registrar General's Social Class (Rose & Elias, 1995). The facts of unequal future salaries, separate budgets for medical and 'non-medical' education and a single pay scale for all health workers except doctors (Agenda for Change, 2002) can also influence the relative status that students perceive when in mixed professional groups.

Thus in addition to educational background, perceived abilities and future position in the workforce, perceptions amongst IPE participants about gender, ethnicity, social status and anticipated pay differential can create social barriers to its effectiveness that need careful consideration.

Teachers and Facilitators

The skills and attitudes of faculty and practitioners towards members of staff and students from other professions can affect the quality of interprofessional learning. Professionals are most likely to have acquired their qualifications in a uniprofessional environment and may have become accustomed to entrenched attitudes towards other health care professionals. Some may feel sceptical about interprofessionalism and its threat to their traditional roles, power and autonomy. Others, who are less hostile, may nevertheless find the idea of working with mixed student groups quite daunting

"…because the diversity of concerns, interests and expertise may well be greater in an interprofessional group. While this diversity can stimulate learning and enjoyment, it can also overstretch the skills of the facilitators or the ingenuity of the curriculum developers who provide trigger material and structure to guide the learners" Freeth (2007, p. 10).

Teachers may also not agree about how students learn. Some prefer a didactic approach and find it difficult to promote student interaction. Others appreciate that students are adult learners who can enquire for themselves and who can be encouraged through facilitation to become reflective life-long learners. One teaching style or preference may dominate in a particular profession and it may be difficult to get uniformity in how to handle heterogeneous groups.

Assessment

Although assessment of IPE is important, this is not a simple matter. Assessing interprofessional learning may encourage student attendance by increasing its perceived value. Students tend to be attracted to subjects that appear to be more relevant, personally appealing or those that are necessary for assessment or examination. But even when IPE is assessed, the weighting accorded to an IPE assessment, relative to other subjects, may vary according to profession (Mitchell et al., 2004), and this may influence the value students attach to the learning. If knowledge-based or other learning is accorded more value, IPE may acquire lower status and lose students' attention.

"For courses leading to academic or professional awards there is a potential conflict between the achievement of learning outcomes that support professional autonomy and those that focus on collaborative working" (Freeth, Hammick, Reeves, Koppel & Barr, 2005, p. 75).

Further, each set of uniprofessional rules must be satisfied. For example only a qualified nurse on the same part of the UK nursing register (NMC, 2006) is permitted to assess a student nurse in practice. This can create problems when a doctor or physiotherapist is best placed to assess a mixed group of students. Similarly collaborative learning and practice are difficult to assess given that most assessments are not team-based. So choosing an assessment protocol that promotes value, fits the regulations and appears to be fair across the professions can be particularly challenging.

Timetabling

The scheduling of IPE can present serious obstacles to its implementation. Almost always, existing timetables have to be modified, occasionally drastically, in order to accommodate IPE and this can present serious obstacles or even lead to resistance.

It may make logistical sense to start with the timetable of one professional group and add others into it. For example it may be tempting to create a common foundation programme for students of several professions from a pre-existing uniprofessional course. But the main danger with this approach is that students or their teachers may perceive they were slotted into a course previously belonging to another profession (Mitchell et al., 2004) and that their timetabling issues are perceived to be less important.

Organising groupings that cut across professional lines to provide opportunities for interprofessional learning is theoretically possible, but separate schools of education, registration bodies, funding streams and employers present formidable logistical challenges. There is no single simple answer to this problem. One strategy may be for curriculum planners to routinely collaborate across all programmes and practice placements – but this is difficult to achieve in a culture where university departments and schools retain their separate hierarchies. A longer view, that might facilitate cross professional planning in education, would be to strive for an interprofessional culture such that faculty and practice staff begin to consider the needs of *all* students when they plan curricula and practice learning.

Culture

Perhaps the most important consideration in successful IPE delivery is the uniprofessional culture of the learning environment in practice and education, which can be the most difficult of all barriers to overcome. Integrated and comprehensive patient care can be severely limited by uniprofessional bias and, unfortunately this model of care can be transmitted to students who then replicate uniprofessional attitudes. Students therefore need to be educated and socialised within an interprofessional environment for them to develop cooperative working relationships across disciplines (Bruder, 2000). But this is not common in health and social care practice and education: profession-centric behaviour tends to be the norm, with each profession holding its preferred view of the world that is reinforced through training.

"Each health discipline possesses its own professional culture that shapes the educational experience; determines the salience of curriculum content, core values, customs, dress, salience of symbols, the meaning, attribution, and etiology of symptoms, as well as what constitutes health, wellness and treatment success" (Pekuconis et al., 2008, p. 420).

Each profession tends to set itself apart from others, seeing themselves positively and more in tune with the real world than others (Pekuconis et al., 2008). Such lack of appreciation for diversity across health and social care delivery promotes competition rather than collaboration and isolation, elitism, and territorialism amongst teachers and role models in professional training. Thus the training environment can be steeped in professional cultures that transmit cultural bias to students and shape their evolving practice attitudes, perceptions and behaviours.

Pekuconis et al. (2008) suggest that promoting interprofessional cultural competence would enable professionals to work effectively in cross-professional situations, just as cultural competence enables people to work in cross-cultural situations, and would enable health care professionals to be comfortable and skilled in working across professions. They suggest several strategies, especially the encouragement of clinical training opportunities that explore the roles of health care team members as a way to rethink students' education so that the separate training institutions can be bridged. Inculcating interprofessional competence in students, as the next generation of health care workers, is suggested for overcoming existing profession-centrism.

But the thing that complicates IPE so much is that it is taught within a *uniprofessional* and not an *interprofessional* climate. This is true of both practice and education. If the time ever comes for students to learn about interprofessional working in an interprofessional environment that has established *interprofessional* attitudes, knowledge and skills, then it will be normal practice for practitioners and educators to role-model interprofessional behaviours every day. But in an environment where uniprofessional cultures dominate, the minority of professionals who become involved in delivering IPE, must both role-model interprofessionalism *and* challenge the prevailing culture. Thus in addition to addressing any interprofessional knowledge or skill deficit, preparation for those delivering IPE needs to include role-modelling interprofessional behaviours and challenging uniprofessional culture and attitudes.

OVERCOMING THE BARRIERS: CRITICAL FACTORS TO CONSIDER WHEN IMPLEMENTING IPE

Contact

The contact hypothesis stipulates that certain conditions must be met in order for people, brought together from opposing sides, to have a positive experience. Contact alone is not enough to reduce the negative attitudes between individuals from different groups (Amir, 1969). Certain conditions must also be satisfied:

1. There must be equal status within the context of the contact;
2. There must be common goals for the group to work on;
3. There must be institutional support;
4. The members must cooperate with each other;

Hewstone and Brown (1986) later added four more conditions:

5. Participants need to have positive expectations;

6.   The joint work must be successful.
7.   Concern must be shown for similarities and differences between group members.
8.   Members brought into contact must be perceived as typical of their group.

But even so, it is difficult to predict which intergroup encounters will be more likely to reduce prejudice (Dickinson & Carpenter, 2005). Firstly, the contact hypothesis may have stipulated too many conditions for positive contact, with the danger of there being a never-ending list. Secondly, it has not been established whether all the conditions or just some are required for effective contact in IPE. Finally, it is not clear which conditions are generic to all IPE situations and which are specific to context.

Another problem is that contact theory does not specify how changes in negative attitudes take place. Pettigrew (1998) identified four possible cognitive processes:

- Contact provides an opportunity for learning about others. Because ignorance about people from another group can promote prejudice (Stephan & Stephan, 1884), getting to know them should promote tolerance. This leads to cognitive dissonance (Festinger, 1957) whereby getting to know someone from another group encourages a person to alter the stereotype held, since it no longer fits.
- Friendships formed in IPE may stimulate empathy and identification that become generalised towards all members of the other group.
- Contact permits insight about one's own group enabling one to reflect on its cultures and behaviours.
- Members of the in-group feel positive towards out-group members who perceive them positively.

But unless change is generalised to other contact situations it is not likely to last long enough to influence future practice. According to Rothbart and John (1985) generalisation can only occur when the out-group behaviour in the contact situation, comes to be seen as typical of the out-group in general. Thus the IPE situation must enable participants to change their perception of who is typical; from those who are out-group members perceived stereotypically because they are not known to the individuals they got to know in IPE. If this shift does not take place, participants can simply re-categorise out-group members according to some characteristic, for example 'the doctor in our IPE session was not arrogant because she was female'.

It is thus possible to see how paying attention to the conditions for quality IPE contact may help an innovation to work. The IPE exercise provides the obvious common goal for the group to work on. Getting students to lead and chair sessions can ensure equal status within the group. It can also encourage all members to listen to, understand and appreciate the different professional concerns. Appropriate sharing of joint tasks can encourage cooperation between the members. Positive expectations can be engendered by appropriate and relevant preparation for students, and by recruiting facilitators who express enthusiasm for IPE. The point that the institution supports IPE needs to be obviously stated as students and faculty alike can often miss it. Finally successful work can encourage the group, who may over time begin to see the other members as typical representatives of the professions rather than the previously held stereotypes.

Social Identity

Understanding the social context can provide important information about how an individual sees him or herself both as an individual and as a member of a group, which is an important social theory for shedding light on the formation of stereotypes. Authors of social interaction theory (Mead, 1934) were interested in how a person acted within the group, whereas social identity theory is concerned with how the group is expressed within the individual.

According to social identity theory, each person constructs a social or collective identity from experiences with members of various groups that are salient to him or her. This contributes to one's self-concept (Tajfel & Turner, 1986) and helps develop an understanding of how to act within the social world. Health and social care personnel thus define themselves not just personally but also as members of their professional group. Each individual strives to maintain his or her self-concept and self esteem by seeking positive social identity through defending and preserving the group values (Abrams & Hogg, 1990).

However, in perceiving him or herself as a group member he or she may make comparisons with other groups and favour in-group members over out-group members (Turner, 2004). Stereotypes can provide members with a framework for interpreting outsiders and predicting uncertain events, but in doing so they can perpetuate group culture by helping to construct 'reality', and solidify self-concept (Hogg, 2000).

Several contact models have been based on Social Identity Theory (Brown & Gardman, 2001). A decategorisation model suggests playing down the differences within the group and making in-group and out-group categorisations less psychologically important by personalising the intergroup situation so participants get to know each other as individuals rather than as members of a group (Brewer & Miller, 1984). A common in-group identity model proposes creating a super-ordinate group identity so that the various members of the group share membership of a new larger category (Gaertner, Dovidio, Anastasio & Bachman, 1993).

Hewstone and Brown (1986) propose a synthesis of the two by making contact both highly intergroup and highly interpersonal. Positive effects of contact are likely to be generalised to the out-group as a whole when the group membership of a person is kept prominent, and optimising conditions for personal contact will encourage individual friendships. IPE group members should therefore be encouraged to be aware of the professional groups to which all members belong and also have the opportunity to engage with out-group members on a personal level.

Organisation Development

In many institutions, implementing IPE requires substantial curricula manipulation and, for that, some degree of organisation development will be needed. Most health and social care curricula did not originate with IPE in mind and it is unusual for a new university to be created into which interprofessional curricula is structured from the beginning, such as that in the University of Linköping (Bergdahl et al., 2005).

Complexity theory is an explanatory model that may contribute to understanding about how apparently chaotic health care organisations operate and change. It proposes three strategies for promoting change in practice and practitioner behaviour: joining, transforming, and learning (Miller, Ross & Freeman, 1999). The clusters of academics, practitioners, students and patients formed around each discipline in uniprofessional education can be seen as belonging to different complex adaptive systems (CAS) with their own dynamic interaction. According to CAS analysis, thinking and operating outside the professional box in the quest to provide interprofessional learning is likely to lead to joining with others, challenging existing structures, transforming the organisations and further interprofessional learning.

Complexity theory recognises that health care institutions comprise professional organisations in which transformations are extremely difficult. These difficulties are caused, in part, by the institutionalised nature of professional organisations, which can be resistant to change. Understanding them as CAS can provide strategies for managing transformations that are not so apparent when more traditional conceptualisations of professional organisations are used (Walls & McDaniel, 1999).

Although there are no proven theoretical frameworks to guide IPE development, Cooper, Carlisle, Gibbs and Watkins (2001) argue that complexity theory, with its focus on connectivity, diversity, self-organisation, and emergence, could provide interprofessional education with a coherent theoretical foundation, freeing it from the constraints of a traditional linear framework, enabling it to be better understood, questioned and challenged as a new paradigm of learning. Applied to IPE, it may offer insights into the behaviour of students and staff in their uniprofessional complex adaptive systems.

Soft systems approach is another methodology for dealing with messy, ill-defined and ill-structured problems. The implementation of IPE is a complex social process that takes place in the context of an environment that is not particularly interprofessional. Through a soft-systems approach, the different viewpoints and assumptions of students, tutors and practitioners can be brought out and articulated in a participatory way. Analysis provided by systems thinking and soft systems methodology may provide understanding about their interrelationships.

Implementation and Facilitation

For successful implementation of IPE it is important for those who are to deliver it to have a sense of ownership and for that they need to be included in the planning of IPE from the beginning. Getting buy-in from various professionals can be helped by designing courses together, inviting the views of all the professions and collaborating on all decisions. Devising a programme of IPE without key stakeholder involvement may lead to resentment and a sense that their ideas might have worked better, had they been asked. Conversely, an inclusive approach will mean that different professionals find themselves meeting new people in other schools or departments, some of whom they may never have met before. They will find themselves in an interprofessional situation, where it is necessary to take responsibility for overcoming obstacles together, which can have an influence on their own culture and behaviours.

Vyt (2009) in arguing for total quality management makes two important points. Including teachers and facilitators in a democratic decision-making process around the devising and organising of IPE will in itself be satisfying for them. Secondly active involvement will be more likely to lead to effective decision-making processes because they will be based on the experience of those delivering IPE. Regular meetings to revise goals and develop the programme will also help sustain it.

Developing confidence for facilitating IPE calls for an interprofessional development programme and team teaching. Those who are to facilitate interprofessional learning need a carefully thought-through programme of training relevant to their varying backgrounds, practice and educational needs. Providing them with the mechanics of the learning exercise will be necessary but not sufficient. They may have (usually unfounded) anxiety about facilitating interprofessional groupings, and fear that gaps in their knowledge might be exposed. Reflecting together and sharing the experience of delivering interprofessional learning can encourage team members to find collective solutions to the problems raised. They can consider whether clinical or profession specific knowledge is sufficient or necessary for delivering IPE, and how to keep the focus on interprofessional matters. They need to feel secure that the point of IPE is not to provide technical or clinical knowledge, but to draw out the different experiences and approaches to the educational task and deal with diversity.

Facilitating IPE students appears to work best when particular principles are applied. Drawing students' attention to their communication skills, a strategy common in all health education, by rewarding good communication and exploring poor communication is especially important in IPE. Teaching listening skills to students and encouraging effective questioning will help them learn how to develop understanding and clarify issues between the professions.

Dealing with diversity by highlighting and discussing similarity and difference between the professions, such as separate cultures, may help them understand and diminish barriers between the professions. Discussing unique or overlapping roles and where these are shared, may help them to identify where gaps might occur. Other areas of commonality or difference that can be explored are professional skills, professional values, professional behaviour, sociological and philosophical understanding.

Helping students to understand how the wider context can impact on interprofessional organisation within health and social care services and what helps or hinders this, is another important aspect of IPE. This can include a critical examination of policy and management decisions, whether hierarchies are helpful, what alternatives there might be, and how one might respond to those perceived to have a higher or lower status.

Discussing stereotyping can be fruitful for raising awareness through drawing attention to common positive stereotypes and why these may be useful. This can be compared with common negative stereotypes and how these might negatively impact on patient care. Providing circumstances and the environment for friendships to develop between the students can be important for positive contact.

CONCLUSION

There have been numerous interprofessional initiatives, and the reforms affecting the delivery of health and social care education have created opportunities for shared teaching and learning. There is emerging evidence that interprofessional collaboration can enhance patient-centred acute and primary care (Barr, Koppel, Reeves, Hammick & Freeth, 2005); it can help patients in addressing their complex needs and it makes sense for clinicians from multiple disciplines to combine resources and strategies for sharing responsibility for their patients (Lorenz, Mauksch & Gawinski, 1999). When doctors and nurses work well together, relationships are positive and disagreements are collaboratively resolved to the benefit of all concerned (Farrell, 2001).

The success of an IPE intervention can depend on several factors. The design and delivery of IPE needs to be based on relevant learning and social theory and to take on board the changes that may be required in the cultural environment of the organisation. Keys to the success of an IPE exercise seem to be addressing the needs of students, satisfying conditions for positive contact, learning in small groups, learning through interaction and practice rather than watching or listening, focussing on skills and behaviour more than knowledge, and where knowledge is included, delivering it contextually through case scenarios, PBL, workshops and discussion groups. For good quality facilitation, planning an IPE activity requires the input of *all* participating faculty and practice professionals, right from its inception and for all staff involved in any IPE activity to undergo a period of training.

REFERENCES

Abrams, D., & Hogg, M.A. (1990). *Social Identity Theory*. New York: Springer-Verlag

Agenda for Change. (2002).

Available at: *http://www.nhsemployers.org/pay-conditions/agenda-for-change.cfm* (Accessed July 14, 2008).

Amir, Y. (1969). Contact hypothesis in ethnic relations. *Psychological Bulletin, 71(5)*, 319-342.

Anderson, E., & Lennox, A. (2004). *Leicester Model of Interprofessional Education: A practical guide for implementation in health and social care*. Medicine, Dentistry & Veterinary Medicine. London: Higher Education Academy.

UK Audit Commission, 2006.

Baldwin Jr., & DeWitt C. (2007). Interview by Lynda d'Avray. *Journal of Interprofessional Care,21* Suppl 1),4-22.

Bandura, A. (1986). *Social foundations of thought and action: A social cognitive theory*. Englewood Cliffs, NJ: Prentice Hall.

Barr, H. (2002). *Interprofessional Education. Today, Yesterday and Tomorrow. A Review*. London: Higher Education Academy, Learning & Teaching Support Network for Health Sciences & Practice.

Barr, H. (2007). *Interprofessional Education in the United Kingdom 1966 to 1997*. Occasional Paper No. 9. Health Sciences and Practice. London: Higher Education Academy.

Barr, H., Koppel, I., Reeves, S., Hammick, M., & Freeth, D. (2005). *Effective Interprofessional Education: Argument, Assumption and Evidence*. Oxford: Blackwell.

Bergdahl, B., Eintrei, C., Fyrenius, A., Hultman P., & Theodorsson E. (2005). Renewed medical education in Linköping. Problem-based learning, basic science and public health intensified (article in Swedish*). Lakartidningen,102(38)*, 2654-2658.

Brewer, M. B., & Miller, N. (1984). Beyond the contact hypothesis: Theoretical perspectives on desegregation. In N. Miller, & M. Brewer (Eds.), *Groups in contact: The psychology of desegregation*. New York: Academic Press.

Brown, R., & Gardman, K. (2001). Social Identity Theory: Past Achievements, Current Problems and Future Challenges. *European Journal of Social Psychology, 30,* 745-778.

Bruder, M. B. (2000). Family-centered early intervention: Clarifying our values for the new millennium. *Topics in Early Childhood Special Education, 20(2)*, 105–116.

Bruner, J. (1966). *Towards a Theory of Instruction*. Cambridge, MA: Harvard University Press.

CAIPE. (1997). *Interprofessional Education – a Definition*. CAIPE Bulletin. London: Centre for Advancement of Interprofessional Education.

Cooper, H., Carlisle, C., Gibbs, T. & Watkins, C. (2001). Developing an evidence base for interdisciplinary learning: a systematic review. *Journal of Advanced Nursing, 35(2)*, 228–237.

Coster, S., Norman, I., Murrells, T., Kitchen, S., Meerabeau, E., Sooboodoo, E., & d'Avray, L. (2008). Interprofessional attitudes amongst undergraduate students in the health professions: A longitudinal questionnaire survey. *International Journal of Nursing Studies, February 2008.*

d'Avray, L., Cooper, S., & Hutchinson L. (2004). *Developing IPE in Practice Report 1: Development, implementation and preliminary evaluation of "process mapping" as an exercise for interprofessional learning in practice*. London: King's College London.

d'Avray, L., Coster, S., & Hall, G. (2005). *Developing IPE in Practice Report 2: Midway progress report and future plans for interprofessional learning in practice*. London: King's College London.

d'Avray, L., Coster, S., & Wade, T. (2006). *Developing IPE in Practice Report 3: Final Report for Learning in Practice 2003-2006*. London: King's College London.

Dahle, L.O., Brynhildsen, J., Behrbohm Fallsberg, M., Rundquist, I., & Hammar, M. (2002). Pros and cons of vertical intergration between clinical medicine and basic science within a problem-based undergraduate medical curriculum: examples and experiences from Linköping, Sweden. *Medical Teacher, 24,* 280-285.

Dewey, J. (1938). *Experience and Education*. Philadelphia: Kappa Delta.

Dickinson, C., & Carpenter, J. (2005). *Contact is not enough: An inter-group perspective on stereotypes and stereotype change in Interprofessional Education*. In H. Colyer, M. Helme, & I. Jones (Eds.), Health Sciences & Practice Occasional Paper No 7: The Theory-Practice Relationship in Interprofessional Education. London: The Higher Education Academy.

Equal Pay Act (1970). Office of Public Sector Information. London: The Stationery Office

Fallsberg, M.B., & Hammar, M. (2000). Strategies and focus at an integrated, interprofessional training ward. *Journal of Interprofessional Care, 4(4),* 337-350.

Fallsberg, M.B., & Wijma, K. (1999). Student attitudes towards the goals of an inter-professional training ward. *Medical Teacher, 21(6)*, 576-581.

Farrell, M., Ryan, S., & Langrick, B. (2001). 'Breaking bad news' within a paediatric setting: an evaluation report of a collaborative education workshop to support health professionals. *Journal of Advanced Nursing, 36 (6)*, 765–775.

Fay, D., Borrill, C.S., Amir, Z., & West, M.A. (2006). Getting the most out of Multidisciplinary Teams: A Multi-sample Study on Team Innovation in Health Care. *Journal of Occupational and Organizational Psychology, 79*, 553-567.

Festinger, L. (1957). *A Theory of Cognitive Dissonance*. Evangston, Il: Row, Peterson.

Finch, J. (2000). Interprofessional education and teamworking: a view from the education providers. *British Medical Journal, 321*, 1138–1140.

Freeth, D. (2007). *Interprofessional education*. In Understanding Medical Education series. Edinburgh: ASME.

Freeth, D., Hammick, M., Reeves, S., Koppel, I., & Barr, H. (2005). *Effective Interprofessional Education: Development, Delivery and Evaluation*. Oxford: Blackwell Publishing.

Freeth, D., Reeves, S., Goreham, C., Parker, P., Haynes, S., & Pearson, S. (2001). 'Real life' clinical learning on an interprofessional training ward. *Nurse Education Today, 21*, 366-372.

Gaertner, S.L., Dovidio, J.F., Anastasio, P.A., & Bachman, B.A. (1993). *The Common Ingroup Identity Model: Recategorisation and the Reduction of Intergroup Bias*. European Review of Social Psychology.

Gyamarti, G (1986). The teaching of the professions: An interdisciplinary approach. *Higher Education Review, 18(2)*, 33-43.

Hammick, J., Freeth, D., Koppel, I., Reeves, S., & Barr, H. (2007). A best evidence systematic review of interprofessional education: BEME Guide no. 9. *Medical Teacher, 29*, 735-751.

Hewstone, M., & Brown, R.J. (1986). Contact is not enough: An intergroup perspective on the 'contact hypothesis'. In M. Hewstone & R.J. Brown (Eds.), *Contact and Conflict in Intergroup Encounters*. Oxford: Blackwell.

Hind, M., Norman, I., Cooper, S., Gill, E., Hilton, R., Judd, P., & Jones, S. (2003). Interprofessional perceptions of health care students. *Journal of Interprofessional Care, 17, (1)*, 21-34.

Hogg, M.A. (2000). Subjective uncertainty reduction through self-categorisation: a motivational theory of social identity processes. *European Review of Social Psychology, 11*, 223-255.

Horsburgh, M., Lamdin, R., & Williamson, E. (2001). Multiprofessional Learning: The Attitudes of Medical, Nursing and Pharmacy Students to Shared Learning. *Medical Education, 35*, 876–883.

Kenny, D., & Field, S. (2003). *Black People Pushing Back the Boundaries II: Key facts on public services and black and minority ethnic people in London*. Greater London Authority.

Kolb, D.A. (1984). *Experiential Learning: Experience as the Source of Learning and Development*. New Jersey: Prentice Hall.

Lave, J., & Wenger, E. (1991). *Situated Learning: Legitimate peripheral participation*. Cambridge: Cambridge University Press.

Lorenz, A.D., Mauksch, L.B., & Gawinski, B.A. (1999). Models of collaboration. *Primary Care, 26*, 401–410.

Mackenzie, A., Craik, C., Tempest, S., Cordingley, K., Buckingham, I., & Hale, S. (2007). Interprofessional Learning in Practice: the Student Experience. *British Journal of Occupational Therapy, 70*, 8.

McCrorie, P. (2001). Tales from Tooting: Reflections on the First Year of the MBBS Graduate Entry Programme at St George's Hospital Medical School. *Medical Education, 35,* 1144-1149.

McMichael, P., & Gilloran, A. (1984). *Exchanging Views: Course in Collaboration.* Edinburgh: Moray House College of Education.

Mead, G. H. (1934). *Mind, self and society.* Chicago: Chicago University Press.

Meads, G., Ashcroft, J., Barr, H., Scott, R., & Wild, A. (2005). *The Case for Interprofessional Collaboration.* Oxford: Blackwell.

Menzies, I.E.P (1970). *The Functioning of Social Systems as a Defence Against Anxiety.* London: Tavistock Institute of Human Relations.

Miller, C., Ross, N., & Freeman, M. (1999). *Shared Learning and Clinical Teamwork: New Directions in Education for Multiprofessional Practice.* London: English National Board of Nursing, Midwifery and Health Visiting.

Mitchell, B.S., McCrorie, P., & Sedgwick, P. (2004). Student attitudes towards anatomy teaching and learning in a multiprofessional context. *Medical Education, 38,*737-748

Parsell, G., & Bligh, J. (1998). 'Interprofessional learning'. *Postgraduate Medical Journal, 74(868),* 89-95.

Pateman C. (1988). *The sexual contract.* Cambridge: Polity.

Pecukonis, E., Doyle, O., & Bliss, D.L (2008). Reducing barriers to interprofessional training: Promoting interprofessional cultural competence. *Journal of Interprofessional Care, 22(* 4), 417 – 428.

Pettigrew, T.F. (1998). Intergroup Contact Theory. *Annual Review of Psychology, 49, 65-85*

Ponzer, S., Hylin, U., Kusoffsky, A., Lauffs, M., Lonka, K., Mattiasson, A., & Nordström. (2004). Working and learning together: Interprofessional training in the context of clinical practice: goals and students' perceptions on clinical education wards. *Medical Education, 38,* 727-736.

Race Relations Act (1965). Office of Public Sector Information. London: *The Stationery Office.*

Race Relations (Amendment) Act (2000) Office of Public Sector Information. London: The Stationery Office.

Reeves, S., Freeth, D., McCrorie, P., & Perry D. (2002). "It teaches you what to expect in future…": interprofessional learning on a training ward for medical, nursing, occupational therapy and physiotherapy students. *Medical Education, 36,* 337-344.

Rose, D., & Elias, P. (1995). The Revision of OPCS social classifications. *Work, employment and society. 9*(3) 583-592.

Rothbart, M., & John, O.P. (1985). Social Cognition and Behavioural Episodes: a cognitive analysis of the effects of intergroup contact. *Journal of Social Issues, 41,* 81-104.

Royal College of Nursing (2007) *Guidance for mentors of nursing students and midwives: an RCN Toolkit.* London. Royal College of Nursing.

Schön, D. (1987). *Educating the Reflective Practitioner: Toward a New Design for Teaching and Learning in the Professions.* San Francisco: Jossey-Bass.

Sex Discrimination Act (1975). Office of Public Sector Information. London: *The Stationery Office.*

Stephan, W.G., & Stephan, C.W. (1984). The role of ignorance in intergroup relations. In N. Miller & M.B. Brewer (Eds.), *Groups in Contact.* New York: Academic Press.

Tajfel, H., & Turner, J.C. (1986). The social identity theory of intergroup behaviour. In W. Worsgel & W. Austin (Eds.),. *Psychology of Intergroup Relations*. Chicago: Nelson-Hall.

Thistlethwaite, J,. & Ridgway, G. (2006). *Making it real: A practical guide to experiential learning*. Oxford: Radcliffe Publishing Ltd.

Turner, J.C. (2004). What the social identity approach is and why it matters. In S.A Haslam (Ed.), *Psychology in Organizations: The Social Identity Approach*. London: Sage.

Vygotsky, L.S. (1978). *Mind in Society: The development of higher psychological processes*. Cambridge, MA: Harvard University Press.

Vyt, A. (2009). *Exploring quality assurance for interprofessional education in health and social care*. Antwerpen/Apeldoorn. Garant.

Wahlström, O., Sandén, I., & Hammar, M. (1997). Multiprofessional education in the medical curriculum. *Medical Education, 31*(6), 425-429.

Walls, M.E., & McDaniel, R.R (1999). Mergers and acquisitions. *Seminars in Nurse Management, 7(3),* 117-124.

Wenger, E. (1998). *Communities of Practice: Learning, meaning and identity*. Cambridge MS: Cambridge University Press.

West, M. (2006). *Managing Change – generating teamwork*, Health estates facilities management association annual conference, Brighton 2006.

In: Sociology of Interprofessional Health …
Ed: S. Kitto, J. Chesters et al.

ISBN: 978-1-60876-866-0
© 2011 Nova Science Publishers, Inc.

Chapter 10

INTERPROFESSIONAL HEALTH CARE AS INTERCULTURAL EXPERIENCE – EARLY YEARS TRAINING FOR MEDICAL STUDENTS

Andrew Russell

ABSTRACT

This chapter uses the experience of 1st and 2nd year medical students at Durham University's Queen's Campus undertaking community placements as a model for the consideration of interprofessional health care training as intercultural experience. Queen's Campus is situated on Teesside, an area in the North East of England with major socio-economic and health inequalities. The approach to intercultural experience used derives from social anthropology, and is distinctive for the in-depth, long-term contact it gives every student with one of a range of non-clinical or unusual clinical health and social care providers. The argument is that interprofessional health care education in such early years medical training is a way of breaking down barriers between professions before medical students have become acculturated to the bounded professional identity that, until relatively recently, has characterised much of medicine.

INTRODUCTION

This chapter argues for the consideration of interprofessional health care training in community settings as intercultural experience. Using theoretical models of intercultural experience developed in social anthropology, I propose that interprofessional health care education, delivered early in the training of medical students, is a way of preventing the formation of barriers between different professions and between professionals and the clients and communities they serve. This is because such training takes place before medical students have become enculturated into the bounded and somewhat impermeable professional identity that, until relatively recently, has characterised much of medicine. Part of the reason for these processes of boundary creation is power. However, I shall argue that another potent reason is fear. The experience of non-clinical health and social care services in community settings at an early stage in their professional development gives students the confidence to develop a professional identity that is more permeable than the traditional 'doctor's shell'. The MBBS Phase I Community Placement scheme at Durham University's Queen's Campus will be used as an example of this theoretical approach. It is an innovative scheme that gives every medical student in-depth, long-term contact with one of a range of non-clinical or unusual clinical health and social care providers on Teesside, a region of profound socio-economic (and therefore health) inequalities in the North East of England. Subsidiary aims of the scheme are to encourage students to remain as practising doctors on Teesside, and to develop a lasting knowledge and understanding of the range of different services available in any community. The underlying premise to this is that the good doctor should be a quasi-anthropologist, making it his or her business to find out more about what is available, wherever they end up practising, in order to be able to direct their patients appropriately. The scheme is monitored and evaluated through a number of different means: evaluations and feedback from the students, including the community placement reports they write at the end of their placements; evaluation forms from, and conversations with, the placement hosts. This chapter draws on a variety of materials to argue for the scheme as a type of intercultural experience.

BACKGROUND

Durham University started delivering the first two years of a five year MBBS (Bachelor of Medicine, Bachelor of Science) degree programme at its Queen's Campus in 2001, a joint venture with the University of Newcastle, UK. Queen's Campus is situated in Stockton, a post-industrial town that is part of the Teesside conurbation, an area with over 500,000 people in the north-east of England marked by wide employment, income and education differentials, and hence profound health inequalities. As Tudor Hart's 'inverse care law' states (1971), "the availability of good medical care tends to vary inversely with the need of the population served", and the most deprived areas of Teesside suffer from a chronic shortage of doctors. Hence the programme at Stockton had a remit to increase the numbers of doctors in the area. Most surveys of medical careers in underserved areas have concentrated on the plight of rural areas, and while the evidence for the impact of training in rural areas on future careers is inconclusive (Ranmuthugala et al., 2007), work by Easterbrook et al. (1999) and Wilkinson, Laven, Pratt and Bailey (2003) suggests that students coming from rural areas are more likely to end up practising in those areas. Thus it is not implausible that likewise students coming from, and familiar with, areas of socioeconomic deprivation and inequality are more likely to end up practicing in these areas. To support this assumption, the Stockton programme has a commitment to widening access to medical school for students from non-traditional backgrounds (cf. Angel & Johnson, 2000). Teesside has traditionally had a relatively low uptake of learners into higher education, and encouraging people from non-traditional backgrounds and the local area onto the programme was seen as an important way of increasing the number of future doctors in the region. Medicine at Queen's Campus now enrols 102 students per year, who complete two years of medical education there, after which they join their counterparts from Newcastle for further clinical work at one of four 'base units' in the northern region of England.

My own progress into medical education (as an educator rather than a medical student) came from my background in medical anthropology. Having taught medical anthropology to undergraduate anthropology students at Queen's Campus for several years, I relished the challenge of imparting the insights and concerns of anthropology to students from another discipline (medicine). Social anthropology deals with the complexity of everyday life amongst disparate social groups through an approach favouring interdisciplinarity and holism. Rather than seeing diversity as something threatening and confusing, social anthropologists celebrate it, both within and across cultures, through a principle of understanding first and judging (assuming judgement is needed at all) later. Social anthropology is particularly concerned with the role of cultural symbols, such as language and ritual, as mediators in people's experience. It is also interested in knowledge – both formalised, authoritative knowledge (such as that imparted through most medical training) and more diffuse, 'muted' and non-formalised knowledge (such as that pertaining to patients and other non-medical, 'lay' persons). Anthropology has also, in recent years, cast off its legacy of colonialism in order to apply insights deriving from the study of 'other cultures' to the study of anthropologists' own societies (Macdonald, 2001; Jackson, 1987).

The concept of culture is central to anthropology's endeavours. Culture is often misunderstood as something static and essential – a 'thing' that can be identified and measured like 'class', 'age', 'sex', or 'ethnicity'. In this formulation, culture is a system of beliefs, values and customs that inhere to and are inherited by membership of a distinct group. It is also something that tends to be perceived as 'other', and culture in this sense has a tendency to be elided into opposition with 'rational', 'non-cultural' practices of the self (or busy professional). This outmoded view is associated with a functional view of society (or a profession) as bounded and impermeable. Such an approach does not give much credence to the possibilities for dynamism and interaction within and between cultural groups, nor to the argument that 'culture' pertains to everyone, not just 'others' such as ethnic minorities.

In more modern formulations of the culture concept, cultural diversity is a characteristic feature within as well as between societies (Leach, 1982), a diversity that is to be found at all levels and in all sectors. Intercultural experience, then, may be gained through contact not only with 'other', non-professional groups such as 'the lay public', but also through interaction with other professional cultures, and with different cultures within the one profession (e.g. medicine). This is important, because intercultural understanding in health care settings is often regarded as being what is required in order to deal with ethnic minority patients in 'culturally competent', 'culturally sensitive' or 'culturally appropriate' ways (e.g. Gibson & Zhong, 2005). The anthropological point about culture is that 'everyone has it', patients (from whatever background) and staff alike. Furthermore, if diversity is a feature of 'professional' as well as 'lay' cultures, intercultural understanding is necessary not only for effective interaction with patients, but for effective working as part of a health care team, which is often made up of people both from within and outside the different health professions. Hall (2005) argues that different and sometimes conflicting professional cultures make effective interprofessional teamwork more difficult, and suggests that doctors, because of the culture of medical profession, find such approaches particularly difficult. My argument is that, by introducing medical students to other professional and non-professional cultures at an early stage in the careers, they can be enculturated in ways that make team working easier and more effective in their future careers.

Medical anthropology has other important messages to impart that feed into the development of appropriate forms of interprofessional conduct. One of these is that health care is not the monopoly of the health care professionals. Rather, there are three sectors of health care – popular, folk and professional. These overlap and interact, and anything between 70 and 90 percent of all care takes place without reference to either of the last two categories (Kleinman, 1980; 1986). Rather than focussing on other professionals, then, to the exclusion of the 'lay' perspective, treatment is more appropriately seen as the domain of the 'therapy managing group' (Janzen, 1978), made up of both professional carers and lay people. An argument could be made that focussing on 'interprofessional training' simply risks shifting the 'self/other' boundary from 'doctors/other health professionals' to 'health professionals/lay people'. The 'expert patient programme' currently being delivered in the UK, despite the consternation it has engendered in some quarters and doubts about its relative effectiveness (Shaw & Baker, 2004; Griffiths, Ramsay, Elridge & Taylor, 2007) further blurs the distinction between 'lay' and 'professional'. Thus, in contrast to much of the literature in medical education that tends to assume that 'community-based learning' is equivalent to learning in general practice settings (e.g. Hart, 1985; Howe, 2002; Oswald, Alderson & Jones, 2001), the medical anthropologist argues that to understand health and social care in the community, one has to step out of the clinic and experience the many ways in which health and health care is delivered in non-clinical contexts, through working not only with professionals in the field but with the clients and their carers they serve.

These messages resonate with pronouncements by the General Medical Council (GMC), the government-appointed regulating body overseeing the conduct of medical education in the UK. In its ground-breaking document 'Tomorrow's Doctors', first published in 1993, the GMC argued for the importance of medical education that would "foster the development of a caring, knowledgeable, competent and skilful medical graduate who broadly understands health and disease of the individual, the family and society, and who is able to benefit from subsequent medical education and adapt to future developments in practice". There has also been more general interest expressed in what constitutes the 'good doctor' (e.g. Calman, 1994; Stewart et al., 1995; Downie & Macnaughton, 1999) and how that person should be trained and assessed. Medicine is currently looking for innovative ways to develop and measure traits such as 'professionalism', 'reflection', and 'patient-centredness' in its practitioners (Arnold, Blank, Race & Cipparrone; 2002, Noble, Kuckack, Marin & Lloyd, 2007; Banos, 2007). Interprofessional education is seen as one vehicle for generating these qualities, either in the classroom (e.g. Thistlethwaite & Nisbet, 2007) or in the community (e.g. Hays, 2007), although the UK Centre for the Advancement of Interprofessional Education (CAIPE) makes no assumption about the venue for such learning in its definition of IPE. However, there is clearly a need to provide "occasions when two or more professions learn with, from and about each other to improve collaboration and the quality of care" (CAIPE, 1992) if we are to fulfil the GMC's further requirement that medical education should produce doctors with "respect for patients and colleagues that encompasses, without prejudice, diversity of background and opportunity, language, culture and way of life" (GMC, 1993). This is a high ideal; the challenge faced by every medical school is how to operationalize such ambitions through the educational process, and at what stage.

The idea of interprofessional health care training as intercultural experience owes much to models of intercultural experience and its educational value promoted by international voluntary work and study abroad schemes. Pusch (1994) suggests five broad qualities that derive from a managed intercultural experience: mindfulness, cognitive flexibility, tolerance of ambiguity, behavioural flexibility, and cross-cultural empathy. These qualities fit neatly into the competencies of the good doctor outlined by the GMC and other bodies. Such qualities are less likely to be generated in the classroom than they are through placement learning; they are a product of personal transformation and development garnered through experiential learning rather than learning through books. Based on a list of reasons why study abroad may be valuable (Pusch, 1996), we could propose that intercultural experience within one's own society offers students the following opportunities, the second of which is specifically interprofessional:

- to become active, reflective learners and draw on their experiences to expand and deepen what they learn in their more formal studies;
- to compare the ways that key issues of health and welfare are approached by different professional and lay cultures;
- to practice new language and communication skills to talk to people from these other cultures;
- to develop the ability to thrive in and adapt to lay and professional cultures different from those with which they are familiar;
- to engage in potentially transforming experiences that challenge their fundamental assumptions about the world;
- to learn to be self-sufficient and resourceful in the face of unexpected challenges.

Thus, it could be argued, there is a strong convergence of interests between medical anthropology and medical education in terms of what the former can offer and the latter requires in order to develop the knowledge, skills and attitudes that constitute the 'duties of a doctor' (GMC, 2006). Through pushing the boundaries of commonly used terms such as 'health and health care', 'professionalism', and 'culture', we can look at new ways of approaching interprofessional practice in early years medical education, through using intercultural experience as a means of influencing the way in which students are enculturated into medicine. I shall now go on to illustrate this with reference to the innovative programme we have established at Queen's Campus that aims to give students experience working in the community, the Community Placement scheme.

THE MBBS PHASE I MEDICINE COMMUNITY PLACEMENT SCHEME AT QUEEN'S CAMPUS

The community placement scheme is the middle part of a 'sandwich' of teaching on the 'Medicine in the Community' strand of the MBBS Phase I Medicine curriculum. At the start of their first year, the medical students at Queen's Campus are introduced to the number and diversity of health and social care providers operating in the local community (Teesside, UK). By the start of their second term, every student is placed with one of a range of participating community-based organisations, which they are expected to work with on a regular basis (around 60 hours in total) for a period of a full calendar year. The aim of the placement is for students to gain in-depth, long-term experience of working with 'their' particular agency. By doing so, they are expected to gain a knowledge and understanding of (and hopefully respect for) the values, organisation and ways of working of the agency in question, and through it a greater understanding of the culture and way of life of the client groups and communities it serves. The scheme also gives students the chance to apply and develop skills learned on campus (such as communication, ethical awareness, cultural competency, personal organisation and time management) in community settings.

Most of the organisations represented in the list of placement providers are non-clinical health and social care agencies in the voluntary or statutory sectors, although a number of what might be called 'unusual' (or 'social') clinical providers (e.g. those offering services to prisoners, substance abusers and immigrants and asylum seekers) are also represented. As well as understanding the organisation in question, students are encouraged to explore its context. Apart from its client groups and communities, students are expected to investigate how the organisation interacts with other agencies and/or health and social care professionals, and how international, national, regional and organisational policies impact at the local level. The community placement scheme is supported by the work of a teaching and placement co-ordinator, part of whose work involves assigning and monitoring placement activities. Students indicate the kind of placement they would like from a list of options using an on-line application form which also asks for any other relevant information such as car availability and preferred times for placement activities. Based on this information, the teaching and placement co-ordinator allocates students to the most appropriate placement for their interests and aptitudes. We currently have over 50 Teesside-based organisations able to take students. The scheme is overseen by a steering committee made up of placement representatives, students and staff.

PLACEMENTS IN PRACTICE

The approach students are encouraged to adopt in undertaking their community placement is modelled on the research method known as participant-observation which, like the concept of culture, is intimately associated with the discipline of social anthropology. Participant-observation within social anthropology has traditionally been characterised by long-term, in-depth fieldwork in what are often exotic and challenging situations. We encourage students to carry on this tradition to a certain extent through being bold in their choice of placements (they can select different types of placement from a range of available options) through making suggestions that take them outside the comfort zone of their prior experience.

Students certainly appreciate moving outside the university environment. "Students are extremely keen to grasp any 'out-of-lecture' experiences they can," wrote two students in a service newsletter after their placement experience (Cameron & Griksaitis, 2002). "It teaches you things which definitely cannot be taught in the lecture theatre", wrote another in the community placement report. However, in terms of intercultural experience, students' first encounter with their placement organisation can be something of a 'culture shock' (Oberg, 1960). The dip in emotional wellbeing associated with such a 'shock' is characteristic of any learning or creative human endeavour, with adjustment involving "the formation of some entirely new role behaviours in the status positions acquired in a new social structure" (Lundstedt, 1963). Culture shock has been described as the "occupational disease of people who have been suddenly transplanted abroad" (Oberg, 1960), but Taft (1977) points out that one does not have to go far away in order to experience some form of cultural transition. Adler (1975) suggests that Americans may be particularly prone to culture shock because they see themselves as somehow 'culture free'. The same may be said of medical students, who carry the added burden of being used to success and functioning at a high level, so that they may feel particularly 'let down' by finding themselves in a situation where, at least at first, there may be little obvious for them to do and their confidence can wane in consequence. Yet culture shock is also "a necessary precondition to change and growth, as individuals strive to regain their inner balance by adapting to the demands and opportunities of the intercultural situation" (Kim & Ruben, 1988, p.310). Sometimes this situation can be a relatively straightforward difference of geography. One student writes of her experience as follows:

> In the beginning, the prospect of going out into the community of Stockton was a very daunting one. I was unfamiliar with Stockton and its inhabitants and had to travel to different schools around the area. The initial stress has definitely been worthwhile though as the things I have learnt could not have been taught in a classroom. I also think that Stockton being the community in question has been of benefit to me. It has a very different culture to the community I was brought up in.

For others, the uncertainty comes from having to deal with an initially unfamiliar and sometimes scary institution or condition:

> I have never known anyone who suffered from Alzheimer's, with my only experience of neurological anomalies being my Aunty's ever-deteriorating Parkinson's disease. I tread carefully initially and stand and observe from the lounge doorways, struck by my inability to actually find an angle or tangible way to go about finding out more about these people. They seem so normal in appearance yet their minds are locked.

As they settle in to their placements, so the students have a chance to explore new ways of relating to the staff and clients they are working with. The manager of an Alzheimer's care home reported that he was locking up his office one evening preparing to go home when he heard some beautiful singing coming from the residents' lounge. A medical student placed at the home had stayed on with one of the older and more unresponsive residents. The student had gathered that the old lady in question used to like hymns, and had decided to sing her a few. As he peered around the door, the manager noticed with a start that the old lady, who had not uttered a word for several months, was moving her lips to the singing. This for him was a magical moment, and it is certainly a magical story – for how many medical students, once qualified, are likely to sing to their patients?

Some students express initial uncertainty as to the likely relevance and value of the placement to their medical education.

> I got from this community placement [a domestic violence support project]...an awful lot more than I was expecting to. It wasn't that I was pessimistic, it was just that I didn't think the placement would be relevant to what we were doing in the rest of the course.

In fact this community placement has taught me an awful lot about communicating with every single type of person. That's the thing about domestic violence, it occurs in all races, classes and affects all ages.

We certainly find evidence of transformative experiences in students writing about their placements. These transformations can be at both a personal and professional level. One student writes, for example:

I feel that my communication skills were enhanced by whilst working here…However, I think that at the beginning of my placement I may have been a bit too quiet, and perhaps didn't make as much of a difference as I could have…My community placement has definitely contributed to my decision to go into psychiatry after medical school…A discussion that some of the members [of the drop-in centre] were having really interested me, they were talking about their GPs and psychiatrists. They were saying that their GPs tended to listen to them more than their psychiatrists. They didn't really like psychiatrists. I thought this was really odd, because they saw their psychiatrists much more than they saw their GP. They gave me tips on what they were looking for in a good psychiatrist and doctor; their main concern was that their psychiatrist didn't listen to them enough and 'only heard what he/she wanted to hear'. This was really useful, because it highlighted to me how important listening to the patient's views about their care is, and how much it affects the effectiveness of their treatment. A lot of them said that they would only go to their psychiatrist if they had to. This discussion made me think about whether I would make a good psychiatrist, and how I would change my practice so that my clients were satisfied with their treatment. Overall, I feel that this placement has been vital to my medical education.

Another student writes about 'Fireworks Night' (November 5th, also known as bonfire night in the UK) as a transformative moment in their placement experience.

Fireworks Night @ Alzheimer's Home
This is a classic example of the biopsychosocial model of medicine we have learnt so much about. But here it is in action. This has happened at a perfect time. I am just coming toward the end of my community placement and this somehow crystallizes the whole purpose of the home, the work of the carers and nurses and also my reason for being there. This is an example of something that cannot be prescribed, possibly has no place in the traditional medical ideology yet seems to be of more benefit than any other intervention that I have seen at the care home… if I could bottle up the spirit, love, generosity, community spirit and caring of all these people here today and prescribe it once I qualify then I would be offering a feel good factor better than any other.

Students also learn about other professionals and their ways of working during their placement activities. This is important, because it is an area in which misunderstandings abound. This point was made to me strongly by a potential placement provider in the social work department of the local council. She talked about how a GP had phoned her once insisting that she take children from a family on her books into care 'immediately'. This, she argued, demonstrated the doctor's complete ignorance about both the methods and measures used in social work. Even had she been able to act 'immediately' in the way the doctor expected (which she wasn't, because her profession, like any other, has procedures to be followed in such cases), her assessment of the family was that they were only 'middling' in terms of their levels of deprivation and difficulty – they were certainly not at a level which would have precipitated such a 'last resort' action on the part of social services that the GP seemed to think was necessary. Because students experience these different ways of working at an early stage of their medical training, they do not necessarily regard them as strange in the way that a qualified doctor without such experience might do.

THE ETHNOGRAPHIC ENCOUNTER

The quotes used above all come from students' anonymous community placement reports which they are expected to write up at the end of their year in the form of a 3,000 word ethnography. The word 'ethnography' baffles many people, particularly those coming from the 'hard science' background that many medical students have followed. It is explained to them as a form of writing that gives the chance to display detailed observational skills as well as an appreciation of the richness and vitality of everyday, 'real life' experience. Given the anxiety that students expressed with regard to ethnographic writing, in 2005 we took the decision to appoint a member of academic staff to run weekly 'drop-in' sessions that focus on students' experiences in their community placement settings and how to write them up. These sessions provide a safe (confidential, non-assessed) environment where students can take the risk of acknowledging their doubts regarding their ability and understanding of the purpose of the project, and to discuss the ways in which they had been and were being challenged by the experience. In 2006-7, about a third of all students (35/109) took up this opportunity.

Even when students do not find their beliefs or values challenged in any direct way (for example by coming into contact with a socio-economically disadvantaged group, or a professional group with values that are different to their own), the placement encourages them to look at the world much more closely, and to some extent in a new way. Asking students to look at a different, unfamiliar world that may challenge the taken-for-granted assumptions they make in their everyday lives (a fundamental precept of culture shock) often produces anxiety. We are asking them to 'achieve' this learning by writing an adequate report of their participant-observation experiences. Yet this form of research calls for a reassessment of one's identity through its somewhat divergent requirements both to conform to a set of norms and practices as part of an organisation through participation within it, whilst maintaining the detachment to observe and reflect on that organisation as individuals. In other words, it fosters simultaneous engagement and detachment, part of the bedrock of reflective practice.

REFLECTIONS ON THE PLACEMENT SCHEME

Our intention, in running the community placement scheme, is that through experiencing health and social care issues at the grass roots, community level, students will be better doctors in whatever branch of medicine they go into in the future. Every doctor has the capacity to become a 'quasi-anthropologist' with the curiosity to gain an in-depth knowledge of the communities they are working in so that they are able to recommend and refer patients to suitable non-clinical agencies where appropriate. However, if this were all the scheme provided, there would be little more to be said and possibly other, more time-effective ways of achieving the desired outcome (e.g. encouraging students to research the nature and range of organisations available on the internet). What we feel the community placement offers is a challenge to the normal forms of enculturation (a term I consider synonymous with socialisation) into medicine.

Enculturation is the process of learning about and identifying with one's own culture. It is slightly different from acculturation, which is the process by which individuals, enculturated into one cultural group, assimilate selected aspects of another culture through their subsequent interactions with it. The linked processes of enculturation and acculturation are vital ways of becoming part of a professional group (Hong, 2001). Enculturation (or socialisation) is a powerful force in the induction of medical students into their profession, involving them "in a new way of seeing the world and a new materially referential language to describe it" (Sinclair, 2000, p. 116). Students develop all sorts of expectations of medical education (and hence medicine) even before their arrival at medical school, a process known as anticipatory socialisation (Sinclair, 1997, p. 80-6). Thus for many students, to come to a medical school which immediately sends them off into the community to find out about non-clinical forms of health and social care may be surprising in its own right, although as our programme becomes established an element of self-selection may come into play with students purposely selecting our degree precisely because of its unusual way of inducting them into medicine.

This early years experience of non-clinical forms of health and social care is also a way for medical students to develop confidence and consideration in dealing with people (either as patients or carers) from backgrounds that may be very different to their own. Some of the placement organisations, for example, give students experience working with prisoners, substance abusers, sex workers, refugees and asylum seekers, and 'children in special circumstances' (such as those who are 'in care'). Bringing students into contact with such people at an early stage in their medical education helps prevent the development of the arrogant, dismissive attitudes all too frequently associated with donning a white coat and stethoscope – the mantle and symbols of professionalism - in later, hospital settings. Sometimes such attitudes are based on fear and insecurity. Doctors are under pressure to behave as if they are wise, knowledgeable and deeply caring, to an extent that lies outside the boundaries of reality (Balint, 1957). Such symbols of professional identity can provide a metaphorical mask for doctors to hide behind. Masks transform, disguise, hide and protect (Lommel, 1970; Napier, 1986). However, the danger of the mask is that it can also act as something of a shell, a barrier that keeps doctors remote and removed (but also protected) from the very same patients they are supposed to serve. Similar barriers can develop between members of different professions, and again the need for early years work to prevent them forming is apparent. Hall (2005, p. 194) talks of "providing interventions early in the professional's education which serve to build bridges between the neophytes before the walls of their silos become so thick and high that reaching across the professions becomes too difficult".

Talking about the mask or shell of the doctor, of course, risks presenting 'doctors' as a single cultural group, whereas I have argued above for the diversity of medical 'culture'. Medicine as a profession is internally diverse – there are over 40 recognised clinical and service specialities recognised by the ten different Royal Colleges in the UK. It is also surprisingly diverse across cultures (Payer, 1990), and through time (Lock, 1980). Furthermore the role of 'medic' is only one of the many roles an individual doctor is likely to inhabit. Focussing on 'enculturation' as if it is a one-way process that engulfs or overshadows an individual's lived experiences ignores the important role of individual agency, personality, or 'personal culture'. However, the process of socialisation into medicine is a deep and powerful one, as writers such as Sinclair (1997) demonstrate.

The symbols and rituals of medicine do a lot to shore up the confidence of individual doctors and may function to inspire the same trust and confidence in patients and their families who have a vested interest in the doctor adhering to the ideal professionalism the mask represents. However, when professional identities are used to separate practitioners from their patients, then the levels of service patients receive are likely to be negatively affected. This will be particularly marked where the cultural distance between the doctor and their patients is greatest, as they are likely to be in the case of the 'hard to reach' groups indicated above.

A subsidiary benefit of the community placement scheme may be to bring to life public health issues that in a formal, taught situation may seem of dubious relevance to most medical students' future careers. For example, Townsend (1988, p. 1) asserts that "inequalities in health are of concern to the whole nation and represent one of the biggest possible challenges to the conduct of government policy". However, as Conroy (2001) puts it, "the topic [inequalities in health] is often dealt with in one mind-numbing undergraduate medical lecture which presents a tedious conveyor belt of statistics". Surely the issue of health inequalities is better dealt with through students' direct experience of the destructive effects of the many inequalities in health and health care that are faced by supposedly 'hard to reach' groups? This accords with what Schmidt et al. (2000, p. 7) describe as community-based education, "an approach...in which students, already in the early phases of their training, are confronted with the health problems of the communities they are supposed to serve in future. It is assumed that through early and extensive contacts with the community, students may become better prepared to deal with those problems in the future". In other words, "it is about putting medical education into a broad context within a wider sphere so that medical students and indeed those that teach them think beyond clinical practice at times to other issues" (Allen, Brown & Hughes, 1997, p. 10).

The placement, then, offers a lot more than the opportunity for students to increase their knowledge and awareness of non-clinical health and social care agencies. It is also a means to transformative learning, enabling some of them to come into contact with aspects of themselves, and others, that they did not know they possessed, or they thought unimportant to the practice of medicine. Whilst the exact mode of self-realisation differs between students and is more striking in some than in others, one can see the process of doing their placement enabling some to become more fully rounded human beings and future doctors. Situational learning has been shown to be a powerful mediator of such change, especially in the development of professional attitudes and motivation to further learning (Hampshire, 1998; O'Sullivan, 2000; Littlewood et al., 2005). Whether it is exposing them to those less fortunate than themselves, being given "opportunities to satisfy altruistic drives" (Gordon, 2003, p. 347) through working in a volunteer role, gaining a broader perspective on the complexity of health issues, or some other stimulus, it is clear that for some, the community placement contributes in significant ways to the construction of an emergent professional identity (Wagne, Hendrick & Hudson, 2007). For some it involves a re-evaluation of often cherished beliefs, for others a shattering of stereotypes. Arnold (2002) argues that it is the satisfactory resolution of such value-conflicts that is the essence of professionalism. Above all the community placement encourages increased emotional and psychological self-sufficiency, broadening knowledge of self and others by a means that is directly related to the extent to which the students have engaged with the community in their placement and are able to write about it afterwards. Since their reports are assessed, we cannot assume that everything we read in them is a true representation of what they think. On the other hand, the descriptions of the work many of them give and the testimonies they present about its effects on their future professional identity indicates the placement has a transformative effect for many students

CONCLUSION

This chapter has presented the MBBS Phase I community placement scheme at Queen's Campus, Stockton, as an opportunity for interprofessional and intercultural learning experience. As such, it provides early years students with an opportunity to develop both personally and professionally. As time goes on, we shall be able to see whether our intentions in establishing such a scheme match reality, at least as far as our students' future attitudes and careers are concerned. It could be that this learning is short lived, given the socialisation pressures from other quarters that may affect students once they move into more clinical settings. Whether of not this happens, however, the community placement scheme opens up public and community health and social care issues to medical students in ways that are vital and often surprising. It certainly establishes 'community-based medical education' as about a lot more than what goes on in GP clinics!

REFERENCES

Adler, P.S. (1975). The transitional experience: an alternative view of culture shock. *Journal of Humanistic Psychology*, 15(4), 13-23.

Allen, I., Brown, P., & Hughes, P. (1997). (Eds) *Choosing tomorrow's doctors*. London: Policy Studies Institute.

Angel, C., & Johnson, A. (2000). Broadening access to undergraduate medical education. *British Medical Journal, 321*,113-118.

Arnold, L. (2002). Assessing professional behaviour: Yesterday, today, and tomorrow. *Academic Medicine, 77*(6), 502-515.

Arnold, E.L., Blank, L.L., Race, K.E.H., & Cipparrone, N. (1998). Can professionalism be measured? The development of a scale for use in the medical education environment. *Academic Medicine, 73*, 1119-1121.

Balint, M. (1957). *The doctor, his patient and the illness*. London: Pitman Medical Publishers.

Banos, J.E. (2007). How literature and popular movies can help in medical education: Applications for teaching the doctor-patient relationship. *Medical education, 41*, 915-920.

CAIPE (1992). *Defining IPE*. Available at: *http://www.caipe.org.uk/about-us/defining-ipe/* (Accessed April 22nd 2009).

Calman, K. (1994). The profession of medicine. *British Medical Journal, 309*,1140-1143.

Cameron, N., & Griksaitis, M.J. (2002). Prison symposium – Medical student placements. *Department of Health and HM Prison Service Prison health newsletter*, (9)19.

Carlson, J.S., & Widaman, K.F. (1988). The effects of study abroad during college on attitudes toward other cultures. *International Journal of Intercultural Relations, 12*(1), 1-17.

Conroy, R. (2001). Book review: 'Poverty, inequality and health: An international perspective, and 'Mind the gap: Hierarchies, health and human evolution. *British Medical Journal, 323*(7306), 239.

Downie, R., & Macnaughton, J. (1999). Should medical students read Plato? *Medical Journal of Australia*, 170(3),125-127

Easterbrook, M., Godwin, M., Wilson, R., Hodgetts, G., Brown, G., Pong, R., & Najgebauer, E. (1999). Rural background and clinical rural rotations during medical training: effect on practice location. *Canadian Medical Association Journal, 160*(8), 1159-1163.

General Medical Council. (1993). *Tomorrow's doctors: Recommendations on undergraduate medical education.* London: General Medical Council.

General Medical Council. (2006). *Good Medical Practice (2006): the duties of a doctor registered with the General Medical Council.* London: General Medical Council.

Gibson, D., & Zhong, M. (2005). Intercultural communication competence in the healthcare context. *International Journal of Intercultural Relations*, 29(5), 621-634.

Griffiths, C., Foster, G., Ramsay, J., Eldridge, S., & Taylor, S. (2007). How effective are expert patient (lay led) education programmes for chronic disease? *British Medical Journal,* 334, 1254-1256.

Hall, P. (2005). Interprofessional teamwork: professional cultures as barriers. *Journal of Interprofessional Care, 19* (S1), 188-196.

Hampshire, A. (1998). Providing early clinical experience in primary care. *Medical Education, 32,* 495-501.

Hart, J.T. (1971). The inverse care law. *Lancet 1*, 405-412.

Hart, J.T. (1985). The world turned upside down: proposals for community based undergraduate medical education. *Journal of the Royal College of General Practitioners 35*, 63-68.

Hays, R. (2007). Interprofessional education in the community: where to begin. *The Clinical Teacher, 4*, 141-145.

Hong, G. Y. (2001). Front-line care providers' professional worlds: The need for qualitative approaches to cultural interfaces. *Forum Qualitative Sozialforschung / Forum: Qualitative Social Research, 2*(3). Available at: http://www.qualitative-research.net/fqs-texte/3-01/3-01hong-e.htm (Accessed: March 16, 2008).

Howe, A. (2002). Twelve tips for community-based medical education. *Medical education, 24*, 9-12.

Jackson, A. (1987). (Ed.) *Anthropology at home.* London: Tavistock.

Janzen, J.M. (1978). *The quest for therapy: Medical pluralism in lower Zaire.* London: University of California Press.

Kim, Y.Y. & Ruben, B.D. (1988). Intercultural transformation. In Y.Y. Kim & W.B. Gudykunst (Eds.), *Theories in intercultural communication.* London: Sage.

Kleinman, A. (1980). *Patients and healers in the context of culture: An exploration of the borderland between anthropology, medicine, and psychiatry.* Berkeley, CA: University of California Press.

Kleinman, A. (1986). Concepts and a model for the comparison of medical systems as social systems. In C. Currer & M. Stacey (Eds.), *Concepts of health, illness and disease: A comparative perspective*. Leamington Spa: Berg.

Leach, E. (1982). *Social anthropology*. London: Fontana.

Littlewood, S., Ypinazar, V., Margolis, S.A., Scherpbier, A., Spencer, J., & Dornan, T. (2005). Early practical experience and the social responsiveness of clinical education: A systematic review. *British Medical Journal*, 331, 387-391.

Lock, M. (1980). *East Asian medicine in urban Japan: Varieties of medical experience*. Berkeley, CA: University of California Press.

Lommel, A. (1970). *Masks, their meaning and function*. New York: McGraw Hill.

Lundstedt, S. (1963). An introduction to some evolving problems in cross-cultural research. *Journal of social issues*, 19(3), 1-9.

Macdonald, S. (2001). British social anthropology. In P. Atkinson, A. Coffey, S. Delamont, J. Lofland & L. Lofland (Eds.), *Handbook of Ethnography*. London: Sage.

Napier, A.D. (1986). *Masks, transformation and paradox*. Berkeley, CA: University of California Press.

Noble, L., Kuckack, A., Martin, J., & Lloyd, M. (2007). The effect of professional skills training on patient centredness and confidence in communicating with patients. *Medical Education*, 41, 432-440.

Oberg, K. (1960). Culture shock: adjustment to new cultural environments. *Practical Anthropology*, 7, 177-182.

O'Sullivan, M., Martin, J., & Murray, E. (2000). Students' perceptions of the relative advantages and disadvantages of community-based and hospital–based teaching: A qualitative study. *Medical Education*, 34(8), 648-655.

Oswald, N., Alderson, T., & Jones, S. (2001). Evaluating primary care as a base for medical education: the report of the Cambridge community-based clinical course. *Medical Education*, 35, 782-788.

Paige, R.M. (1993). *Education for the intercultural experience*. Yarmouth, ME: Intercultural Press.

Payer, L. (1990). *Medicine and culture: Notions of health and sickness in Britain, the U.S., France and West Germany*. London: Gollancz.

Pusch, M.D. (1994). The chameleon capacity. In R. D. Lambert (Ed.), *Educational exchange and global competence*. New York, NY: Council on International Education Exchange.

Pusch, M.D. (1996). Where credit is due; recognizing the benefits of intercultural experience. Availble at: *Transitions abroad magazine*
http://www.transitionsabroad.com/publications/magazine/9703/study_abroad_benefits_o f_intercultural_experience.shtml (Accessed March 16, 2008).

Ranmuthugala, G., Humphreys, J., Solarsh, B., Walters, L., Worley, P., Wakerman, J., Dunbar, J.A., & Solarsh, G. (2007). Where is the evidence that rural exposure increases uptake of rural medical practice? *Australian Journal of Rural Health* 15(5), 285–288.

Schmidt, H., Magzoub, M., Feletti, G., Nooman, Z., & Vluggen, P. (2000). *Handbook of community-based education: Theory and practices*. Maastricht: Network Publications.

Shaw, J., & M. Baker (2004). 'Expert Patient': dream or nightmare? *British Medical Journal*, 328, 723-724.

Sinclair, S. (1997). *Making doctors: An institutional apprenticeship*. Oxford: Berg.

Sinclair, S. (2000). Disease narratives: constituting doctors. *Anthropology and Medicine*, *7*(1), 115-134.

Stewart, M., et al. (1995). *Patient Centred Medicine*. London: Sage.

Taft, R. (1977). Coping with unfamiliar cultures. In N. Warren (Ed.), *Studies in Cross-Cultural Psychology, Vol 1*. London: Academic Press.

Thistlethwaite, J., & Nisbet, G. (2007). Interprofessional education: what's the point and where we're at. *The Clinical Teacher, 4*(2), 67-72.

Townsend, Davidson, P. N., & Whitehead, M (1988). *Inequalities in health: The Black Report and the Health Divide*. Harmondsworth: Penguin.

Wagner, P., Hendrick, J., & Hudson, V. (2007). Defining medical professionalism: a qualitative study. *Medical Education*, 41, 288-294.

Wilkinson, D., Laven, G., Pratt, N., & Beilby, J. (2003). Impact of undergraduate and postgraduate rural training, and medical school entry criteria on rural practice among Australian general practitioners: national study of 2414 doctors. *Medical Education, 37*(9), 809–814.

In: Sociology of Interprofessional Health …
Ed: S. Kitto, J. Chesters et al.

ISBN: 978-1-60876-866-0
© 2011 Nova Science Publishers, Inc.

Chapter 11

COMPETITION THE NEW COLLABORATION? EMPLOYING INTER-TEAM COMPETITIVENESS TO MOTIVATE HEALTH STUDENTS TO LEARN TOGETHER

Monica Moran, Rosalie A. Boyce and Lisa Nissen

ABSTRACT

In the health workforce, competition between the professions for recognition and professional status has long been seen as an impediment to the development of interprofessional teams (Light, 1988; O'Reilly, 2000). Entrenched professional hierarchies have tended to favour some professional groups leading to professional growth and significant financial and status rewards, while others have experienced lower status and perceived or indeed real lack of recognition (Salhani & Coulter, 2009). The pattern of jostling for supremacy begins as soon as a student steps into his/her professional training program and appears to be well developed by the time the new health professional reaches the workplace. How then can educators in the health professions motivate students to see beyond their own professional boundaries, and develop collaborative ways of valuing and working with others outside their own professional groups: to negotiate ways of power sharing rather than power struggling (Salhani & Coulter, 2009)? This chapter will explore the mobilizing aspects of competition as a driver to motivate health sciences students to learn with and about one another in an interprofessional team structure. It will draw on student feedback and reflection on participation in an interprofessional team competition where groups of students representing up to nine health professions compete against one another for a prize and public recognition. The literature around teams, competition and social learning theories will be used to provide a multifaceted lens in which to explore the student experience.

INTRODUCTION

Teamwork has become the preferred model for delivery of health care services over the past decade. The influence of the *'Learning together to work together for health'* World Health Organisation (WHO, 1988) report cannot be overestimated as a catalyst for generating a new direction in health care delivery. Educators have come to realise that neither increasing the numbers of graduates, nor enhancing the quality of their degree will prepare students for the reality of professional practice in a rapidly changing world. The provision of relevant education leading to the graduation of practitioners able to take on the professional mantle has never been more challenging (Corbett & Corbett, 1999). Barnett, writing from the higher education field, talks of 'learning for an unknown future' in a societal environment of 'supercomplexity' where it is no longer possible to predict what learning and understandings will be required let alone what skills will be demanded (Barnett, 2004). Coupled with this unknown future is a societal and economic expectation that higher education programs will become increasingly accountable for the quality of their professional graduates, and their contribution to the national quality of life (Gibbons, 1998). Inclusion models of community growth and development are fuelling the demand for health and social care professionals to involve themselves in the creation of environments and opportunities that promote equal participation for all members of societies (WHO Ottawa Charter for Health Promotion, 1986). As a result the capacity to identify and collaborate with health care workers and service stakeholders requires the emerging health professional to have a much more nuanced understanding of the workplace and its dynamics than any previous generation of graduates.

However, training students of the various health sciences to work together in interprofessional settings continues to be problematic for educators. The quest to provide authentic interprofessional teamwork learning activities has led to the rise of novel and alternative mechanisms of teamwork training (Johnson et al., 2006; Moran, Boyce, O'Neill, Bainbridge & Newton, 2007). These activities are often characterized and articulated by two key features:

- They are designed to augment and enhance, rather than displace existing and often congested educational programs;
- They provide exposure to practical, real life learning experiences in an interprofessional milieu.

While many authentic and reality based short learning interventions have been described in the IPE literature this chapter is concerned with a particular group of learning experiences that might perhaps at first glance appear in conflict with the collaborative principles of interprofessionalism – that is competition based learning activities. The use of competition as a driver for learning is not unusual; learning may be motivated by individual competition for achievement of higher grades or entry to limited advanced study opportunities, for example admission to honours degree streams. But can competition be utilised to promote learning that is not so much focused on the individual striving for superiority or the acquisition of limited prizes but that is focused on the need to know and understand another in order to reach the prize of that understanding? A number of health education settings are developing competitively styled health team challenges to attempt to answer this question. The Health

Care Team Challenge (HCTC), the subject of this chapter, is one such project which will be examined in detail. But before the mechanics of the HCTC are unpacked it is worthwhile investigating the learning theories which may be identified as underpinning such an activity.

THEORIES SUPPORTING INTERPROFESSIONAL LEARNING

Contact Hypothesis

The 'contact hypothesis' developed by Allport (1954) has been suggested as a congruent social theory to underpin interprofessional learning (Hean & Dickinson, 2005). Its tenets of reducing stereotyping and negative between-group attitudes mesh well with the aspirations of interprofessional educators. Additionally its attention towards reducing conflict between hostile groups by creating a set of circumstances where they may learn about and work with one another (the contact) can be seen in many learning settings both within and beyond the health education arena. The conditions proposed by Allport that facilitate successful contact include:

- The need for institutional support to bring together and support the team members,
- The importance of having frequent meetings in order for conflicting team members to become more familiar with one another,
- The need for an external goal that all team members can work towards, and,
- Clear understanding of the equal nature of each team member in the specific situation.

While this theory has been widely used it is not without its critiques. Concerns regarding the utility of the 'contact hypothesis' have included an issue that is also frequently raised as a barrier in the IPE literature: the challenge to find a time and place for contact to occur (Amichai-Hamburger & McKenna, 2006). Creating an environment and opportunity for student groups to meet is extremely challenging in their already congested uniprofessional programs. Another concern raised by Hewstone and Brown (1986) is the capacity of positive contact experiences to be generalized from the individual to the larger group they may represent. In other words negative stereotypes and hostile attitudes may be extinguished towards an individual representing an alternate group during contact but the positive re-framing may only be perceived towards that individual. In order to manage this risk Hewstone and Brown (1986) emphasize the importance of individuals being explicitly identified with the group they represent in order for attitudinal changes to be generalized beyond the interpersonal contact. This at least is an easier condition to fulfill in interprofessional education as students come together explicitly to represent their professional groups and act as ambassadors for their cognate disciplines.

Communities of Practice

Another social learning theory, that of communities of practice (or learning communities), has reached into educational and workplace settings (Pfaff & Huddleston, 2003; Wenger, 2003). The concept of communities of practice develops the idea that learning and indeed knowing involves participation; and that though participation community identities are learned that involve knowledge and competence. Wenger (2003) identifies three dimensions that link practice with community:

Mutual engagement

'Practice resides in a community of people and the relations of mutual engagement. Practice does not exist in the abstract… but in actions whose meanings they negotiate with one another' (Wenger, 2003, p. 73).

A joint enterprise

… 'is the result of a collective process of negotiation…that involves learning to live with differences and coordinating respective aspirations' to achieve a common enterprise' (Wenger, 2003, pp. 77-79).

A shared repertoire

Within a community of practice this can involve the development of shared language, beliefs, communication and shared ways of dealing with ambiguity.

This theoretical framework offers a broad platform for the development of interprofessional learning activities. It acknowledges the complexity within communities including the need for negotiation, shared and individual aspirations and differences in ways of professional knowing.

CHALLENGES OF USING TEAM ACTIVITIES IN HEALTH EDUCATION

Students frequently feedback to their educators their fears and frustrations around team based learning activities (Pfaff & Huddleston, 2003). This feedback is often focused on their experiences of team activities where conflicts over role confusion, workload inequalities and perceived watering down of final outcomes have created negative impressions. This is a major stumbling block for heath educators striving to introduce authentic interprofessional team learning activities.

The structure and format of the HCTC has enabled educators to mitigate some of these common experiences of student group work. Counter-intuitively it has taken a competitive model to bring students to real collaborative learning. The following section of the chapter will unpack some of the components of the HCTC to demonstrate how the barriers discussed above have been managed.

THE HEALTH CARE TEAM CHALLENGE (HCTC) STRUCTURE

The HCTC is held each year at the University of Queensland in Australia and the University of British Columbia in Vancouver, Canada. A similar student team competition called Clarion runs annually at the University of Minnesota. A number of other universities in countries from Singapore to New Zealand are planning to introduce HCTC styled events. While the finer organisational details of project implementation differ slightly from one university and country setting to another, the fundamental structure remains consistent. The HCTC is in essence an extra-curricular voluntary activity for students training in the health professions. Its goals are:

1. To complement existing learning experiences with an authentic interprofessional experience.
2. To enhance students' knowledge of roles and values of other health professions.
3. To increase students' understanding of how IPE contributes to patient care.
4. To enhance student attitudes towards working in IP teams
5. To overcome university logistical barriers to IPE through an innovative extra-curricula strategy.
6. To contribute to the evidence base for short, extra-curricula IPE learning activities.

HCTC FORMAT

The HCTC is a time limited, extra-curricula, voluntary learning activity for students enrolled in health science programs. Students are typically in their final year of pre-registration study. They will have had some supervised fieldwork or clinic exposure, however their previous level of contact with other health professionals or health students may range from zero contact to a setting with fully integrated interprofessional clinical teams.

Final year students are briefed by academic staff about the HCTC and encouraged to volunteer by emailing their names to the project manager. Once volunteers are received from all the health professions they are randomly allocated into mixed professional teams and provided with a complex health biography of a real patient. The teams are challenged to develop an interprofessional health management plan over a 2-3 week planning period for presentation at a public event in front of an audience of peers, academics, clinicians and family. The focus during this pre-event developmental stage is on interprofessional communication and collaboration within each student team. Students are supported with a web-based learning platform where they have access to useful references and contact details for community based professionals who are available to assist with any problems relating to the case study.

On-line communication and learning platforms have been identified as positive tools to improve interpersonal and intergroup relationships in the early stages of group formation as they provide a low anxiety, low cost, equal status forum for meeting (Amichai-Hamburger & McKenna, 2006). Students are then expected to organise face to face meetings and work as an interprofessional team for their patient during the pre-event developmental phase. Student team size varies from institution to institution but generally accommodate between six and ten students depending on the number of health profession groups in the specific university setting.

At the public event which is the culmination of the HCTC, teams compete against one another to present the best management plan as judged by an interprofessional team of experienced clinicians from the community. The communication and interprofessional collaboration skills each team has developed over the planning period are crucial to success as they are challenged by a series of previously unseen extension questions that further complicate the case study and to which they must respond in real time.

ACADEMIC LEADERSHIP

A major element of the HCTC organisation is the involvement of a cohesive team of academic leaders from all of the academic training programs whose students are involved. These leaders promote the project to students and faculty, recruit student participants, contribute to the overall planning of the event and ensure that the case study developed for the challenge contains health biography detail that represents a sphere of concern for each student health professional involved. A perhaps more powerful but less obvious influence of the academic leadership team is its capacity to reflect for students a functional interprofessional team made up of individual academic leaders they each know and respect from their training programmes.

CASE DEVELOPMENT

The fundamental learning tool of the HCTC is the complex case study provided to interprofessional student teams to stimulate the collaborative process. The academic leadership team spends a prolonged period creating a comprehensive health biography that encompasses the following features.

- The case study presents a wicked problem (Rittel & Webber, 1973). That is a problem that is characterized by complexity and ambiguity. It may be difficult to articulate or indeed identify and is often embedded with other equally complex issues (Drinka & Clark, 2000). It has no clear or simple solution. Wicked problems reflect the complexity of health care delivery for clinicians in the real world.
- In creating a 'wicked problem' the biographical details and experiences of a real patient are used. This collaboration with volunteer patients has allowed the academic team to create rich and authentic case studies that reflect the life experiences of our clients. With their permission, photos and excerpts of video footage of the patient are collated along with detailed histories and in some cases additional comments from family members to provide students with a rich picture of the patient's life.
- Case studies are peer reviewed by community based clinicians prior to being released to the student teams.
- Each case is designed to facilitate the involvement of a large team of health professionals so that students from all the disciplines in each team can make a

meaningful contribution and allow other disciplines to see where their profession fits in the health delivery continuum.

- The patient and his/her family are situated at the centre of the case and become part of the students' learning community.

STUDENT REWARDS

The HCTC is a voluntary, extramural activity and as such the academic team must create a range of possible rewards or motivators that will attract students to participate. Students have many calls on their time and will choose to involve themselves in this activity over another based on the possibility of obtaining a meaningful reward or return for their commitment.

The following list itemizes some of the material and non-material rewards that have been identified as meaningful and attractive to participating students:

- Representation of their student cohort and their profession;
- Opportunity for a high-profile public speaking activity;
- Prospect of meeting and learning more about other health professionals;
- Experience of interprofessional collaboration in preparation for professional practice post graduation;
- In-depth experience of the complex experiences of patient and significant others
- Exposure to a large audience of academics, health professionals and the public
- Reputational benefits – participation can be recorded on future resumes or curriculum vitas;
- Certificate of participant involvement to evidence their teamwork contribution
- Trophy and prize for each member of the winning team;
- Opportunity to meet prestigious public and professional representatives at the challenge event.

In the sports literature we are presented with the idea of reward. Reward is used to identify superiority between teams. Luschen (1970) talks about the sports contest as a 'zero-sum game – what one side wins, the other loses'. The HCTC while identifying one overall winning team acknowledges the participation and enthusiasm of all students. Apart from the trophy and prize participating students on all teams have access to the rewards listed above. In post event focus groups students have consistently identified both their motives to participate and the benefits (rewards) they gained transcended a trophy or prize.

I suppose working together with people from other faculties and students that were like in their final year of uni and so they're more than likely to be your colleagues in the next few years and I think the more people that you meet now out before you get out into the field you know the friendly faces you meet in a big hospital or wherever really does help.

(Student comment)

It really gave us an opportunity to actually see just what sort of caring people do, to actually get to see exactly what their treatment plan would be, and try to sort of work really holistically together was I thought it was just a really good opportunity to have a go at doing that before we graduate. Student comment

And it was amazing to see how many different perspectives you can take on the one case and what everyone can bring to the table. You have no idea at your student level just how limited your knowledge can be until you meet other people and put it all together. Student comment

(Student Comment)

In my field I feel like there is almost a very closed atmosphere. We don't know much about the other professions. It is going to be more important for me working in a rural setting. Student comment

JUDGING THE EVENT – MAKING IT REAL

In order to reflect authentic real life practice, student case presentations and responses to extension questions are evaluated by a team of community based health professionals who have experience both of interprofessional practice and service delivery models as well as expert knowledge of the 'wicked problem' embedded in the case study. Whenever possible the person with the most expert understanding of the 'wicked problem', the patient, is invited to be part of the judging panel.

The judging panel ranks the presentation of each team and their responses to extension questions using a series of items and also provides qualitative feedback for each team. Examples of both the ranking sheet and judges' comments are illustrated in table 1 and table 2.

Table 1. HCTC Judging Sheet

	Question (Measured on a 1-7 Likert scale)	Team 1	Team 2	Team 3
1	Students demonstrated a good understanding of the central role of the patient in guiding management plan			
2	Ethical decision making and recommendations for practice were explicit in presentations			
3	Presentations indicated a good understanding of others roles and prioritization of professional input for best practice			
4	Open and respectful communication among team members appeared to take place as plans were being formulated			
5	The team displayed high quality communication skills in presenting the initial management plan			
6	The team displayed high quality communication skills in presenting the extension questions management plans			
7	Decision making responsibilities appeared to be shared among team members			
8	The team demonstrated an innovative approach to engaging the audience			
9	Overall team functioning and collaboration			
Overall Total				

The qualitative feedback is particularly useful and valued by students as it taps into their desire for genuine and authentic advice on how to improve their practice as they prepare to enter the professional world. It is provided to students in written form within a week of their participation as a summary document.

Table 2. Example of HCTC Judges' Additional Feedback

Team 1	Team 2	Team 3
• Think about what supports could you engage in the community? • Remember the ICF! • Medical model heavy. • Consider whose goals are you looking at? • Think about Jim's ADLs and interests. • Need to consider Jim's wife? • Medically oriented-not patient centred. • Little consideration of carer (ann) and local support groups. • Not significant collaborative practice. • Need to increase the client centred focus. • Jim and family need further consultation. • Addressed arm pain. • A lot of information regarding medical management. • Not much mention of or consideration for family needs. • Extension question 2 involved all team members.	• Considered family and wife. • Short and long term plans. • Support groups- good use of community support groups. • Good interdisciplinary approach. • Checked eligibility for ACAT. • Consider disability services in Queensland? • No mention of the arm pain. • Good research on community services. • Extension question 2: good knowledge of community supports and funding options, home visiting suggestions were good.	• Continuum of care- short/med/long term goals. • In extension: focus on patient and goal setting. • Good team and collaborative approach. • Consider disability services QLD? • HACC services are very hard to get and most provide only 2-8hours a week. No mention of the arm pain. • Equipment like hoists were mentioned- no lift techniques.

AUDIENCE PARTICIPATION AND RESPONSE

The presence of an audience is central for the success of the event. It transports student learning from primarily a semi-private academy based activity to a public event. Students know they are presenting themselves as novice professionals to a mixed group of peers, future professional colleagues, family and academic representatives. Having family and friends from outside their professional training programs in the audience was highlighted by many students as a momentous event as it was the first time they were seen in their professional role by their significant others. Similarly many audience members were vocal in their appreciation of the student teams' presentations. At each event an audience evaluation is conducted to garner feedback on the value of the event to a public audience and to tap into suggestions on how the event might be improved from an audience perspective.

CHALLENGES AND STRENGTHS OF COMPETITION AND TEAMWORK

A major strength of the competitive HCTC model is the excitement and novel learning opportunities it provides to students both as participants and as audience members. However competitive team activities are not without their challenges. The opportunity of presenting in a public audience with prestige professional representatives may over-ride team allegiance for some members and drive them to prioritise their own presentation over the needs for the team to look good. These conflicting demands may create social dilemmas for team members. Once this competitive behaviour starts in a group it is often modeled by other members thereby reducing the overall cohesion and success of the group effort and performance. Factors that enhance group cooperation and collaboration in a mixed motive situation include the dynamic of members 'feeling that their contributions to the team are relevant and valued, they believe that other members are acting in the same way and there is a high degree of trust amongst team members leading to greater commitment' (Levi, 2007, pp. 74-75).

Focus group comments from students who have participated in HCTC activities reflect some of the strategies they used to enhance their group cohesion and avoid potential problems.

> It is probably one of the most motivated and most diligent groups that I have ever worked with. One of the best groups in terms of team work as well. Anytime…it is true. Anytime anyone was …anytime anything needed to be done, someone would put their hand up for it. And anytime they volunteered to do something followed through and it was fine. I think it was because everyone really chose to be there and everyone wanted to be there o it was a good experience. (Student comment)

HCTC AS A MECHANISM TO PROMOTE TEAMWORK

The health and management literature is awash with definitions of teamwork and it is worthwhile to interrogate the capacity of the competitive HCTC to meet the constructs embedded in concept of teamwork. A very recent and comprehensive definition of teamwork was developed by Xyrichis and Ream (2008) using a concept analysis methodology that reviewed the health and management literature over the past 20 years. Their resulting definition proposes that 'teamwork is a dynamic process involving two or more health care professionals with complementary backgrounds and skills, sharing common health goals and exercising concerted physical and mental effort in assessing, planning, or evaluating patient care. This is accomplished through interdependent collaboration open communication and shared decision-making, and generates value-added patient, organisational and staff outcomes' (Xyrichis & Ream, 2008, p. 239).

Based on the feedback of students both immediately after the UQ HCTC event and at follow up focus groups eight weeks post-event we can argue that all but the final outcomes in this definition of teamwork related to service delivery are achieved. This competitive activity creates opportunities for new contacts between students and the development of new dynamic communities of practice that motivate and energise students to work together in interprofessional teams. It fulfils many of the conditions of the 'contact hypothesis'. Students meet regularly and spend time getting to know one another both on an interpersonal and a professional level.

> Well we had dinner a lot (laughter). Yeah, lots of food and there was a lot of communication between our group members like we sent so many emails. But they weren't just about the actual case. We asked each other questions about what our roles were. Like there were a whole heap of emails where we had "a day in the life of our profession" so the dentist the OT and the speechie all sent everyone so we were more aware of what each others role was. That also helped to form us as a group. We hung out afterwards because we all respect each other. (Student comment)

Students also reflected on how the experience had increased their confidence in their own professional roles providing a sense of validation and reducing professional anxiety.

> It did actually change my own views about my own specialty. Well I kind of went in going, well I looked at the case and thought, what can nursing really offer? I didn't really think there was that much to offer from the nursing side of things but as we figured out the case more I really realized what I had to offer. And that I did, I had a valuable perspective to add to the case. So that was really good. It kind of boosted my own confidence in my own specialty. (Student comment)

> When I first walked in I though well what am I doing here? There is nothing in this case for me to be here for. But as I actually started talking about it, I realized that there was a part that the audiologist does play and um…the other group members were really supportive too. They said "no, no, no, you do have a part to play we just need to sit down and think about it, what it is that you do". The group members really came together and supported me so I felt much better after that and started to relax a bit. And bring in my profession. (Student comment)

MIXED MOTIVE SITUATIONS

Amongst the common problems associated with assessable team work activities is the conflict of mixed motive situations when individual goals conflict with team goals. The HCTC creates a mixed motive situation where cooperation within the team is encouraged and intra-group competition is replaced with inter-group competition. The clinical case study is carefully designed by an interprofessional team of educators to ensure that every student professional has a contribution to make.

> … it was amazing to see how many different perspectives you can take on the one case and what everyone can bring to the table. You have no idea at your student level just how limited your knowledge can be until you meet other people and put it all together. (Student comment)

Involving a real volunteer patient as the foundation for the case study also had a strong impact on the student teams' sense of the relevance and value of their contributions.

> I wasn't expecting a real patient and then this video came out and I was like oh my goodness this is actually some person's life here. I thought it was excellent that we got a real patient. That was above and beyond my expectations. (Student comment)

Students found the competitive framework of the challenge motivating.

> I think the fact it was a competition for us really motivated us and kept us on the goal. Because it could have been quite easy just to get carried away and um have more of a good time rather than being so like focused on what we were working towards. (Student comment)

> And a bit of friendly rivalry between your colleagues from the other teams as well was also good. (Student comment)

CONCLUSION - INTO THE WORKPLACE

Feedback from graduates who have participated in HCTC events indicate that they are generalising their learning to the workplace and modifying the way they approach their professional practice to be more team focused. This encouraging evidence of enduring change supports the use of carefully designed learning activities that incorporate competition as valuable learning tools for interprofessional education.

> I think for me it just also highlights the importance of making time when you start in a new workplace and getting to know the roles of each individual health care professional. (Graduate comment.)

> The HCTC forces you to look beyond stereotypical roles and boundaries of different professions. It promotes an understanding of different roles and enhances your ability to look at problems as a team. It is upon entering the workforce that I have developed a deeper understanding of the long-term effects of the HCTC. The skills which I gained by participating in this event I utilise in everyday practice. (Graduate comment)

> I hope to see this competition live on strong and grow so to help students learn more about their other health profession colleagues. Potentially this could change the future of our health care system, we are after all the future health care providers of this country. (Graduate comment)

ETHICS APPROVAL

All student and graduate comments were collected as part of a longitudinal research and evaluation project that received ethical approval from the University of Queensland.

ACKNOWLEDGMENTS

This project could not have developed without the cooperation and commitment of students who agreed to participate in the HCTC and the subsequent research project, and the academic representatives of nine professions who worked together to make it a reality. The authors are most grateful for their involvement and support for interprofessional education.

REFERENCES

Allport, G. (1954). *The nature of prejudice*. Reading, MA: Addison-Wesley.

Amichai-Hamburger, Y., & McKenna, K. Y. A. (2006). The contact hypothesis reconsidered: Interacting via the Internet. *Journal of Computer-Mediated Communication, 11*(3), 825-843.

Barnett, R. (2004). Learning for an unknown future. *Higher Education Research & Development, 23*(3), 247-260.

Corbett, K., & Corbett, J. C. (1999). The new professional: The nexus of healthcare trends. *Canadian Journal of Occupational Therapy*, 66(3), 111-115.

Drinka, T. J. K., & Clark, P. G. (2000). *Health care teamwork: Interdisciplinary practice and teaching*. Westport, CI: Auburn House.

Gibbons, M. (1998). Higher education relevance in the 21st century. Proceedings from UNESCO World Conference on Higher Education, Paris, Oct 5-9 1998.

Hean, S., & Dickinson, C. (2005). The Contact Hypothesis: An exploration of its further potential in interprofessional education. *Journal of Interprofessional Care*, 19(5), 480 – 491.

Hewstone, M., & Brown, R. J. (1986). Contact is not enough: An intergroup perspective on the Contact Hypothesis. In M. Hewstone & R. J. Brown (Eds.), *Contact and Conflict in Intergroup Encounters* (pp. 1-44). Oxford: Blackwell.

Johnson, A. W., Potthoff, S. J. Carranza, L., Swenson, H. M., Platt, C. R., & Rathbun, J. R. (2006). CLARION: A novel interprofessional approach to health care education. *Academic Medicine*, 18(3), 252-256.

Levi, D. (2007). *Group dynamics for teams*, (2nd edn), Thousand Oaks, Sage.

Light, D. W. (1988). Turf battles and the theory of professional dominance. *Research in the Sociology of Health Care*, 7, 203-225.

Lüschen, G. (1970). Cooperation, association and contest. *The Journal of Conflict*, 14(1), 21-35.

Moran, M., Boyce, R., O'Neill, K., Bainbridge, L., & Newton, C. (2007). The healthcare team challenge: a case-study for interprofessional engagement. *Focus on Health Professional Education: A Multi-disciplinary Journal*, 8(3), 47-53.

Newton, C., Bainbridge, L., Moran, M., & Boyce, R, (2008). The Health Care Team Challenge: the key to implementing interprofessional education in an inter-organizational, international setting. Paper presented at *All Together Better Health IV Conference*, 1-5 June, Stockholm, Sweden.

O'Reilly, P. (2000). *Health care practitioners: An Ontario case study in policy making*. Toronto, ON: University of Toronto Press.

Pfaff, E., & Huddleston, P. (2003). Does it matter if I hate teamwork? Student attitudes towards teamwork. *Journal of Marketing Education*, 25(1), 37-45.

Rittel, H., & Webber, M. (1973). Dilemmas in a general theory of planning. *Policy Sciences*, 4(2), 155-169

Salhani, D., & Coulter, I. (2009). The politics of interprofessional working and the struggle for professional autonomy in nursing. *Social Science & Medicine*, 68(7), 1221-1228.

Wenger, E. (2003). *Communities of practice; Learning, meaning and identity.* Cambridge: Cambridge University Press.

World Health Organization, (1986). Ottawa charter for health promotion. Health Promotion, 1, pp. iii–v.

World Health Organisation, (1988). *Learning together to work together for health. Report of a WHO study group on multiprofessional education of health personnel: the team approach.* Geneva, World Health Organisation Technical Report Series 769, pp. 1–72.

Xyrichis, A., & Ream, E. (2008). Teamwork: a concept analysis. *Journal of Advanced Nursing*, 61(2), 232–241.

In: Sociology of Interprofessional Health …   ISBN: 978-1-60876-866-0
Ed: S. Kitto, J. Chesters et al.   © 2011 Nova Science Publishers, Inc.

Chapter 12

PREPARING EDUCATORS FOR INTERPROFESSIONAL LEARNING: RATIONALE, EDUCATIONAL THEORY AND DELIVERY

Jill Thistlethwaite and Gillian Nisbet

ABSTRACT

The growing literature on interprofessional education (IPE), learning and practice mainly focuses on evidence for the effectiveness of education and practice, while describing educational activities taking place around the world. There has been less emphasis on the need for the development of educators and facilitators of IPE, the specific challenges of 'training the trainers' for interprofessional activities and models of professional development. In this chapter we discuss the attributes required of effective interprofessional facilitators and consider whether they should still be clinical practitioners. Facilitators have to ease learners through the process of professional socialisation and acculturation while ensuring that they develop skills and behaviours for working and collaborating with other professionals and within interprofessional teams. Faculty development is vital to prepare and hone the skills of facilitators who may have a wide experience of working uniprofessionally and therefore find interprofessional activities challenging. Both sociological and learning theories are important to provide a firm base for educational delivery. We describe a module we have developed for health professionals wishing to become involved in IPE and explore the difficulties associated with the evaluation of educational developments and delivery.

INTRODUCTION

Necessary attributes of an interprofessional educator have been defined as being "attuned to the dynamics of interprofessional learning (IPL), skilled in optimizing learning opportunities" and the educator should value "the distinctive experience and expertise which each of the participating professions brings" (Barr, 1996, p. 244). Moreover as Interprofessional education (IPE) involves "the application of principles of adult learning to interactive group-based learning, which relates collaborative learning within a coherent rationale which is informed by understanding of interpersonal, group, intergroup, organisational and interorganisational relations and processes of professionalisation" (Barr, 2002, p. 24) it is obvious that we are asking a lot of our facilitators. However while facilitator/educator preparation and development are of paramount importance for the introduction and continuing delivery of high quality interprofessional learning, the exact nature of such preparation has not been defined (Oandasan & Reeves, 2005). The majority of published reports relating to faculty development programs focus on university/faculty tutors, with few concentrating on practising health professionals and/or clinical educators/facilitators (Steinert, 2005).

When IPL as a concept is applied to health professional education, learning activities may take place within the classroom (university-based) and/or within the workplace (clinical setting). This adds complexity to an already difficult pursuit as educators within these two settings have varying levels of teaching expertise, varying degrees of recent clinical experience, different levels of commitment and time availability for teaching and are often employed by different institutions, who define their roles and responsibilities. While university-based teachers are employed in part to teach, educators in the clinical setting often have education as a secondary or even tertiary role after clinical service commitment and research. Therefore defining the pedagogical needs of this diverse group of educators and providing staff development activities to meet these needs is problematical. Add to this the necessity for uniprofessional or profession-specific professional development and it becomes clear that preparing educators for IPL is fraught with difficulty.

Defined learning outcomes for participants in different settings are also likely to vary, as is their status (pre-qualification or post-qualification), their motivation for learning (mandated or voluntary) and their prior experience of learning 'with, from and about' other professions – the hallmark of interprofessional learning (CAIPE, 1997). Interprofessional learning outcomes may not be included for generic professional development but the skilled IPL facilitator will make these explicit by ensuring that participants are aware of the 'added value' of learning interprofessionally. Thus facilitators need to be as skilled in relating to and developing the process of learning in interprofessional groups as well as delivering content as outlined in curricula.

THE ATTRIBUTES OF AN EFFECTIVE INTERPROFESSIONAL LEARNING FACILITATOR

If we could draw up a wish list of attributes these would be likely to include:

- Up-to-date knowledge of educational theory including adult learning theories;
- Up-to-date knowledge and skills relating to the theories of team work and team building;
- Recent or current experience of working in a health care team – ideally interprofessional rather than multiprofessional;
- Experience of collaborative practice and ability to promote this within the workplace;

- Knowledge of others' professional roles and responsibilities and awareness of boundary issues including the debate around blurring of professional roles;
- Knowledge of the process of professional socialisation and how this might impact on interprofessional learning;
- Skills in facilitation and conflict resolution;
- Enthusiasm and dedication to interprofessional practice – being an IPE champion;
- Knowledge of the evidence for IPE and IPP and ability to distil and disseminate this to faculty and learners;
- An understanding of the arguments relating to the underlying philosophy of and rationale for IPE, timing of activities and possible outcomes.

Freeth, Hammick, Reeves, Koppel and Barr (2005) suggest a similar list as does Bray (2008), the latter developed through a Delphi process to ascertain 'expert opinion on the complexities of facilitating IPL (p. 30). The five themes arising from this process include: awareness and use of self as a facilitator (personal qualities with emphasis on reflective practice), dealing with difference and conflict, group process and relationships, awareness and understanding of power dimensions within the group and between the facilitator and the group, and context and planning (sessions are best if pre-planned) (Bray, 2008).

Within medical education clinical teachers have been said to have four roles: physician, teacher, supervisor and supporter (Ullian, Bland & Simpson, 1994). Translated into the IPE milieu the first of these may be translated as clinical practitioner. How important is it that IPL facilitators are still practising in a clinical setting or that they have working relations with practitioner colleagues? Being an active health professional ensures that knowledge is up-to-date and that the educator is aware of current health trends and service provision changes, particularly in relation to interprofessional practice. Active service adds to the credibility of the facilitator and increases the role modelling effect. The educator will also have a bank of clinical anecdotes to draw upon – students enjoy hearing these tales from the front line and stories help them begin to understand the environment in which they will be working. However, university based teachers may be at a disadvantage if they have given up clinical practice for full-time academia. Learners need to be exposed to skilled IPL facilitators both in the classroom and the clinical setting. Co-facilitation involving an expert facilitator and clinical expert is one way to achieve this balance.

The teacher role is self-evident. Supervision involves watching and giving feedback to students undertaking IPL activities. For IPL there is the additional observation of how students interact and collaborate, and includes the supervisor giving feedback on team processes and facilitating reflection on roles, responsibilities and language. Support may involve encouraging students in their IPL activities, particularly if these are not compulsory, not all students are undertaking them or if they are in addition to other timetabled sessions.

PROFESSIONAL IDENTITY AND ACCULTURATION

All of these roles require an understanding of the nature of professional socialisation and how this might impact on student learning during different stages of their education as well as its effects on educators as they begin to facilitate interprofessional activities. Professional socialisation occurs during a student's progress from novice to professional and includes a social acculturation into a professional group (Ajjawi & Higgs, 2008). Individuals bring existing values into the learning process which are refined and developed through their interactions with the professionals they learn from and work with, so that a health professional eventually identifies with his or her profession both externally and through a process of internalization (Davis, 1968; Mackintosh, 2006).

In the current educational climate where there is a growing awareness that "professionalism must be taught" (Cruess & Cruess, 1997), a discussion with health professional educators (and later with students) about what it means to be a professional and what a profession is can be a stimulating interprofessional interactive group activity. The six elements of a profession have been defined as: the presence of skill based on specialist knowledge; provision of training and education; the means of testing for competence; organisation of members, adherence to a code of conduct; and the provision of an altruistic service not just for financial reward (Johnson, 1972).

In its broad sense acculturation is the process of learning to live within another culture and the exchange of cultural features between peoples. Sociologically we could say that interprofessional practice has similar features to multiculturalism, which is a public policy in Australia (Australian Government, 1989) and which as a concept has many definitions including the process whereby the distinctive identities of the cultural groups within a society are maintained or supported (Soanes & Stevenson, 2003) but with an added emphasis on living and working together with respect and in collaboration. The three dimensions of multicultural policy (Australian Government, 1989) may be adapted to the interprofessional environment, substituting health professional for Australian:

- Professional/Cultural identity: the right of all health professionals, within carefully defined limits, to express and share their individual professional heritage, including their language;
- Social justice: the right of all health professionals to equality of treatment and opportunity;
- Economic efficiency: the need to maintain, develop and utilize effectively the skills and talents of all health professionals, regardless of background.

In the health professions different cultural features include professional language (or jargon) and different models of care such as nursing and medical. Thus, while multiculturalism and interprofessional practice stress the importance of an individual's culture/practice, there is no reason why some crossover of custom (or blurring of roles) cannot occur – though certainly these concepts do not advocate a total blending with subsequent loss of cultural identity or worse a dominant culture overwhelming the minority. Educators need to be aware that students may be grappling with acculturation into their chosen profession – and then in addition they are asked to learn to collaborate across cultures/professions. Even before starting a university program some students already have stereotypical attitudes about their own and other professions (Rudland & Mires, 2005).

Three major conceptual frameworks, derived from social and health psychology, have been described to help the process of acculturation in migrants and refugees (Herman, 1992). These may be applied to IPL activities and may help facilitators understand the process of professional acculturation and its potential problems and challenges in IPE. The first is attention to the affective component – social (and educational) support to help the learner through the stresses of professional socialisation and change. The second is a behavioural approach – facilitation of the learning of specific skills to help the learner in everyday professional situations, for example learning the 'jargon' of different professionals. Students are often just beginning to get to grips with their own situated language practices (Lave & Wenger, 1991), their profession specific discourse, which helps socialize them into their own profession. Now they must also develop the skills to enable them to communicate within an interprofessional learning group or working team. Finally the cognitive framework focuses on establishing professional identity and learning to work through the conflicts that may occur between different professions.

THE INTERPROFESSIONAL FACILITATOR

When asked about their own experience of education, teachers remember their 'good' teachers and the motivation that such skill engendered. A major source of understanding about the teaching role thus comes from the observation of teachers when one is a learner oneself (Irby, 1993). However, very few, if indeed any, potential IPL facilitators will have had experience of interprofessional education themselves as students and therefore this source of knowledge is lacking.

Who decides to become involved in IPE? The literature makes frequent reference to champions in terms of the clinicians and educators who introduce and maintain interest in IPL within an organisation. We have met and heard of champions from all professional backgrounds whose motivation has been stimulated by their experiences of receiving, giving and teaching health care. For some collaborative teamwork is just the right (and only) way to practise. Champions enthuse others but their sphere of influence depends on their position in the hierarchy. Some affect other educators and practitioners through the educational activities that they deliver, while more senior staff can affect organisation change through university and health service processes.

Not all who are requested to take part in interprofessional facilitation may have the same values or even enthusiasm for IPE or Interprofessional practice (IPP). One study from Canada of the attitudes of faculty members (medicine, nursing, pharmacy and social work) showed that medical professionals were less positive than nurses to IPE within the academic setting. Positive attitudes were more likely if a respondent had had previous experience of IPE but did not appear to be affected by age or experience as a health professional (Curran , Sharpe & Forrestall, 2007). This study, albeit small, does suggest that the more educators are exposed to IPE, the more they are likely to want to become engaged with it. The concept of IPL without actual previous exposure may be off-putting to some.

Not all facilitators are hired specifically because of their expertise and enthusiasm for IPL. Some are plucked from uniprofessional education and asked to take on new tasks – often without professional development for their new role. The institution may decide to set up an interprofessional education unit and bring in experts, who can then train facilitators across faculties and schools. But this can also lead to problems – such units may be seen as separate, not integrated within any particular profession and therefore outside all; or they may be seen as located within a particular profession and thus favoring their colleagues. The location of the 'interprofessional education team' will continue to be a problem while there are separate faculties and departments.

AN OVERVIEW OF FACULTY DEVELOPMENT

The term faculty development strictly refers to programmes and activities based within the university for faculty members. A comprehensive development programme should include: orientation to the institution and to faculty roles; educational/teaching improvement and mentoring; leadership development; and organisational development such as an understanding of policies and procedures (Wilkerson & Irby, 1998). All of these may incorporate an interprofessional focus but for IPL perhaps the most pertinent of these is teaching improvement.

A record of attending teaching development sessions is mandatory in some institutions, and indeed universities are now beginning to require evidence of educational expertise through staff gaining certificates or diplomas in higher education teaching delivery. Learning outcomes will usually focus to begin with on the generic principles of learning and teaching. Such activities may include advice on how to give a lecture, facilitate small groups, assess students and evaluate teaching. More advanced study will explore curriculum design and delivery, the scholarship of learning and teaching and perhaps educational research. Then there may be additional profession/discipline specific outcomes. Experiential learning (from patients and in the clinical workplace), working with simulations and simulated patients, teaching clinical skills and problem-based learning fall into this category. These topics may also be incorporated in sessions for clinicians, including those who do not hold university appointments.

Development of this type may often be offered across faculties and involve participants from different disciplines with the university, such as law and the arts as well as medicine, nursing and health sciences. This mix may be referred to as interdisciplinary, however faculty development rarely considers such interdisciplinary teaching as a topic itself to be discussed. Moreover professional development may be restricted to within the faculty, or even individual schools, reducing the potential of learning from and with others from outside one's own subject areas.

FACULTY DEVELOPMENT FOR INTERPROFESSIONAL LEARNING

Staff who become involved in IPL may already be experienced educators. But such experience and recognition as a skilled facilitator within uniprofessional education does not mean that the transition to interprofessional education will be smooth (Freeth et al., 2005). Moreover, academic staff, who originally trained as health professionals, may no longer work in their primary occupation, and have little recent experience of clinical work. They thus may only have a theoretical knowledge of interprofessional practice and/or collaborative practice. Tutors in clinical settings, who themselves work as clinicians with a service commitment for part of their time, will also have variable experiences of interprofessional practice, depending on their workplace and specialty. The role of interprofessional modelling as a fundamental component of educational development may therefore need some thought.

A 'train the trainer' approach to IPL facilitator development may offer an effective way to prepare facilitators. Ideally train the trainer sessions should involve participants from two or more health professions learning 'from, with and about' each other not only to tutor and facilitate IPL activities but also to gain experience of the nature of interprofessional learning through modelling what they themselves will provide to students in future. The traditional model of 'train the trainer' involves the novice trainers learning how to deliver pre-existing material in a set format. If there is time, ideally IPL facilitator sessions should allow the novice trainers to set their own learning outcomes and develop their own ways to deliver IPE.

Constructivism theory is useful in looking at how learning should happen and views each learner as a unique individual with a unique background. Social constructivism moves on from this and resonates with IPL as it emphasizes that we learn through interactions with others and the environment in which we work. There should be active engagement with the roles, beliefs and culture of other professionals. Furthermore collaborative learning is important – collaboration in tasks and discussions to achieve shared understanding (Duffy & Jonassen, 1992), and in terms of practice, shared goals. According to social cognitive learning theory, which takes a more behavioural approach, the social or interactive components of learning are also highly important for adult learners (Bandura, 1986). In their own learning sessions, the fledging IPL facilitators need not only to participate in but also to observe the interactions around them. The expert facilitator needs to alert them to the process of interaction and how one's own profession or background impinges on this process. If possible having two facilitators from different professions also helps with the modelling process and aids vicarious learning, i.e. the observation that two different health professional educators can perform well together helps the novice realize that he or she can also teach this way. The personal experience of the learner (in this case the fledging facilitators), the learning and working environment and the type of learning activities all interact on teaching behaviour.

The concept of communities of practice introduced by Lave and Wenger in 1991 and incorporating the theory of situated learning is also useful in this context (Lave & Wenger, 1991). Think of interprofessional students moving from the periphery of their own profession into a greater understanding of their role within it, and then interacting with other professions first as observers and then full members of the team. Educators who have been through a similar process in their clinical workplace will have an understanding of how this happens, through learning, experience, reflection and feedback, and know ways in which to facilitate the process. Knowledge exchange and knowledge transfer are key components (Kaufman & Mann, 2007), and fit within the learning 'with, from and about' paradigm.

Learning sessions should include a time for self-reflection. The literature on reflection in education and reflective practice is immense. Reflection, discussion, an environment in which to test ideas and a skilled facilitator enable 'transformative learning' and the transfer of new learning into practice (Moon, 1999). Moon (1999) gives one example of transformative learning that is relevant to IPL: "I can see that my view was biased in the past. Now I am reconsidering the situation" (p. 146). The theory of transformative learning views learning as the construction and internalization of a new or revised interpretation of one's own experience through a social process (Kaufman & Mann, 2007). This reinterpretation is again important within interprofessional activities. Adapting Mezirow's description of transformative learning (Mezirow, 1990), we may say that transformative IPL reveals distorted assumptions (or stereotypes). IPL facilitators must be open to alternative points of view and to be empathic to how other professionals work, think and feel. They need to ensure equal participation by all students in discussion, while being mindful of the similarities and differences between them. For example, students from different health professions may come together at different stages of their training, and have markedly different knowledge and skills. Similarly facilitators will have varying degrees of both educational and practice experience.

Following formal IPL facilitator training sessions and then active IPL facilitation in the field, best practice advocates a time for participants to reconvene and discuss their experiences: what went well, what they would do differently and why. Boud et al. suggest three phases to this process. In this case, firstly there is the interprofessional teaching experience, followed by reflection and discussion of positive and negative outcomes and feelings (Boud, Keough & Walker, 1985). This interaction should generate new perspectives on teaching, with a commitment to change behaviour for the next group of students or teaching activity. In reality such group reflection is rare, but hopefully it is happening on a personal scale.

Facilitator training sessions involve activation of prior learning – this may also involve participants unlearning some of their stereotyping or prejudices about other health professionals. If disparaging remarks are made about one's colleagues during a learning session, the optimum scenario is if one of the participants draws attention to this and challenges the speaker. Failing this, the facilitator needs to initiate feedback and encourage participants to comment on why such remarks are made, their potential effects and how they would handle such incidents amongst their own students.

POTENTIAL BARRIERS

Within the IPE literature barriers to successful implementation of professional development programmes tend to focus on logistics and timetabling – just getting staff together might be too much of a challenge. But there are also factors such as lack of support from teachers/tutors for IPL generally, who certainly do not see the effort required to put the students in the same space at the same time is merited. Institutional and organisational buy-in is so important; the trickle down effect of motivated champions who enthuse others with their passion and belief in IPL as a means to enhanced interprofessional teamwork and practice is paramount to engage educators in a new way of working. Many of these educators will remain to be convinced of the evidence for IPL and will become disaffected if 'forced' to teach in this way. Active resistance to change might take the form of doing as little as possible to ensure success or even actively sabotaging the process; indifference may be more insidious including apathy (Gelmon, White, Carlson & Norman, 2000). A concise, well-written summary of the evidence should be part of the development package, highlighting the move of health service delivery to a patient-centred/client-centred team approach. Negotiation and collaboration are key components of the change process, mirroring the skills needed for interprofessional practice itself.

Given the competing pressures on educators, there needs to be some tangible benefit for educators firstly to attend IPL facilitator programs and, secondly, to put this into practice by developing and/ or running IPL programs for their students or colleagues. One incentive may be to have facilitator programs accredited and to attach (continuing professional development) CPD points. Incorporating IPL into performance development systems is another option worth exploring.

Another potential problem for IPE and facilitator development is the perceived academic elitism and stereotyping of professions, found not only in students but in their teachers. As with undergraduate education, there may be a prevailing culture of deferring to medical doctors, for example for opinion, decision-making and expertise. This may be resented by some health professionals. If such attitudes and behaviour emerge during sessions, the trainer should draw attention to the process and ask the participants why they think this is happening and ways that it should be tackled. The solutions should then be those that the facilitators could themselves use when running IPL activities as it is likely that similar situations will occur with students and other learners.

Perceived power and status differences between the professions can impact on the success of facilitator development programs; this is often accentuated when there is unequal representation from each of the professions. However, this can be turned around as a teaching and learning discussion point and explored early on by participants as one of the real practical challenges when facilitating IPE programs; again, the role modelling of a process that facilitators could use themselves to tackle 'up-front' the issues of power differences is useful in preparing future IPL facilitators. Strategies generated from our own experience include the establishment of 'ground rules' to encourage participation by all and encouraging reflection on both positive and negative experiences from practice.

EXAMPLES OF IPL PROFESSIONAL DEVELOPMENT PROGRAMS

A Staff Development Workshop

IPL has been developing at the University of Sydney since the early part of the twenty-first century. Following the successful implementation of a pilot work-based pre-qualification interprofessional activity (Nisbet, Henry, Rolls & Field, 2008), a need for facilitator development was recognized if the programme was to expand. The subsequent workshop design and development was based on existing literature (Nisbet & Thistlethwaite, 2007). As well as enhancing the quality of IPL programmes offered through staff training, we anticipated that the workshop would increase the knowledge of clinical educators relating to IPL and would therefore attract more into offering and supervising IPL programmes and activities. The workshop learning outcomes are listed in Box 1.

Feedback from the workshops indicated that participants were receptive to increasing IPL opportunities for students and could identify areas within their workplace setting where IPL could be implemented. Unfortunately, due to a low response rate, long term follow up to determine the extent of *actual* implementation could not be gauged.

Box 1. IPL facilitator workshop learning outcomes

1. Identify characteristics of effective interprofessional teams as it relates to a workplace setting.
2. Apply understanding of IPL to a clinical/ practice education setting.
3. Identify benefits and barriers to interprofessional learning as it relates to your own workplace education setting.
4. Within the practice setting apply knowledge of IPL to explore interprofessional learning opportunities.

MASTERS OF MEDICAL EDUCATION

Since 2006, a unit of study titled 'Promoting Interprofessional Learning' has been offered as part of the University of Sydney Masters of Medical Education program. The full Masters requires eight units of study to be completed. Attracting local and international students, this unit is targeted towards university based and clinically based educators and clinicians with an interest in developing, implementing and evaluating interprofessional learning initiatives within their local context. Although the Masters program is part of the Faculty of Medicine, it is open to students from a range of backgrounds. This is particularly relevant and appropriate as there is interprofessional learning occurring as Masters students learn "from, with and about" each other in an interactive, safe environment.

Learning outcomes of the program are listed in Box 2.

Box 2. IPL unit of study learning outcomes – Master of Medical Education

- Design and implement a checklist/ guideline for evaluating interprofessional teamwork.
- From the literature identify the benefits of and barriers to interprofessional learning as it relates to clinical and classroom teaching environment.
- Within the workplace setting apply knowledge of the interprofessional learning literature and educational strategies to design interprofessional learning opportunities.

The unit of study has a scholarly focus, covering evidence and rationale for interprofessional practice and learning, and the pedagogical considerations for developing IPE. The content covers the theoretical and practical aspects of teamwork within modern health care delivery. The practical application is further promoted as students discuss, debate, and attempt to address the well documented barriers to implementing and sustaining IPL initiatives. The summative assessment task for this unit of study is a written proposal to a curriculum committee or workplace management committee advocating for the introduction of an IPL initiative.

To date, approximately 25 students have completed the unit of study. Submitted assessments have produced IPL initiatives covering a range of contexts, for example an IPL initiative within a general practice setting involving practice nurses, general practitioners and administrative staff; undergraduate IPL workshops focusing on teamwork skill development;

integration of IPL activities within clinical placements, learning activities involving medical students and theology students, and medical students and law students; and postqualification continuing professional development within the Emergency Department.

Although the unit of study does not specifically cover skills for facilitating IPL, it provides a strong base for the attributes of an IPL facilitator listed earlier. Students not only have the opportunity to learn from other health professions, but they also experience interprofessional facilitation "in action" through the role modelling occurring through the unit convenors/facilitators; intentionally, these convenors are from two different professional backgrounds.

A re-occurring theme that invariably surfaces through discussion is the need for cultural change amongst educators and clinicians in regard to an altered paradigm of health professional education. Students of this unit of study potentially can act as change agents in this cultural shift through themselves facilitating IPL activities and promoting the IPL concept with others.

WHAT WE HAVE LEARNT FROM RUNNING THIS UNIT

The unit is focused on IPL but our students tend to be medical educators in that, though they themselves come from different professional backgrounds (mainly medical, nursing and midwifery), they are involved in teaching medical students and junior doctors in their home institutions. For the majority IPL is a new concept, sometimes difficult to grasp and therefore students can take time to engage with the material. While by the end of the semester's work they are able to propose IPL activities to be included within curricula across their health professional faculties, they have very little experience to draw on in planning compared to other units which are grounded in their day-to-day educational development and delivery. Moreover, the question remains as to where IPL will be prioritized in relation to their other teaching requirements.

It would certainly be interesting to track the three cohorts who have taken this unit and see what difference if any their study has made in a practical way to their educational responsibilities. Ideally the Masters program will be aimed in future at all health professional educators, ensuring a more lively interprofessional discussion and debate. The material needs to speak to the participants, and be both academic and practical. Even collaborative teamwork is a novelty idea for participants from some overseas countries.

As the unit is offered both on-line and blended (on-line and face-to-face sessions) it is important to ensure that all students engage in discussion so that different professional views are put forward. At least as the two facilitators we model interprofessional facilitation, coming as we do from nutrition and medical backgrounds.

EVALUATION OF TEACHING AND FACILITATOR DEVELOPMENT

Universities have instituted systems for collecting student evaluation and feeding this back to teachers so that the teachers may act on the results and plan their further educational development. In regards to clinical education, such institutional feedback is often not helpful as it is impossible to link it to individual educators, or even activities. Educators within the clinical setting therefore may use their own or departmental evaluation forms to gather student feedback. However we have known for a long time that written feedback of this kind within any university department is ineffectual in stimulating change (Centra, 1973); tutors are more likely to seek to improve their teaching through a form of appraisal with support from a superior or peer who suggests improvements. Peer review through observation of teaching is also worth considering – but is even more difficult to organize and is labour intensive.

There is no reason why the above teaching evaluation methodologies cannot be applied to the IPL context. However, thought is required as to how this is logistically managed; how feedback is provided if sessions are co-facilitated; and what IPL considerations are to be included in the evaluation. For example one aspect to be explored may be how well the facilitator included the perspectives of all professions present.

IMPACT OF FACULTY DEVELOPMENT PROGRAMMES

The UK Centre for the Advancement of Interprofessional Education (CAIPE) has developed a model of evaluation for outcomes of IPE, derived from Kirkpatrick, whose original model was developed in 1959 (Kirkpatrick, 1994; Barr et al., 2000). Kirkpatrick defined four levels to evaluate the effectiveness, impact and quality of educational interventions: essentially the reaction of the student, the increase in knowledge, behaviour change including any enhancement of capability and finally the effects on the environment. For the fourth level CAIPE included the effects on the final stakeholders of any health professional education – the patient and the health service organisation. We have adapted these further for IPL facilitator programmes (see Box 3). These programmes have an added level of complexity in that the 'students' are now the educators being trained, and the stakeholders include their own students who are being taught. As faculty development should have an impact on the learning experience of students who interact with the facilitators, level 4b therefore should involve not only patients/clients but the recipients of education from the facilitators who have undergone educational development. When advocating that faculty enhance their capabilities through development programmes, we need to be able to show that such programmes meet their objectives. However most of the literature in this field focuses on descriptions of learning activities, usually with some short term participant evaluation from post intervention questionnaire data. There is little written about the impact of the programmes on subsequent teaching delivery and efficacy, and whether there are any longer term changes in terms of student behaviour and attitudes.

Box 3. Model of outcomes of IPL 'train the trainer' programs

1. Reaction Participants' views on the learning experience and its interprofessional nature.

2a. Modification of attitudes/behaviour Changes in reciprocal attitudes or perceptions of participant health professional educators.

2b. Acquisition of knowledge/skills Includes knowledge & skills linked to interprofessional education and collaboration in practice.

3. Behavioural change   Transfer of interprofessional learning to practice setting resulting in changed professional and teaching practice.

4a. Change in organisational practice Wider changes in organisation, education & care delivery.

4b. Benefits to patients/clients Improvements in health or well-being of patients/clients and students Improvements in learning experience for students and their subsequent capabilities for interprofessional practice.

'Student' here may refer to qualified health professionals. Important evaluation outcomes for them and their organisations might include enhanced capability to work collaboratively and subsequent improved patient care and satisfaction, as well as positive changes in terms of workforce recruitment and retention.

A BEME (Best Evidence in Medical Education) systematic review of faculty development initiatives designed to improve teaching effectiveness in medical education in 2006 analysed 53 papers (Steinert, Nasmuth, Daigle & Franco, 2006). An inclusion criterion was that outcomes beyond simple participant satisfaction had to be reported. Only this small number, from 2,777 abstracts, was therefore read in full. As this review focuses on medical education it is not surprising that only one paper is listed as involving 'mixed health professions', though these are still mainly physicians and the workshop described is to help staff work with problem residents (junior doctors in training) (Steinert et al., 2001). However this work is useful in its conclusions as to what is needed in this field; these conclusions may be applied to interprofessional faculty development:

- Further exploration of which elements work from the wide range of learning activities offered;
- A better understanding of teachers' educational practices and the difficulties they face;
- The development of more longitudinal programmes to allow for continuing professional growth;
- A re-examination of what should be voluntary and what should be mandatory for educators.

From this literature the following outcomes were evident:

- High satisfaction with the development programmes undertaken;
- Changes in attitudes towards teaching and professional development;
- Enhancement of knowledge and skills;
- Changes in teaching behaviour.

Changes in subsequent student behaviour were rarely mentioned – highlighting again that such longer term evaluation is difficult and costly.

CONCLUSION

Faculty and educator development for the development and delivery of effective and sustainable IPL has been neglected as a topic in the IPE literature to a large extent, though this is likely to change in the next few years. Any program of development should be constructed with a sound educational base and evaluated for impact on the participants themselves, as well as longer term impact on their learners and subsequently, ideally, on patient care.

However, the influence of professional identity and acculturation cannot not be ignored when considering how best to extend and enhance professional development in IPL. We need to recognize that interprofessional learning is a relatively new concept for many educators and consequently, identification with their profession and its culture will likely be dominant. This, however, does not preclude cross pollination of cultures and sharing of experiences and knowledge between professions. The development of educators and facilitators of IPL provides an important means by which to achieve this, whilst at the same time enhancing the learning experience for students of IPL.

REFERENCES

Ajjawi, R., & Higgs, J. (2008). Learning to reason: A journey of professional socialisation. *Advances in Health Sciences Education*, 13, 133-150.

Australian Government, Department of Immigration and Citizenship (1989). National Agenda for a Multicultural Australia. October 2008, Availabe at: *http://www.immi.gov.au/media.* (Accessed October 2008).

Bandura, A. (1986). *Social Foundations of Thought and Action.* Englewood Cliffs, NJ: Prentice-Hall.

Barr, H. (1996). Ends and means in interprofessional education: towards a typology. *Education for Health*, 9, 341-352.

Barr, H. (2002). *Interprofessional Education. Today, Yesterday and Tomorrow. A Review.* London: LTSN, HS&P.

Barr, H., Hammick, M., Freeth, D., Koppel, I., & Reeves, S. (2000). *Evaluations of interprofessional education: a United Kingdom review for health and social care.* London: CAIPE/BERA.

Boud, D., Keogh, R., & Walker D. (Eds.) (1985). *Reflection: turning experience into learning.* London: Kogan Page.

Bray, J. (2008). Interprofessional facilitation skills and knowledge: evidence from a Delphi research survey. In: E. Howkins & J. Bray (Eds.), *Preparing for interprofessional teaching. Theory and practice.* (pp. 27-39). Oxford: Radcliffe Medical Publishing.

CAIPE, (1997*). Interprofessional education: a definition.* London: Centre for the Advancement of Interprofessional Education.

Centra, J. A. (1973). Effectiveness of student feedback in modifying college instruction. *Journal of Educational Psychology*, 65, 395-401.

Cruess, S. R, & Cruess, R, L. (1997). Professionalism must be taught. *British Medical Journal,* 315, 1674-1677.

Curran, V. R, Sharpe, D., & Forristall, J. (2007). Attitudes of health science faculty members towards interprofessional teamwork and education. *Medical Education,* 41, 892-896.

Davis, F. (1968). Professional socialisation as subjective experience. The process of doctrinal conversion among student nurses. In H. Becker & B. Geer. (Eds.), *Institutions and the person* (pp. 235-251). Chicago, IL: Aldine.

Duffy, T. M., & Jonassen, D. H. (1992). *Constructivism and the technology of instruction: A conversation.* Hillsdale, NJ: Lawrence Erlbaum Associates.

Freeth, D., Hammick, M., Reeves, S., Koppel, I., & Barr, H. (2005). *Effective Interprofessional Education. Development, delivery and evaluation.* Oxford: Blackwell.

Gelmon, S. H. White, A. W, Carlson, L. & Norman, L. (2000). Making organizational change to achieve improvement and interprofessional learning: perspectives from health professions educators. *Journal of Interprofessional Care*, 14(2), 131-146.

Herman, J. (1992). *Trauma and Recovery.* New York, NY: Basic Books.

Irby, D.M. (1993). What clinical teachers in medicine need to know. *Academic Medicine,* 69, 333-342.

Johnson, T. J. (1972). *Professions and power.* London: Macmillan Press.

Kaufman, D. M. & Mann K.V. (2007). *Teaching and Learning in Medical Education: How theory can inform practice.* Edinburgh: ASME.

Kirkpatrick, D. (1994). *Evaluating training programs: The four levels.* San Francisco: Berrett-Koehler.

Lave, J., & Wenger, E. (1991). *Situated learning: legitimate peripheral participation.* Englewood Cliffs, NJ: Prentice Hall.

Mackintosh, C. (2006). Caring: The socialisation of pre-registration student nurses: A longitudinal qualitative descriptive study. *International Journal of Nursing Studies*, 43, 953-962.

Mezirow, J. (1990). *Fostering critical reflection in adulthood.* San Francisco, CA: Jossey-Bass.

Moon, J. A. (1999). *Reflection in Learning and Professional Development. Theory and Practice.* London: Kogan Page Limited.

Nisbet, G., & Thistlethwaite, J. E. (2007). Preparing our educators for interprofessional learning: a framework for a work-based interprofessional learning staff development workshop. *Focus on Health Professional Education*, 8, 95-101.

Nisbet, G., Hendry, G., Rolls, G. & Field, M. (2008). Interprofessional learning for pre-qualification health care students: an outcomes-based evaluation. *Journal of Interprofessional Care*, 22(1), 57-68.

Oandasan, I., & Reeves, S. (2005). Key elements for interprofessional education. Part 1: The learner, the educator and the learning context. *Journal of Interprofessional Care,* 19(Supplement 1), 21-38.

Rudland, J. R,. & Mires, G. J. (2005). Characteristics of doctors and nurses as perceived by students entering medical school: implications for shared learning. *Medical Education,* 39, 448-455.

Soanes, C. & Stevenson, A. (Eds.) (2003). *Oxford Dictionary of English*. Oxford: Oxford University Press

Steinert, Y. (2005). Learning together to teach together. *Journal of Interprofessional Care*, 19(Supplement 1), 60-75.

Steinert, Y., Nasmith L., Daigle N. & Franco E. D. (2001). Improving teachers' skills working with 'problem' residents: a workshop description and evaluation. *Medical Teacher*, 23(3), 284-288.

Ullian, J. A., Bland, C. J., & Simpson, D. E. (1994). An alternative approach to defining the role of the clinical teacher. *Academic Medicine,* 69, 832-838.

Wilkerson, L., & Irby, D.M. (1998). Strategies for improving teaching practices: a comprehensive approach to faculty development. *Academic Medicine,* 73, 387-396.

In: Sociology of Interprofessional Health …
Ed: S. Kitto, J. Chesters et al.

ISBN: 978-1-60876-866-0
© 2011 Nova Science Publishers, Inc.

Chapter 13

HEALTH WORKFORCE REFORM: DYNAMIC SHIFTS IN THE DIVISION OF LABOUR AND THE IMPLICATIONS FOR INTERPROFESSIONAL EDUCATION AND PRACTICE

*Rosalie A. Boyce, Alan Borthwick,
Monica Moran and Susan Nancarrow*

ABSTRACT

Reform of the health care workforce has become a central component of Government health policy initiatives across many of the Anglophone nations in recent years (Willis, 1983; Nancarrow & Borthwick, 2005; Allsop, 2006; Coburn, 2006). Innovative steps to ensure a health care workforce that is 'fit for purpose' are necessary to successfully address a looming crisis in health care provision (Boyce, 2008; Cameron & Masterson, 2003; Sibbald, Shen & McBride, 2004). In this chapter we explore health workforce reform from the perspective of the sociology of the professions and the inherent difficulties that the jurisdictional, boundary and competitive positions that underpin the notion of profession posits for implementing authentic interprofessional education and practice. By examining key features of the international workforce reform agenda together with the motivations of professions that are revealed from a sociological analysis, we show that the division of labour in health care is in a state of intense and dynamic change. These changes create a new challenge for interprofessional education and practice through an increased complexity of the health workforce arising from shifting boundaries, new roles and new types of workers.

INTRODUCTION

In both the UK and Australia, health care services face critical labour shortages, whilst unmet demand continues to rise in line with population ageing (Department of Health, 2000; Richards, Carley & Jenkins, Clarke, 2000; Appel & Malcolm, 2002; Foot & Gomez, 2006).

Within a wider, global context, further pressures are being brought to bear which underpin the call for radical workforce redesign. Solutions to the problems posed by an ageing population, rising health care need and ongoing technological developments have implications for the nature of the workforce required (Sibbald & Chen, 2004; Nancarrow & Borthwick, 2005).

In addition, new measures in purchasing, organising and regulating the health workforce are also emerging as the health care workforce is 'modernised' to meet these demands (Nancarrow & Borthwick, 2005). Furthermore, the continued ascendancy in neoliberal political values evident across the anglophone world continue to emphasise economic rationalist policies, stressing enhanced effectiveness and efficiency in the delivery of 'patient centred' services, and a disdain for what has been perceived as self-serving professional agendas (Alaszewski, 1995; Ham, 2004; Allsop, 2006; Willis, 2006). Mistrust of the professions, in the wake of a number of medical scandals, has led to a questioning of professional self-regulatory privileges, and to a series of further policy reforms aimed at enhancing professional accountability, transparency and governance (Kennedy, 2001; Allsop & Saks, 2002; Baggott, 2002). In the UK, European Union Working Time Directives, which imposed limitations on the permissible working hours for doctors, have further edged the health care workforce to the brink of its functional capacity (Simpson, 2004; Goodwin, Pope Mort & Smith, 2005).

POLICY SHIFTS IMPACTING ON HEALTH WORKFORCE

By the late 1990s, in the UK and Australia as elsewhere, subtle ideological changes underpinning the policy agenda began to increasingly stress 'user empowerment' and greater professional accountability as a means to enhance service effectiveness. These shifts had the dual effect of increasing the centrality of patient-centredness to decision-making, whilst reducing the 'power' of the health care professions in defining health care needs and how these were to be met (Baggott, 2002).

Faced with an ongoing climate of policy change aimed at containing costs and diluting the authority of the professions, it was, perhaps, unsurprising that the professions broadly considered these reforms as hostile in intent. Demands for a change to the regulatory status of the professions, coupled with a relative loss of public trust, have resulted in a notable realignment in the nature of the relationships between the health professions and the state – in which the role of the state has moved from 'enabling' to 'managing' professional regulation (Larkin, 2002; Moran, 2002). Medical power has, in particular, been viewed as in retreat, assailed by the relentless pursuit of economic viability by market–orientated, entrepreneurial government policies (Coburn, 2006; Dent, 2006; Willis, 2006).

In combination, the many changes in ideological, regulatory, demographic and technological developments impacting on the health care workforce have acted to force upon it a new agenda, to which it has been compelled to respond. Under increasing political pressure to reconfigure the design of the professional workforce, without an obvious, underpinning "guiding vision...deeper than an impatience with the legacy and ethos of current patterns of professional regulation", the challenge for the professions is now clear (Larkin, 2002). They must adapt to demands for 'new ways of working', which 'cross traditional professional boundaries', and which may involve the loss of existing roles, the adoption of new roles, and the sharing of yet others (Department of Health, 2000).

SOCIOLOGY OF THE PROFESSIONS AND THE "PROFESSIONAL PROJECT

New professional groups are set to emerge, as existing groups are required to reshape and reform (Saks & Allsop, 2007). It is, therefore, incumbent on the professions to find new ways of negotiating relationships with each other, the public and the state. Yet, adapting to these demands is particularly problematic for the professions, as one of their most enduring - indeed defining - features has been the use of exclusionary and monopolistic strategies to attain high social status and other societal rewards (Larson, 1977; Macdonald, 1995; Saks, 2003). That is, they function by working constantly to compete in a market place for scarce resources – in terms of remuneration, autonomy and prestige – and are not, therefore, easily disposed to interprofessional 'sharing', particularly where sought-after privileges are at stake (Freidson, 1970a; Freidson, 1970b; Øvretveit, 1985; Saks, 2003).

Conceptually, this is captured neatly within the notion of the 'professional project', first described by Larson (1977) and elaborated upon later by MacDonald (1995). Central to the professional project is the idea that the social rewards generally accepted as being granted to professions – upward social mobility and high status alongside market control and enhanced remuneration – are not simply the result of the acquisition of special expertise, skill or knowledge, but the outcome of a successful 'project', which is, rather, an ongoing campaign of action to secure and maintain these privileges (Larson, 1977; Macdonald, 1995). The 'professional project' is about persuading others of the justification of claims to professional status, and thus its rewards, through the use of the resources of expert knowledge and skill (Larson, 1977). It is dependent for success upon the ability of the profession collectively to persuade its key audiences of the merit of their claims to exclusivity and privilege – most notably the state and the public.

CONTEMPORARY PROFESSIONALISM

Interprofessional education and practice stand in challenge to established understandings of professionalism that constitute the 'professional project'. To more fully understand the nature and magnitude of the challenge posed by the policy reforms alluded to above, as well as professional responses to those challenges, it is essential to examine the nature of professionalism in a contemporary context. In doing so, both the obstacles to change, and the adaptive strategies required (and undertaken) to enable such change, may be better appreciated. These issues lie at the heart of the obstacles to interprofessional education and practice; interprofessional practice may, at one level, offer a 'solution' to the problems facing the health care workforce, yet an unproblematic, seamless operationalisation is unlikely in the face of those forces and tensions which characterise and motivate the professions.

Where doctors are under pressure to assume new roles, in the wake of technological developments requiring greater specialisation, or to reduce working hours, it seems eminently sensible that government reforms should seek to transfer some of the burden to other suitably trained professions. In terms of economic viability, it is a seemingly sensible approach. One key contemporary example is the way in which the prescribing of medicines, once unique to medicine alone, has become part of the role of specialist allied health practitioners (Lawrenson, 2005; Hogg et al., 2007; Borthwick, 2008). Yet, to assume that such a policy could be effortlessly enacted would be to fail to appreciate the nature of professionalism and the contemporary dynamic of the 'expert' health care division of labour (Larkin, 2002; Saks, 2003).

As Larkin has pointed out, professions have *'thrived on their sense of separateness'*, built upon an identity which has been constructed around the ownership of certain task and knowledge domains, and which are defended vigorously when challenged by competitors (Larkin, 1993; 1995; 2002). Interlopers must be repelled if role boundaries, and thus task domains, are to be retained intact.

Alternatively, professions may seek to adapt to the loss of exclusivity in one arena by encroaching upon the exclusive domain of another, or by developing new domains of knowledge and control (Nancarrow & Borthwick, 2005). However, although dynamic and adaptable, professions nevertheless do not yield territory without some response, which has clear implications for the broader health care workforce and particularly for workforce planning within the organised health services. It is unlikely, in these circumstances, to conceive of an unproblematic reshuffle in professional roles, nor an unremarkable collaboration between professions in the execution of roles that have previously been exclusive to only one.

Increasing complexity and the emergence of new professional or support worker groups adds to the uncertainty and challenge (Humphris & Masterson, 2000; Saks & Allsop, 2007). How then do professions adapt, reform and redefine themselves in the face of policy demands for change? How do they respond to calls for the immediate development of collegiate interprofessional practices when they have been accustomed to competing for ascendancy in these areas? Evidence from the literature suggests how some professions are deploying adaptive strategies, and these will be discussed in this chapter.

WORKFORCE CHANGE AGENDAS

First, it is important to draw attention to the tendency to conceptualise current demands for workforce change as a purely contemporary phenomenon, which should, perhaps, be viewed with some caution. Shifting trends in workforce alignments are not new, nor are some of the forces suggested in the literature as producing pressures unique to the contemporary world (Nolan, 2004). For example, the impact of occupational specialisation on the health division of labour was evident during the latter half of the 20th century in the UK, as the National Health Service was becoming established and new roles developed, and led to a perceived need to engage with both interprofessional teamwork and role flexibility.

"occupational boundaries of very recent origin had quickly somehow acquired an aura of inevitable permanence…At the same time anxieties about whether occupational specialisation in medicine has been excessive in the light of changing health needs have grown in recent years. These anxieties, however, have usually been associated with calls for 'flexibility' and 'teamwork'...rather than any systematic analysis of the tensions of the resulting division and re-division of labour" (Larkin, 1983, p. vi).

As Larkin (1983) cogently observed at the time, calls for enhanced teamwork and role flexibility may not have been informed by a coherent policy appreciative of the need to consider the 'tensions' that would emerge within the professional division of labour as a result.

Workforce Shortages

Workforce shortages remain a particularly potent driver for change in the health services internationally. Looming shortages inform government policies relating to workforce redesign, and, in particular, the desire to enable a re-alignment in role boundaries between professions (Department of Health, 2000; Duckett, 2005; Sanders & Harrison, 2008). This shortfall has been addressed, to some extent, through international recruitment, with up to one half of new professional registrations of doctors and nurses in the UK emanating from practitioners trained overseas Saks & Allsop, 2007).

Cost of Labour, Flexibility and Cheaper Substitutes

As labour costs constitute a central component of health care funding, accounting for up to two thirds of all health care expenditure, there is an economic imperative which has led to a growth in 'cheaper' forms of labour, through 'role enhancement, substitution, delegation and innovation' (Saks & Allsop, 2007). Furthermore,

'the customary boundaries between professional tasks and the form of registration, based on the legal entitlement to use a particular title to practise, are seen as rigidities that prevent workforce flexibility, changes in skill mix and team working' (Saks & Allsop, 2007, p. 167).

Indeed, workforce supply is recognised as only one facet of the problem – ensuring workforce flexibility is also a key concern, stemming from fears of overspecialisation and the inefficient use of skilled staff (Duckett, 2005). As Duckett, (2005) asserted,

"the current assignment of roles for health professionals is perceived to be inefficient either because more staff are employed than would be required in an efficient organisation of roles, or staff at higher pay classifications being used to perform tasks which could be performed by staff at lower pay levels". (p.1).

Regulatory Rigidities and Inflexible Skill Mixes: Barriers to Change

Less recently, Larkin (1983) also noticed that *specialisation promotes a measure of interdependency as well as hierarchy*". Both points are consistent with the logic behind the introduction of health workers in support roles (McKee, Dubois & Sibbald, 2006; Saks &

Allsop, 2007). Further barriers to health care 'modernisation' and the incorporation of new and support worker roles into the workforce are felt to include the stark lines of demarcation that exist between professions, as are particularly manifest in their distinctive educational and career pathways (Saks & Allsop, 2007). As a result, new 'foundation' degrees, more generic health courses and interprofessional modules within established unidisciplinary programmes have been increasingly introduced to provide greater 'diffusion' of opportunities (Humphris & Masterson, 2000; Saks & Allsop, 2007).

Thus, a range of important drivers for change have amplified the challenge to professional identity, and bring into sharp relief the magnitude of the readjustment to be made by professions. Within the literature of the sociology of the professions, the Weberian concepts of social closure, professional dominance and autonomy underpin explanations which illuminate the nature of interprofessional conflicts based on education, role boundaries and task domains (Larkin, 1983; Saks, 1983; Larkin, 1988; Elston, 1991; Hugman, 1991; Witz, 1992; Turner, 1995). Before providing an explanatory workforce model to aid an understanding of the adaptive strategies available to professional groups within the health division of labour, it will be helpful to reiterate those elements of professionalism which both inform and potentially undermine seamless, interprofessional practice.

UNDERSTANDING PROFESSIONAL BOUNDARIES: THE DEFENCE OF PROFESSIONAL TERRITORY

As noted in Larson's (1977) model of the 'professional project', professions, acting as a collectivity, characteristically engage a range of strategies to ensure exclusive control over specific forms of knowledge and skill, which are legitimized by key audiences such as the public and the state (Abbott, 1988). In particular, Larson acknowledges that, once these goals are achieved, ongoing effort to maintain and extend these privileges is required, as circumstances change and other competitors enter the arena (Larson, 1977; Macdonald, 1995). Broadly, the Weberian concept of 'social closure' provides a theoretical backdrop to much of the literature analysing the professions (Parkin, 1979; Murphy, 1986).

SOCIAL CLOSURE AND THE PROFESSIONS

Social closure effectively explains the way professions act to 'close off' opportunities and rewards to other, 'outsider' groups, thus retaining the privileges of monopolisation within a 'charmed circle' (Parkin, 1982; Pilgrim & Rogers, 1993). A key maxim of closure theory is the desire and intent of a given collectivity to ensure that other (occupational) groups seeking a similar role are excluded from doing so, in order that the rewards gained from exclusive control are maintained (Pilgrim & Rogers, 1993).

Parkin's (1979) elaboration of the theory recognises exclusionary, usurpationary and dual closure dimensions to the strategies adopted to enforce social closure, which are further developed by Witz (1992) in her seminal work on the professions of medicine, nursing and radiography, to include demarcationary closure. These merit exploration, as they anticipate the evident hierarchical arrangements and power relations that pervade the division of labour, most clearly within the notion of 'professional dominance' (Freidson, 1970a; 1970b; Larkin, 1983; 1988; Saks, 1983; 1995).

PROFESSIONAL DOMINANCE THEORY

Professional dominance, also referred to as 'professional authority', describes the power and authority of the superordinate profession of medicine within the hierarchy of health care professions, where it enjoys not only autonomy over its own working practices, but also power over other professional groups, that are subjected to forms of subordination, exclusion or limitation of their practices (Freidson, 1970a; 1970b; Larkin, 1983; Willis, 1983; Turner, 1995). Elston (1991) identified two central elements of professional dominance, social and cultural authority, each allowing the dominant profession to shape societal views to conform to its own (also referred to as 'professional sovereignty' by Willis (1983).

In health care, medicine is viewed as the most successful profession and one which exercises the power of dominance over the other health care professions (Freidson, 1970a; 1970b; Willis, 1983). Indeed, even as the power of the medical profession, and its 'dominance' in the field of health care, is felt to be in decline, there is little doubt that it retains a broadly stable position within the health care professional hierarchy, albeit weakened in its relationship with the state (Allsop, 2006; Coburn, 2006; Dent, 2006; Willis, 2006).

EXCLUSIONARY AND USURPATIONARY STRATEGIES

Medical dominance is an important factor in explaining the 'tensions' in the health care workforce, and is a component of the exclusionary and usurpationary elements of social closure theory when it is applied. Exclusionary closure strategies are those usually adopted by the more powerful professions, such as medicine, to ensure continuity and maintain the preservation of privileges (such as high social status and remuneration). They are designed to exclude others groups from gaining the status and authority already won.

Usurpationary strategies are those most commonly deployed by less powerful groups intent on gaining the privileges enjoyed by the more powerful groups. This strategy resonates with the aims and activities of the allied health or nursing professions, possibly exemplified in their eagerness to assume 'extended' roles in domains once exclusive to the medical profession (Parkin, 1979; Larkin, 1983; Hugman, 1991; Borthwick, 2000).

DEMARCATIONARY STRATEGIES

For Witz demarcationary strategies are mechanisms aimed at inter-occupational control: they are "concerned with the creation and control of occupational boundaries between occupations" (Witz, 1992, p. 46). They equate, in Witz's view, to the concept of 'occupational imperialism' adopted by Larkin (1983). For Larkin, occupational imperialism "refers to attempts by a number of occupations to mould the division of labour to their own advantage, or, as Kronus (1976) puts it, to extend normative and legal boundaries as far as possible in their own interests. It involves tactics of 'poaching' skills from others or delegating them to secure income" (Larkin, 1983, p. 15).

OCCUPATIONAL IMPERIALISM

Larkin (1983) favoured the use of the concept of occupational imperialism to explain the dynamic within the health care hierarchy, in preference to medical dominance, which he regarded as 'over muscular' and focused on 'zero-sum' conflict, where the success of medicine equated directly to the failure of the other professions. This is an important point, for it reminds us that non-medical professions are also capable of operating similar mechanisms of control in a bid to advantage their own collective positions, and that interprofessional conflict in health care is not exclusively a reflection of tensions between doctors and the non-medical professions.

Whereas Turner (1985; 1995) described three ways in which the dominance of the medical profession might be expressed – through the subordination, limitation or exclusion of others professions – other authors have identified similar strategies adopted by the 'paramedical' professions (Larkin, 1983; Hugman, 1991). In the typology outlined by Turner (1985), some professions, such as nursing or radiography, were restricted to practices which were subject to the direction of physicians, where tasks might be delegated under instruction, thus limiting 'paramedical' independent decision-making (subordination). Others were either confined to the development of expertise in discrete areas of the body, such as the eyes or teeth (optometry or dentistry), or particular task areas, such as dispensing medicines (pharmacy), or simply marginalised. In the latter case, those professions excluded from mainstream health care provision were somehow tainted with an aura of charlatanism or quackery, unable to enjoy the status of a legitimate health care provider (Turner, 1985; 1995).

On the other hand, both Hugman (1991) and Larkin (1983) explored the ways in which these strategies might also be used by the non-medical health care professions, deployed against each other as well as the medical profession. In particular, Larkin's use of the 'occupational imperialism' framework was justified in part by his concern that "the expansionist tactics of para-medical groups" had drawn little attention from sociologists, possibly because of an "assumption that they are liberating rather than repressive, as in the case of doctors" (Larkin, 1983, pp. 15-16). Yet it is precisely because these concepts deal with professions as relatively homogenous collectivities that they perhaps lack the subtleties of micro-level analyses, which allow for local or individual influence (Sanders & Harrison, 2008).

IMPORTANCE OF THE WORKPLACE DOMINANCE STRATEGIES AND BOUNDARY DISPUTES

It is in the workplace itself where individual professionals often resolve boundary disputes, and where the "day to day exigencies of getting work done mean that formal professional boundaries cannot be strictly maintained", possibly in spite of official policies which may tend to stress the opposite (Sanders & Harrison, 2008). Abbott's (1988) work identified and acknowledged that jurisdictions are contested in three spheres – the public arena, legal system and the workplace – and that in the latter instance, jurisdictions are governed by 'situation specific rules' (Abbott, 1988; Sanders & Harrison, 2008; Theberge, 2008). Within specific contexts in the workplace, clear boundaries between professions may become clouded. For Abbott (1988) jurisdictions in the workplace constitute a 'simple claim to control certain kinds of work', which may alter when demand outstrips supply. For example, 'if there is too much professional work, non professionals do it', leading to a form of workforce assimilation.

Abbott (1988) recognised five forms of jurisdictional settlement that reflect professional concerns and help to explain why role transfer or work substitution may meet with resistance. Professions may settle jurisdictional conflicts through subordination (often through cognitive dominance, where practical skills are delegated) such as in the attempts by the UK Royal College of Surgeons to recognise non-medical surgical practitioners as technicians, operating under the direction of medically qualified surgeons (Borthwick, 2000).

Professions may split a jurisdiction, or share elements of it, or allow an advisory role for one profession, as it supervises another (Abbott, 1988). However, in the health care sphere, many of these options retain the pre-existing hierarchy in which medicine is pre-eminent, and that, as a result, they do not invoke hostility. However, where challenges to medical hegemony exist, conflict often does result. Many such contemporary examples still exist, and demonstrate the degree to which the maintenance of exclusive professional boundaries remains an important professional goal (Collins, Hillis, Stitz, 2006; Yong, 2006; Stevens, Diederiks, Grit & van Der Horst, 2007). Indeed, it has been suggested that conflict of this type arises particularly in situations where new professional provider groups arise and assume roles that have not been vacated by existing providers. This may also be relevant in policy initiatives such as in the case in non-medical prescribing (Weiss & Fitzpatrick, 1997; McCartney, Tyrer, Brazier & Prayle, 1999; Bradley, Hynam & Nolan, 2007).

Thus, the protection and maintenance of professional boundaries remains a relevant and potent driver in contemporary health care. The tension created by the logic of the market, with its focus on 'flexibility and boundarylessness', may actually contribute to the reconstitution of modified professional boundaries, rather than simply ensure the erosion of traditional boundaries (Fournier, 2000). Examples of the way in which professions may reconstruct their roles and boundaries in response to the challenges posed by neoliberal market forces will illustrate the adaptability of the professions. Before addressing some of these strategies, however, a deeper context can be provided by offering an account of four key strategic approaches which help to explain how the health care workforce responds to the challenges identified above (Nancarrow & Borthwick, 2005).

WORKFORCE FUSION AND FISSION

Nancarrow and Borthwick (2005) have developed a taxonomy to describe the way that health worker professional boundaries can change through the identification of new areas of work, or adoption of roles normally undertaken by other providers. They describe movement of the workforce in four directions:

- diversification,
- specialisation,
- horizontal substitution and
- vertical substitution.

Diversification and specialisation involve the expansion of professional boundaries within a single discipline, or intra-disciplinary change. Vertical and horizontal substitution (sometimes termed 'encroachment') involve expansion beyond traditional professional boundaries to take on tasks that are normally performed by other health service providers, or inter-disciplinary change.

Intra-Disciplinary Change

Diversification

Diversification involves the identification of a novel approach to practice by a particular disciplinary group such as the creation of a new task, or a new way of performing an existing task, which results in the expansion of the role for that discipline. Professional groups create new language to describe or define the new task or role, and often rely on regulation to legitimise or 'own' a new technology.

There are several examples of diversification by professional groups, including;

- The growth of complementary medicine, which suggests a willingness to embrace philosophies of care that are differentiated from those of conventional medicine (Saks, 1995; 1999);
- The language and concepts of podiatric biomechanics (Borthwick,1999);
- The early ownership of antibiotics and anaesthetics by doctors (Willis, 1983).

The ability of the health professions to diversify is influenced by several factors, the most important of which has been medical hegemony. The influence of the medical profession over other health and related disciplines has been described by several commentators (Johnson, 1972; Larkin, 1983; Kenny & Andrews, 2006).

Other factors that may influence the ability of a discipline to diversify include:

- their access to new research knowledge;
- their ability to control or regulate the new technology (Larkin, 1983);
- gender dominance within a particular discipline (Witz, 1992; Davies, 1995);
- the willingness of third party payers and funders to purchase services from particular types of workers; and
- the indemnity risks posed by a discipline undertaking a particular type of task.

Specialisation

Specialisation is defined as the "adoption of an increasing level of expertise in a specific disciplinary area that is adopted by a select group of the profession and legitimised through use of a specific title, membership to a closed-subgroup of the profession, and generally involves specific training" (Nancarrow & Borthwick, 2005, p. 907). Specialisation differs from diversification in that the specialist tasks are only accessible to a select group of the profession.

Medicine has well established systems for training and rewarding specialists, through membership to professional colleges that have restrictive entry criteria, require rigorous and extensive training and bestow a title to the member of that college. Other professional groups differ widely in their approaches to, and recognition of specialisms. For instance, in 2001, the Chartered Society of Physiotherapy argued that definitions of speciality restrict the practitioner and patient (Chartered Society of Physiotherapy, 2001). More recently, however (in the UK), new systems have been introduced across nursing, allied health and general practice, that enable the introduction of extended roles. The specialisms within these disciplines are not as formally implemented or recognised as the traditional medical specialisms, nor are they always associated with greater rewards.

Specialisation is often associated with increased status within a professional group. By specialising, workers have less time to undertake the more routine, mundane or less skilled components of their task. Thus the ability of the professional group to discard the less pleasant or lower status roles is an important component of specialisation (Larkin, 1983). Examples of this are most clearly seen in medicine, with the development of medical specialties where specialised tasks are the sole domain of specialist providers and the more routine aspects of care have historically been undertaken by general practitioners (Freidson, 1988).

The move to a specialist role, and the discarding of unwanted roles or tasks can bring risks to professional groups. When tasks are discarded by one discipline and adopted by one or more other disciplines, the discarded tasks can not easily be reclaimed by their original 'owner'. This risk is most likely to arise when the need for the specialist role diminishes.

INTERDISCIPLINARY CHANGE

Disciplinary boundaries in the health workforce can be changed by taking on work traditionally performed by other disciplines, or substitution. The term 'substitution' acknowledges that task transfer can be mutually agreed or involve contested boundary disputes in which transfer may be resisted. The terms vertical and horizontal refer to the level of training, expertise or status between the practitioners. There has been explicit support for the concepts of interdisciplinary working and training over the past decade, resulting in an (unquantifiable) increase in the amount of vertical and horizontal substitution between different types of workers (Nancarrow, 2004).

VERTICAL SUBSTITUTION

Vertical substitution involves the delegation or adoption of tasks between workers from different professional backgrounds, and with different levels of training and / or expertise. Examples of vertical substitution include the growth of non-medical prescribing in the UK by pharmacists and allied health professionals (McCartney, Tyrer, Brazier & Prayle, 1999). Therapy assistants and support workers are often delegated roles by therapists and nurses in rehabilitation settings (Nancarrow, 2004). The substituted roles are often adopted as a natural extension of the task repertory of the existing provider group; however this may be determined locally, and informally. Thus roles adopted by a therapy assistant in one setting may not be permissible in other settings (Nancarrow & Mackey, 2005).

In some cases, that increased role may be limited to a specialised part of that group. For instance, non-medical prescribing is limited to practitioners with specific training, enabling these practitioners to form a sub-specialty within their own discipline through vertical substitution. In this case, the vertical substitution involved the adoption of tasks normally owned by the medical profession. The extent and nature of vertical substitution tends to be controlled by the more powerful discipline, with the formation of a 'technically subordinate' group (Freidson, 1988).

HORIZONTAL SUBSTITUTION

Horizontal substitution refers to the sharing of tasks between providers with similar level of training and expertise, but from different disciplinary backgrounds. Horizontal substitution implies a mutually agreed transfer of tasks or negotiated boundary changes (Kreckel, 1980), rather than contested boundary disputes (Abbott, 1988). There are several examples of horizontal substitution, including the training of physiotherapy and occupational therapy assistants to become generic assistants (Rolf, Jackson, Gardiner, Jasper & Gale, 1999). Sharing of tasks around physical functioning and transfers by occupational therapists and physiotherapists, is an example of horizontal substitution (Booth & Hewison, 2002; Nancarrow, 2004).

Horizontal substitution does not appear to be associated with an increase in professional status, power or income, thus these boundary shifts are more likely to occur in response to situational factors such as staff shortages, or the setting of care (such as home based care), when it makes pragmatic sense for another practitioner to deliver an intervention (Nancarrow, 2004). The extent and success of horizontal substitution is likely to be influenced by the accessibility and proximity of staff. For instance, staff performing home visits as part of a multidisciplinary team may be more likely to perform the roles of other team members if they have the appropriate skills and knowledge. In contrast, in a hospital setting, a wider range of staff are likely to be accessible, thus role boundaries are more likely to be more rigidly defined.

Other factors that are likely to influence the roles of staff members within teams include the attitudes and support by management, structures of team meetings and access to interprofessional education. Horizontal substitution is more likely to occur where practitioner roles are similar. The potential for substitution increases when the tasks are less well defined, not protected through regulation and do not involve access to restricted technology.

Vertical and horizontal substitution has the advantages that when there are workforce shortages at particular levels, some tasks can be undertaken by other workers (Nancarrow, 2004). This model fits well with the adoption of competency based skills and knowledge frameworks adopted by the Department of Health in England for training staff.

WORKFORCE REFORM: NEW ROLES, NEW BOUNDARIES, NEW IDENTITIES?

Within the contemporary sociological literature, there are several examples of the ways in which health care professions are responding to the demands for change. Within the health division of labour, pressures for workforce redesign have already involved a significant reshaping in professional roles and boundaries (Weller, 2006; Oldmeadow, et al., 2007; Smith, 2007, Smith & Baird, 2007). New roles for established professions (specialisation), role transfer between established professions (such as drug prescribing), emergent new professional groups (such as respiratory therapists or assistant practitioners), and a surge in support worker roles have characterised these changes (Sewell, 2006; Weller, 2006; Saks & Allsop, 2007; Frossard, Liebich, Brooks & Robinson, 2008).

In some instances the professional organisations have been cautiously supportive of these developments, in others much less so (Collins, Hillis & Stitz, 2006; Kenny & Andrews, 2006; Sewell, 2006; Van der Weyden, 2006; Yong, 2006). Freidson once spoke of the 'core' practices of medicine as being central to the identity of medicine, roles which the profession would particularly seek to defend if challenged, and therefore roles which it would be least likely to relinquish by choice (Freidson, 1970a). '*Autonomy of technique*' was, he argued, at the core of what is unique about a profession, and medicine exemplified this through the "physician's right to diagnose, cut and prescribe...the physicians authority and responsibility in that constellation of work are primary" (Freidson, 1970a, p. 69)

Thus, it is when those areas of medical authority are challenged that the greatest resistance to change is likely to arise. Indeed, there is ample evidence to demonstrate the strategic responses of the medical profession to the advent of non-medical practitioners assuming roles within these spheres. Acceptance of non-medically trained practitioners adopting surgical roles, for example, is inevitably contingent upon the demand that doctors retain ultimate control of the diagnosis, and direct the surgical interventions of the non-medical operator (RCS, 1996; Borthwick, 2000; Collins et al., 2006). Even the adoption of titles which imply independence on the part of the non-medical practitioner may give rise to conflict, where, for example, podiatrists using the title 'podiatric surgeon' are decried as mischievous, and where the medical authorities become willing to acknowledge the role only if the title adopted reflects a delegated, technician-like status, such as 'podiatric surgical practitioner', ' operative podiatrist' or even 'podiatric proceduralist' (RACS, 2006; Laing, Ribbans, Parsons, Wilson et al., 2007).

Role Transfer – Critical Case – Non-Medical Prescribing

One of the most important aspects of role transfer to date has involved the legitimization of non-medical prescribing (Weiss & Fitzpatrick, 1997; McCartney, Tyrer et al., 1999; Taylor, 1999; Borthwick, 2001; Britten, 2001; Bradley Hynam & Nolan, 2007). Nurses, pharmacists and optometrists lead the way with new 'independent' prescribing roles in the UK, with podiatrists, physiotherapists and radiographers adopting 'supplementary' prescribing roles since 2005 (Borthwick & Nancarrow, 2005; Borthwick, 2008). Within Australia, funding for pharmaceutical provision is largely secured via the national PBS scheme (Pharmaceutical Benefits Scheme), which covers 80% of current prescriptions issued and is expanding by 10-15 % each year (ACT Health, 2007). As yet, however, only optometrists have achieved a budget under this scheme, and this is vociferously opposed by the Australian Medical Association, arguing that "the slippery slope to doctor pretenders is well and truly with us…It is part of a much broader push towards task substitution…The AMA is opposed to the budget decision to allow optometrists to prescribe on the PBS" (O'Dea, 2007).

In the UK, supplementary prescribing is a constrained through its dependence upon physician approval through the creation of 'clinical management plans', in which initial diagnosis is first established by the doctor (Bradley et al., 2007). Non-medical 'independent' prescribing does not permit practitioners access to certain categories of controlled drugs or unlicensed medicines, unlike doctor prescribing, which allows free access to all such medicines (Dawson & Hennell, 2007).

Boundary Disputes in Role Transfers

It is apparent that task transfer within these areas, although supported by regulatory and legislative changes as part of wider, government-sponsored, health workforce redesign measures, is not amenable to easy transition. Stevens et al. (2007) examined the issue of exclusive expertise in the case of optometrists and ophthalmologists (and GPs) in the Netherlands. As elsewhere, the advent of enhanced roles in prescribing for optometrists in the Netherlands is a relatively recent development. Legislation establishing optometry as an autonomous primary care health profession was enacted as late as 2000, including rights to prescribe drugs for diagnostic purposes. As a consequence, boundary disputes emerged with ophthalmologists, which hinged upon the degree to which the disputed jurisdictions involved task overlap, shared 'expert' knowledge or where professional boundaries were seen to be 'diffuse'. Stevens et al. (2007) argued that perceptions of the exclusiveness of expertise were more firmly embedded in the medical profession and its specialities than in the non-medical professions, such as optometrists. Their findings did not suggest that the 'rise of optometry' simultaneously signal a decline in the power of the ophthalmologists, as supervision by the latter was retained, at least in hospital settings.

Boundary-Blurring and Boundary-Spanning Strategies

Several recent case studies highlight a range of strategies adopted by those professions engaged in role expansion into domains previously exclusive to the medical profession, in which some degree of accommodation is involved. Allen (1997) utilised negotiated order theory to explain how some nurses undertook roles beyond their formal jurisdictions, a form of boundary-blurring that involved 'breaking the rules'. Such practice models are an unsatisfactory solution, bearing in mind the more recent demands for enhanced regulation, governance and 'performativity' required of the professions (Allsop & Saks, 2002; Dent & Whitehead, 2002; Moran, 2002).

Boundary-spanning is another mechanism deployed by non-medical professions when faced with potential disputes over the exercise of authority and expertise in contested areas of practice. For example, Tjora (2000) explored the ways nurses in a specific environment (emergency communication centres) exercised discretionary judgement in giving medical advice and establishing diagnoses, rather than deferring to doctors codified instructions. Tjora's (2000) point, however, is that whilst nurses may, in certain circumstances, undertake diagnostic roles, they do not 'take ownership' of this activity.

Goodwin, Pope, Mort and Smith (2005), in exploring anaesthetic room practices, found a similar pattern of activity, in which nurses or operating department practitioners were denied 'legitimate participation' in key decision-making, and were consequently forced to resort to tactics of persuasion (of doctors) in order to initiate the required action. Thus, although in possession of a relevant form of professional knowledge, and therefore expertise, their lack of cultural authority or legitimacy in the anaesthetic room hierarchy demanded they attempt to persuade or influence the doctor, often in a 'diplomatic and sensitive' way, to act in response to their assessment of the situation. In these cases, medical hegemony, and dominance, remains intact.

In a not dissimilar fashion, Theberge (2008) noted the way in which chiropractors apparently successful integration into sports medicine 'teams' was contingent upon the use of tactics designed to circumnavigate contested knowledge and skill boundaries through a reduction in their claims. Specifically, this meant asserting only that their treatment constituted a mechanical form of manual therapy, and not a medical intervention underpinned by medical diagnosis and knowledge.

Incorporation

In another case, Carmel (2006) identified a new strategy of 'incorporation' adopted by health care professions faced with interprofessional boundary work, through a micro-analysis of the dynamic within intensive care environments. In this strategy nurses and doctors emphasise organisational identity over occupational identity, thus avoiding boundary disputes in the rarefied environment of intensive care units. The relationships between nurses and doctors become "characterised more by convergence and incorporation than by competition" (p. 155), in which an allegiance to the 'unit' takes precedence over an allegiance to the profession. For Carmel (2006), the occupational division of labour is 'obscured', where the organisational division of labour is 'reinforced'. In practical terms, this situation nevertheless continues to acknowledge a medical hegemony, with the dominant role of medicine in intensive care preserved, although the work of both groups tends to be viewed as a collective 'jointly executed strategy' aimed at reducing the likelihood of conflicts arising, whether deliberate or inadvertent.

Another example from the UK is the recently established 'nurse endoscopy clinics', in which nurses carry out the surgical procedures associated with exploratory endoscopy, are now said to be 'successfully implemented' (Cash, Schoenfeld & Ransohoff, 1999; Goodfellow, Fretwell & Simms, 2003). The emergence of new roles for 'surgical care practitioners', engaged in the harvesting of saphenous veins for coronary artery bypass procedures, acknowledges non-medically trained personnel actively participating in surgery, through a joint UK curriculum framework agreed between the Royal College of Surgeons of England and the National Association of Surgical Care Practitioners (RCS, 1999; Department of Health, 2006).

CONCLUSION

What is at stake in each of the cases discussed, and their accompanying strategies, appears to be the preservation, in one form or another, of a medical hegemony and a hierarchy in which medicine retains key elements of care – most notably the diagnosis and its associated decision-making. The transfer of tasks of a complex nature can, albeit reluctantly, be negotiated under pressure from policy imperatives, but that retention of the exclusive right to establish a diagnosis and to direct subsequent care is a requirement for smooth transition in role boundaries. This is most evident in the case of the practice of surgery by non-medically qualified practitioners.

In these workforce reform initiatives there is, however, a common corollary – that 'technical' and operative interventions occur under "defined levels of supervision" by doctors (de Crossart & Graham, 2004). The evidence suggests that in both the UK and Australia that any attempt to establish or maintain independent surgical practice by non-medically qualified practitioners, outside the overarching authority of medicine, is unlikely to gain the support of medicine and is, on the contrary, likely to lead to intense interprofessional conflict (Borthwick, 2000; Hillis et al., 2006). In these circumstances the opposition takes several forms, ranging from demands that such activity be subject to accreditation by medical authority rather than independent authority (notably via the Australian Medical Association rather than the Joint Accreditation System of Australia and New Zealand – the 'JAS-ANZ'), to the limiting of practices to 'minor procedures', and the restriction in the use of professional titles to reflect a subordinate, technician-like role (RACS, 2006).

New 'physician assistant' roles and surgical care practitioner roles demonstrate the effectiveness of policy content and emphasise the urgency involved in reconfiguring the workforce. Central to the argument deployed by the medical profession is that although role and task boundaries may be crossed, the underpinning knowledge required to ensure the medical hegemony is still exclusive. What is debatable, perhaps, is the degree to which this position is sustainable in a climate of change that demands radical workforce redesign measures in a health care system which will ensure a health service fit for the 21st century. The intensity of calls for a 'new professionalism' through the implementation of authentically embedded interprofessional education and practice remains one of the most potent policy developments capable of further eroding the bedrock of traditional conceptualisations of the division of labour in health care.

REFERENCES

Abbott, A. (1988). *The system of professions - An essay on the division of expert labour.* Chicago: University of Chicago Press.

ACT Health. (2007). *Non-Medical Prescribing.* Canberra: ACT Health.

Alaszewski, A. (1995). Restructuring health and welfare professions in the United Kingdom - The impact of internal markets on the medical, nursing and social work professions. In T. Johnson, G. Larkin & M. Saks (Eds.), *Health Professions and the State in Europe* (pp. 55-74). London: Routledge.

Allen, D. (1997). The nursing-medical boundary: A negotiated order? *Sociology of Health and Illness,* 19(4), 498-520.

Allsop, J. (2006). Medical dominance in a changing world: the UK case. *Health Sociology Review,* 15(5), 444-457.

Allsop, J., Jones, K., & Baggott, R. (2004). Health consumer groups in the UK: a new social movement? *Sociology of Health and Illness,* 26(6), 737-756.

Allsop, J., & Saks, M. (2002). Introduction: the regulation the health professions. In J. Allsop & M. Saks (Eds.), *Regulating the Health Professions.* London: Sage.

Appel, A., & Malcom (2002). The triumph and continuing struggle of nurse practitioners in New South Wales, Australia. *Clinical Nurse Specialist,* 16(4), 203-210.

Bach, S., & Winchester, D. (2003). Industrial Relations in the Public Sector. In P. Edwards (Ed.), *Industrial Relations: Theory and Practice* (pp. 285-313). Oxford: Blackwell.

Baggott, R. (2002). Regulatory politics, health professionals, and the public interest. In J. Allsop & M. Saks (Eds.), *Regulating the Health Professions.* London: Sage.

Beck, U. (2000). *The brave new world of work.* Cambridge: Polity Press.

Borthwick, A. (2000). Challenging medicine: the case of podiatric surgery. *Work, Employment and Society,* 14(2), 369-383.

Borthwick, A. (2001). Drug prescribing in podiatry: radicalism or tokenism? *British Journal of Podiatry,* 4(2), 56-64.

Borthwick, A. (2008). Professions allied to medicine and prescribing. In P. Nolan & E. Bradley (Eds.), *Non-Medical Prescribing - Multi-disciplinary Perspectives* (pp. 133-164). Cambridge: Cambridge University Press.

Borthwick, A., & Nancarrow, SA. (2005). Promoting health: the role of the specialist podiatrist. In A. Scriven (Ed.), *Health Promoting Practice.* Basingstoke: Palgrave Macmillan.

Bradley, E., Hynam, B., & Nolan, P. (2007). Nurse prescribing: Reflections on safety in practice. *Social Science and Medicine,* 65, 599-609.

Bridges, M. (1995). *Job shift - how to prosper in a workplace without jobs.* London: Nicolas Brearley.

Britten, N. (2001). Prescribing and the defence of clinical autonomy. *Sociology of Health & Illness,* 23(4), 478-496.

Cameron, A., & Masterson, A. (2003). *Reconfiguring the clinical workforce.* Basingstoke: Palgrave Macmillan.

Carmel, S. (2006). Boundaries obscured and boundaries reinforced: incorporation as a strategy of occupational enhancement for intensive care. *Sociology of Health and Illness,* 28(2), 154-177.

Casey, B., Metcalf, H., & Millward, N. (1997). *Employers' use of flexible labour.* London: Policy Studies Institute.

Cash, B., Schoenfeld, PS., & Ransohoff, DF. (1999). Licensure, use, and training of paramedical personnel to perform screening flexible sigmoidoscopy. *Gastrointestinal Endoscopy*, 49, 163-169.

Coburn, D. (2006). Medical dominance then and now: critical reflections. *Health Sociology Review*, 15(5), 432-443.

Collins, J., Hillis, DJ., & Stitz, RW. (2006). Task transfer: the view of the Royal Australasian College of Surgeons. *Medical Journal of Australia*, 185(1), 25-26.

Cooper, R. (2006). Quality among a diversity of health care providers. *Medical Journal of Australia,* 185(1), 2-3.

Dawson, J., & Hennell, S. (2007). *Practical prescribing for musculoskeletal practitioners.* Keswick: M&K Publishing.

de Crossart, L., & Graham, R. (2004). Curriculum development for surgical care practitioners. *Annals of the Royal College of Surgeons of England*, 86(Suppl), 354-355

.Dent, M. (2006). Disciplining the medical profession? Implications of patient choice for medical dominance. *Health Sociology Review,* 15(5), 458-468.

Dent, M., & Whitehead, S. (2002). *Managing professional identities - knowledge, performativity and the 'new' professional.* London: Routledge.

Department of Health. (2000). *The NHS Plan.* Available at: http//www.dh.gov.uk (Accessed May 13, 2008).

Department of Health. (2006). *The Curriculum Framework for the Surgical Care Practitioner.* Available at:http//www.dh.gov.uk (Accessed March 14, 2008).

Duckett, S. (2005). Interventions to facilitate health workforce restructure. *Australia and New Zealand Health Policy*, 2(14).

Elston, M. (1991). The politics of professional power: medicine in a changing health service. In J. Gabe, M. Calnan & M. Bury (Eds.), *The Sociology of the Health Service.* London: Routledge.

Foot, D., & Gomez, R. (2006). Population ageing and sectoral growth: the case of the UK 2006-2026. *Oxford Journal of Business and Economics*, 5(1), 85-94.

Fournier, V. (2000). Boundary work and the (un)making of the professions. In N. Malin (Ed.), Professionalism, Boundaries and the *Workplace.* London: Routledge.

Freidson, E. (1970a). *Profession of medicine - A study of the sociology of applied knowledge.* London: University of Chicago Press.

Freidson, E. (1970b). *Professional dominance: The social structure of medical care.* New York: Atherton Press.

Frossard, L., Liebich, G., Hooker, RS., Brooks, PM., & Robinson, L. (2008). Introducing physician assistants into new roles: international experiences. *Medical Journal of Australia,* 188(4), 199-201.

Goodfellow, P., Fretwell, I.A., & Simms, J.M. (2003). Nurse endoscopy in a district general hospital. *Annals of the Royal College of Surgeons of England,* 85, 181-184.

Goodwin, D., Pope, C., Mort, M., & Smith, A. (2005). Access, boundaries and their effects: legitimate participation in anaesthesia. *Sociology of Health and Illness*, 27(6), 855-871.

Ham C. (2004*). Health policy in Britain*. Basingstoke: Palgrave Macmillan.

Hogg, P., Francis, G., Mountain, V., Pitt, A., Sherrington, S., & Freeman, C. (2007). Prescription, supply and administration of medicines in radiography: current position and future directions. *Synergy News - Imaging and Therapy Practice (December)*, 26-31.

Hugman, R. (1991). *Power in the caring professions*. Basingstoke: Macmillan.

Humphris, D., & Masterson, A. (2000). *Developing new clinical roles - A guide for health professionals*. Edinburgh: Churchill Livingstone.

Kennedy, I. (2001). *Learning from Bristol - The Report of the Public Inquiry into children's heart surgery at the Bristol Royal Infirmary* 1984-1995. HMSO.

Kenny, L., & Andrews, MW. (2006). Addressing radiology workforce issues. *Medical Journal of Australia*, 186(12), 615-616.

Laing, P., Ribbans, B., Parsons, S., & Winson, I. (2007). *BOFAS business plan for development of foot and ankle surgery with podiatry*. London: British Orthopaedic Foot and Ankle Society.

Larkin, G. (1983). *Occupational monopoly and modern medicine*. London: Tavistock.

Larkin, G. (1988). Medical dominance in Britain: image and historical reality. *The Millbank Quarterly,* 66(Suppl 2), 117-132.

Larkin, G. (1993). Continuity in change: medical dominance in the United Kingdom. In W. Hafferty & J. McKinlay (Eds.), *The Changing Medical Profession: An International Perspective*. Oxford: Oxford University Press.

Larkin, G. (1995). State control and the health professions in the United Kingdom: historical perspectives. In T. Johnson, G. Larkin & M. Saks (Eds.), *Health Professions and the State in Europe*. London: Routledge.

Larkin, G. (2002*).* Regulating the professions allied to medicine. In J. Allsop & M. Saks (Eds.), *Regulating the Health Professions*. London: Sage.

Larson, M. (1977). *The rise of professionalism - A sociological analysis*. London: University of California Press.

Lawrenson, J. G. (2005). Recent changes in the use and supply of medicines by optometrists. *Optometry Today* (3rd June), 28-32.

Macdonald, K. (1995). *The sociology of the professions*. London: Sage.

McCartney, W., Tyrer, S., Brazier, M., & Prayle, D. (1999). Nurse prescribing: radicalism or tokenism? *Journal of Advanced Nursing*, 29(2), 348-354.

McKee, M., Dubois, C., & Sibbald, B. (2006). Changing professional boundaries. In C. Dubois, M. McKee & E. Nolte (Eds.), *Human Resources for Health in Europe*. Maidenhead: Open University Press.

Moran, M. (2002). *The* health professions in international perspective. In J. Allsop & M. Saks (Eds.), *Regulating the Health Professions*. London: Sage.

Murphy, R. (1986). Weberian closure theory: a contribution to the ongoing assessment. *British Journal of Sociology*, 37, 21-41.

Nancarrow, S., & Borthwick, A. (2005). Dynamic professional boundaries in the healthcare workforce. *Sociology of Health & Illness,* 27(7), 897-919.

Nolan, P. (2004). The changing world of work. *Journal of Health Service Research and Policy,* 9(Suppl 1), S1:3 - S1:9.

O'Dea, J. (2007). An eye for an eye. *Australian Medicine* (June).

Oldmeadow, L., Bedi, H., Burch, H., Smith, J., Leahy, E., & Goldwasser, M. (2007). Experienced physiotherapists as gatekeepers to hospital orthopaedic outpatient care. *Medical Journal of Australia*, 186(12), 625-628.

Øvretveit, J. (1985). Medical dominance and the development of professional autonmy in physiotherapy. *Sociology of Health and Illness*, 7(1), 76-93.

Parkin, F. (1979). *Marxism and class theory: A bourgeois critique*. London: Tavistock.

Parkin, F. (1982). *Max Weber*. London: Routledge.

Pilgrim, D., & Rogers, A. (1993). *A sociology of mental health and illness*. Buckingham: Open University Press.

RACS. (2006). *Royal Australasian College of Surgeons submission to NSW Health concerning the performance of podiatric surgery in New South Wales*. Sydney: Royal Australasian College of Surgeons.

RCS. (1996). *Invasive Procedures Undertaken by Non-medically Qualified Health Professionals Without Delegation*. London: Royal College of Surgeons of England.

RCS. (1999). *Assistants in Surgical Practice: A Discussion Document*. London: Royal College of Surgeons of England.

Richards, A., Carley, J., & Jenkins-Clarke, S. (2000). Skill mix between nurses and doctors working in primary care delegation or allocation: a review of the literature. *International Journal of Nursing Studies*, 37, 185-197.

Rolfe, G., Jackson, N., Gardner, L., Jasper, M., & Gale, A. (1999). Developing the role of the generic healthcare support worker: phase 1 of an action research study. *International Journal of Nursing Studies*, 36, 323-334.

Saks, M. (1983). Removing the blinkers? A critique of recent contributions to the sociology of professions. *Sociological Review*, 31(1), 1-21.

Saks, M. (1995*). Professions and the public interest: medical power, altruism and alternative medicine*. London: Routledge.

Saks, M. (1999). The wheel turns? Professionalisation and alternative medicine in Britain. *Journal of Interprofessional Care*, 13(2), 129-138.

Saks, M. (2003). The limitations of the Anglo-American sociology of the professions: a critique of the current neo-weberian orthodoxy. *Knowledge, Work and Society*, 1(1), 13-31.

Saks, M., & Allsop, J.(2007). Social policy, professional regulation and health support work in the United Kingdom. *Social Policy and Society*, 6(2), 165-177.

Sanders, T., & Harrison, S. (2008). Professional legitimacy claims in the multidisciplinary workplace: the case of heart failure care. *Sociology of Health and Illness*, 30(2), 289-308.

Sewell, J. (2006). Task transfer: the view of the Royal Australasian College of Physicians. *Medical Journal of Australia*, 185(1), 23-24.

Sibbald, B., Shen, J., & McBride, A. (2004). Changing the skill mix of the health care workforce. *Journal of Health Service Research and Policy*, 9(Suppl 1), S1:28 - S21: 38.

Simpson, P. (2004). *The Impact of the European Working Time Directive to Junior Doctors Hours on the Provision of Service and Training in Ananesthesia, Critical Care and Pain Management*. Available at: http://www.rcoa.ac.uk/docs/ewtd.pdf (Accessed April 29, 2008).

Smith, A. (2007). Competency for new prescribers. *Australian Prescriber*, 30(3), 58-59.

Smith, T., & Baird, M. (2007). Radiographers' role in radiological reporting: a model to support future demand. *Medical Journal of Australia*, 186(12), 629-631.

Stevens, F., Diederiks, J., Grit, F., & van der Horst, F. (2007). Exclusive, idiosyncratic and collective expertise in the interprofessional arena: the case of optometry and eye care in The Netherlands. *Sociology of Health and Illness*, 29(4), 481-496.

Taylor, R. (1999). Partnerships or power struggle? The Crown review of prescribing. *British Journal of General Practice*, 49(442), 340-341.

The Lancet, editorial (1995). Who is a surgeon. *The Lancet,* 345(8951), 663-665.

Theberge, N. (2008). The integration of chiropractors into healthcare teams: a case study from sport medicine. *Sociology of Health and Illness*, 30(1), 19-34.

Tjora, A. (2000). The technological mediation of the nursing-medical boundary. *Sociology of Health and Illness*, 22(6), 721-741.

Turner, B. (1985). Knowledge, skills and occupational strategy: the professionalisation of paramedical groups. *Community Health Studies,* 9(1), 38-47.

Turner, B. (1995). *Medical power and social knowledge* (2nd ed.). London: Sage.

Van der Weyden, M. (2006). Task transfer: another pressure for evolution of the medical profession. *Medical Journal of Australia*, 185(1), 29-31.

Weiss, M., & Fitzpatrick, R. (1997). Challenges to medicine: the case of prescribing. *Sociology of Health and Illness, 19(3),* 69-89.

Weller, D. (2006). Workforce substitution and primary care. *Medical Journal of Australia,* 185(1), 8-9.

Willis, E. (1983). *Medical dominance: The division of labour in Australian healthcare.* London: George Allen and Unwin.

Willis, E. (2006). Introduction: taking stock of medical dominance. *Health Sociology Review,* 15(5), 421-431.

Witz, A. (1992). *Professions and patriarchy.* London: Routledge.

Yong, C. S. (2006). Task substitution: the view of the Australian Medical Association. *Medical Journal of Australia,* 185(1), 27-28.

In: Sociology of Interprofessional Health …
Ed: S. Kitto, J. Chesters et al.

ISBN: 978-1-60876-866-0
© 2011 Nova Science Publishers, Inc.

Chapter 14

RE-IMAGINING INTERPROFESSIONALISM: WHERE TO FROM HERE?

Simon Kitto, Scott Reeves, Janice Chesters and Jill Thistlethwaite

INTRODUCTION

In the introduction to this book, we suggested that the recent emphasis on interprofessional education and practice by (primarily) western neo-liberal governments has, up until to this point, avoided a critical sociological analysis. In this edited collection we have tried to redress this gap by bringing together an eclectic group of clinicians from varying backgrounds across the health and social care spectrum, alongside an equally diverse group of social science academics from the UK, Australia and Canada, to begin to critically engage with the current concept(s) and practice(s) of interprofessionalism. In doing so however, we recognised the commitment of these professionals to improving interprofessional practice and that this may have, quite naturally, led to the book containing a crypto-normative interprofessional theme. Nevertheless, we have attempted, wherever possible, to ensure that contributors draw upon the critical threads which underpin sociological thought.

As editors, the question we must ask ourselves of this book is have we gone far enough in interrogating interprofessionalism? Typically, the sociological approach asks what is happening? Why? What are the consequences? How do we know? And most importantly how could it be otherwise (Willis, 2004)? As noted above, this book has begun to critically explore aspects of interprofessionalism and as a result we have been partially successful in answering these questions. Overwhelmingly, and quite rightly, our contributors have stayed within the brief of critically analysing interprofessional issues, meditations, case studies, evaluations and theoretical reflections on the practice of interprofessional collaboration in health and social care. The idea behind this book was to move beyond instrumental and descriptive evaluations of interprofessional education, learning and practice, to examine the core social, cultural, psychological, professional and educational issues that underpin both the barriers and facilitators to interprofessional health care practice. Significantly, we also asked our authors to offer possible solutions to the problems they identified. No easy task. For the most part, this book has centred in on micro and meso cultural and structural issues existing within the domain of the health care system to produce a useful resource for teachers, policy makers, practitioners and students engaged in interprofessional practice education, practice and learning health and social care activities.

In this chapter we wish to move to a more macro level to briefly reflect on what it is that we have asked our contributors to re-imagine; the very nature of interprofessionalism. As noted above, we want to ask: what is happening? Why? What are the consequences? How do we know? And most importantly how could it be otherwise? But with a view to understanding the emergence of interprofessionalism and why it has taken hold (at least at a policy level) in countries such as the UK, Canada and Australia. We suggest a governmentality approach might provide valuable insights into these questions.

INTERPROFESSIONALISM AS A FORM OF GOVERNMENTALITY

The notion of governmentality was originally employed by Foucault (1979) as a way to explain the shaping of the conduct of individuals and populations at the micro-level, at-a-distance within a matrix of political reason (Rose, 1999a). The prevailing political rationalities of recent times are embedded within advanced liberal practices of rule, which attempt to activate the choices individuals/agencies make, while simultaneously setting normative standards to evaluate their respective performances. Within this approach, the notion of the 'free' individual/agency is always context-bound as they are always situated in organised networks of governing (Dean, 1999). In this sense, advanced liberal government operates through a range of rationalities, technologies and agencies concerned with, as Dean (1999, p. 166) notes:

> "Structuring, shaping, predicating and making calculable the operation of our freedom, and of working off and through diagrams of free subjects constituted by forms of governmental and political reasoning".

How though does the notion of governmentality relate to our concerns with interprofessionalism?

In the late 1980s and early 1990s we saw the emergence of discourses of interprofessionalism on a global scale, particularly in the UK, US, the Nordic countries, Canada and Australia (CAIPE, 1997; WHO, 1988). In the last decade, there has been a consolidation of these discourses within both governmental and non-governmental health policy and practice in the UK, US and Canada, and again to a lesser extent in Australia. Through a variety of policies developed by interprofessional government and non-government agencies it is possible to identify the emergence of a specific discourse of interprofessionalism that in short, seeks to create shared decision making within a 'community of equals' who work within the health care system and are free to learn from each other to improve quality of health and social care.

From a governmentality perspective, this can be understood as being a discursive process of 'government through community' - a type of advanced liberal form of governing through policy programs designed to activate the capabilities and resources of communities predicated upon responsibilised notions of self-help. It often encourages mutual self-regulation and moments of spontaneous solidarity (Rose, 1996). Typically, this kind of governmental activity has historically been targeted toward health consumer groups, but interestingly, in relation to interprofessionalism, we see it now being targeted towards the occupations and professions which make up health and social care as well as the wider community. For example, the UK CAIPE specifically:

"Calls for collaboration amongst government departments, employing authorities, statutory and regulatory bodies, universities and colleges, professional associations and service users and carers... No one profession, working in isolation, has the expertise to respond adequately and effectively to the complexity of many service users' needs and so to ensure that care is safe, seamless and holistic to the highest possible standard" (CAIPE, 2009).

Similarly, in Canada, the Interprofessional Education for Collaborative Patient-Centred Practice (IECPCP) movement holds the following values:

"Interprofessional education has been described as learning together to promote collaboration. It involves: socializing health care providers in working together, in shared problem solving and decision making, towards enhancing the benefit for patients, and other recipients of services; developing mutual understanding of, and respect for, the contributions of various disciplines; and instilling the requisite competencies for collaborative practice' (Health Canada, 2009)."

This could be construed as a direct attempt by government (and indirectly as well through professional partners such as CAIPE) to constitute and govern professions, occupations, individuals and other 'stakeholders' within the heath and social care systems at an integrated 'community' level. As Rose (1999b, p. 145) points out:

"By acting upon these associations, networks, cultures of belongingness and identity, by *building networks, enhancing trust* relations, *developing mutuality and cooperation* – through a new relation between *ethical citizenship* and *responsible community* fostered by, but not administered by, the state – citizens can now be 'governed through community."

Arguably, nowhere is this discourse of governing more explicit than within CAIPE's principles of IPE as stated on their website:

"IPE is more than common learning, valuable though that is to introduce *shared concepts, skills, language and perspectives* that establish common ground for interprofessional practice. It is also comparative, *collaborative* and interactive, a test-bed for interprofessional practice, taking into account respective roles and responsibilities, skills and knowledge, powers and duties, value systems and codes of conduct, opportunities and constraints. This cultivates *mutual trust* and *respect*, acknowledging differences, dispelling prejudice and rivalry and confronting misconceptions and stereotypes" (CAIPE, 2009).

We would argue that such statements have created a powerful global discourse about the need to *think* and *act* in an interprofessional manner through communities that contain a diversity of health care professionals. As a result, it is possible to argue that these discourses have created a sense that interprofessionalism is a 'natural' and logical part of the health and social care landscape. Such discourses mask the situatedness of interprofessional practices – that are located within a specific socio-political epoch. The challenge it creates is the struggle to think otherwise. How do we truly understand the nature of this movement while we ourselves are positioned within such a pervasive and globally dispersed liberal political paradigm? The adoption of a governmentality approach may help us to look underneath the surface level, to probe why these movements are happening, and begin to explore the associated consequences.

WHERE TO FROM HERE?

As the chapters in this book have demonstrated, a sociological lens can generate a range of potentially useful ways of thinking about interprofessional education and practice. This book has offered an initial sociological analysis. An analysis albeit, which requires further exploration, examination and refinement. As we argued above, the use of a governmentality approach can provide a helpful way of examining the nature of interprofessionalism as it offers a much needed critical perspective. It can begin to question and unpack some of the common (largely positive) assumptions the interprofessional community holds about interprofessionalism. Only through the adoption of such critical approaches can we develop a more sophisticated and richer understanding of the nature of interprofessional education and practice which can provide answers to our sociologically-informed questions of what is happening? Why? What are the consequences? How do we know? And how could it be otherwise? Through making the familiar strange (Macionis, 2007) we can start to appreciate where we have come from differently, and more importantly, where we are currently in the development of interprofessionalism. We would argue that such an ongoing enterprise can help provide a positive and self-reflexive commitment to improving health care practice into the future.

REFERENCES

CAIPE, (1997). *Interprofessional education - A definition*. London: Centre for the Advancement of Interprofessional Education.
CAIPE, (2009). About Us: Defining IPE. Available at :http://www.caipe.org.uk/about-us/defining-ipe/ (Accessed 15th August 2009).
Foucault, M. (1979). 'On governmentality'. *I&C*, 6, 5-21.
Health Canada. (2009). Interprofessional Education for Collaborative Patient-centred Practice. Available at: *http://www.hc-sc.gc.ca/hcs-sss/hhr-rhs/strateg/interprof/index-eng.php* (Accessed XX August 2009).
Macionis, J. (2007). *Sociology*. Upper Saddle River, NJ: Prentice Hall Publishers.
Rose, N. (1999a). *Powers of Freedom: Reframing Political Thought*. Cambridge: Cambridge University Press.
Rose, N. (1999b). Inventiveness in politics. *Economy and Society*, 28, 467–493.

Rose, N. (1996). The death of the social? Refiguring the territory of government. *Economy and Society, 25*(3), 327-356.

WHO. (1988). *Learning together to work together for health. Report of a WHP study group on multiprofessional education of health personnel: the team approach.* Geneva: World Health Organisation

Willis, E. (2004). *The Sociological Quest: An Introduction to the Study of Social Life* (4th Ed.). St Leonards, New South Wales: Allen and Unwin.

In: Sociology of Interprofessional Health … ISBN: 978-1-60876-866-0
Ed: S. Kitto, J. Chesters et al. © 2011 Nova Science Publishers, Inc.

Contributor Biographies

Editorial Team

Simon Kitto

Simon is a Scientist at the Li Ka Shing Knowledge Institute at St. Michael's Hospital focussing on educational research related to knowledge translation. He is also a Scientist at the Wilson Centre for Research in Education; Assistant Professor in the Department of Surgery; Direcctor of Education Research in the Office of Continuing Education and Professional Development, Faculty of Medicine, University of Toronto. Simon is also an Adjunct Senior Lecturer in the Department of Surgery, Monash University. His core research interests lie in the areas of medical and surgical culture as related to knowledge translation, continuing education, and situated performances of interprofessionalism and their inter-relationships with profession-specific standards/protocols.

Janice Chesters

Janice is currently Acting Director of the Monash University Department of Rural and Indigenous Health in Moe Victoria. Janice chairs the Board of a psychiatric disability support and recovery service, co-chairs the All Together Better Health 5 conference committee and is a board member of a large rural stand alone community health service. Janice's principal research area is rural mental health and wellbeing, especially research into non clinical mental health services. As a rural health academic she has broadened her career beyond mental health research to investigate rural workforce issues, interprofessional education and practice, theoretical and applied health education, rural health in general and Indigenous issues. Her teaching, research and publications highlight the connectedness of physical and mental health and stress the complexity and diversity of health care in rural places.

Scott Reeves

Scott is a Scientist at the Li Ka Shing Knowledge Institute at St. Michael's Hospital and the Wilson Centre for Research in Education. He is also Director of Research at the Centre for Faculty Development, St. Michael's Hospital and an Associate Professor in the Faculty of Medicine, University of Toronto. His main research interests are exploring and evaluating the processes and outcomes related to interprofessional education and practice by use of ethnographic, mixed methods and systematic review. He was recently appointed as the new Editor-in-Chief of the Journal of Interprofessional Care.

Jill Thistlethwaite

Jill is Professor of Clinical Education and Research at Warwick Medical School, UK, and is a general practitioner. She is a member of the WHO study group on interprofessional education (IPE). In 2009 she became an adjunct professor of IPE at Auckland University of Technology (AUT). She previously worked at James Cook University and the University of Sydney. She is associate editor of the Journal of Interprofessional Care and president of InterEd, the international association for interprofessional education and collaborative practice. Jill has co-authored four books and published widely in health professional education.

Clare van den Dolder

Clare is an assistant at the Monash University Department of Rural and Indigenous Health, Victoria, Australia. She has provided administrative and editorial support for this book, and other projects within the department since 2005.

Authors
Lesley Bainbridge

Lesley Bainbridge is the Director, Interprofessional Education in the Faculty of Medicine and Associate Principal in the College of Health Disciplines at the University of British Columbia. Her areas of special interest in which she has published and presented include interprofessional health education (IPE), collaborative practice, shared decision making, leadership, evaluation of IPE, curriculum development related to IPE, interprofessional practice education and other areas related to IPE such as rural health, geriatrics, health human resources and underserved populations. She was one of the principal authors of a Health Canada funded report entitled Accreditation of Interprofessional Health Education in 2009.

David Beckett

David Beckett is an Associate Professor in Education, and an Associate Dean in the Melbourne School of Graduate Research, The University of Melbourne. He publishes in adult and vocational learning, philosophy of education and education policy.

Alan Borthwick

Alan is a Senior Lecturer at the School of Health Sciences, University of Southampton, UK. His research has largely focused on the contemporary and historical sociology of the allied health professions in the UK and Australia, and in particular on the profession of podiatry. His most recent work includes a comparative study of allied health professionals access, administration and prescribing of medicines in the UK and Australia.

Rosalie A. Boyce

Rosalie A. Boyce is the Principal Research Fellow within the Centre for Rural & Remote Area Health, University of Southern Queensland. She also has an appointment in the School of Health & Rehabilitation Sciences in her role as a joint program director on the Health Fusion Team Challenge. Rosalie's primary research interests are on the management and organisation of the allied health professions, workforce reform, interprofessional education, and building international collaborative policy networks.

Mollie Burley

Mollie comes from an extensive background in rural nursing, management, qualitative research and education. She holds a Senior Lectureship in the Monash University Department of Rural & Indigenous Health. Her main interests are developing and implementing interprofessional collaborative practice in rural Victoria, Australia, as convener of the Health & Social care Interprofessional Network (HSIN) and is part of two research teams exploring interprofessional collaborative practice. Currently Mollie works as a consultant in a community health service assisting with the development, enhancement and implementation of effective student placements and facilitating and enhancing education and research for staff, founded on interprofessional collaboration.

John Carpenter

John Carpenter is Professor of Social Work and Applied Social Science at the University of Bristol, where 25 years ago he designed, ran and evaluated one of the first pre-registration programmes of interprofessional education (IPE) in England. Since then, he has worked at Kent and Durham universities, returning to Bristol in 2005. He has led major evaluations of the outcomes of IPE for community mental health and child protection. He is co-author of Interprofessional Education and Training Policy Press (2008).

Julia Coyle

Julia, who qualified as a physiotherapist in London in the United Kingdom, came to Australia in 1985. Twenty years clinical experience in metropolitan but more predominantly in rural areas fostered in her a commitment to improving health care for inland communities of Australia. Since 1999, Julia has drawn upon this clinical experience to inform her work at Charles Sturt University. In particular, she has focussed on research into health care teams and inland health services and the development, with teams of equally committed people from the School of Community Health, of innovative curricula for allied health founded on principals of integrated practice and community partnership. .

Vernon Curran

Vernon Curran is an Associate Professor of Medical Education and Director of Academic Research and Development with the Faculty of Medicine, Memorial University. He is also Co-Director of the Centre for Collaborative Health Professional Education, Memorial University and has led the development and establishment of an interprofessional education curriculum across the health and human service programs at Memorial. Vernon also holds a cross-appointment with the Faculty of Education at Memorial University and teaches in the undergraduate and graduate degree programs in Adult Education and Post-Secondary Studies. He holds undergraduate and graduate degrees in psychology, adult education, distributed learning and rural extension studies.

Lynda d'Avray

Lynda d'Avray is a Lecturer in Interprofessional Development for Medical and Healthcare Education, St George's, University of London and leads the development of interprofessional education for students of medicine at St George's, University of London. Lynda also leads on the implementation and expansion of the Interprofessional Practice Placement where mixed teams of students give hands-on care to patients receiving care in South West London interprofessional training wards. She is an enthusiastic supporter of interprofessional education, interested in promoting interprofessional experiences for all health care students across faculty and practice learning, and the development of staff to support this. She is currently involved in several IPE research projects including joint research with colleagues in Denmark.

Claire Dickinson

Claire Dickinson is a Research Associate at the Institute of Health and Society at Newcastle University. Claire developed her interest in interprofessional education whilst working on her PhD, supervised by John Carpenter, on interprofessional education in community mental health. Claire's current interests include working relationships in health and social care.

Joy Higgs

Joy was appointed as the Strategic Research Professor in Professional Practice in Research Institute for Professional Practice, Learning & Education (RIPPLE) and the Director of The Education for Practice Institute at Charles Sturt University in 2007. Before joining CSU she worked for over 25 years as an educator, scholar, researcher and research supervisor at The University of New South Wales and The University of Sydney. She has held appointments as visiting scholar and consultant to a number of Australian and international tertiary institutions. In 2004 Joy received a Member of the Order of Australia award for service to health science education through course development, academic and administrative contributions and research into teaching methods. Her primary role at CSU is the advancement of practice-based education through collaborations in research, scholarship, student supervision and education.

Lindy McAllister

Associate Professor Lindy McAllister, Ph.D. is Deputy Head of the Medical School at The University of Queensland, responsible for the Office of Teaching and Learning as well as other leadership and management roles in the School . She was previously the head of the speech pathology program at Charles Sturt University. Her research and scholarship interests are in professional issues, ethics, clinical education, assessment, and the applications of qualitative research to practice development.

Peter McCrorie

Peter McCrorie is Professor of Medical Education and the Head of the Centre for Medical and Healthcare Education at St George's, University of London. He is Director of the new 4-year MBBS Graduate Entry Programme and has been involved in its design, organisation and implementation. He is Head of the Centre for Medical and Healthcare Education and

Associate Dean for International Affairs (Education). His main interest is in the assessment of competence, in its widest sense, and with curriculum development, in particular problem-based learning, community-oriented learning and graduate entry. He is an enthusiastic supporter of interprofessional education and has presented his ideas in the UK, Australia, Brunei, the Czech Republic, Canada and, most recently, Japan.

Monica Moran

Monica is a senior lecturer in the division of Occupational Therapy, Faculty of Health Sciences, at the University of Queensland, Brisbane. She is joint program director of HealthFusion Team Challenge, an Australia wide project to encourage best practice in student teams. Within UQ she contributes to the planning, delivery and evaluation of interprofessional education throughout the faculty. Her research interests include communication and culture, graduate entry and accelerated learning models in the health professions and client centred practice.

Susan Nancarrow

Susan is a health services researcher and Principal Research Fellow at the Centre for Health and Social Care Research at Sheffield Hallam University. She has a background as a podiatrist, and her recent research has explored workforce dynamics, in particular models of interprofessional working in older peoples' services and she is currently the project lead on two large Dept of Health (England) studies.

Gillian Nisbet

Gillian Nisbet has a professional background in Nutrition and Dietetics and has worked within NSW public hospitals in clinical, education and management positions. More recently Gillian led a project to introduce interprofessional learning (IPL) into curricula for students from allied health, medicine and nursing professions at the University of Sydney. Gillian was instrumental in setting up an interprofessional teamwork module that introduced health care students to the concept of teamwork within health, and in establishing an IPL clinical placement program for senior year health care students. Through these positions Gillian has developed an interest and expertise in the area of interprofessional learning, particularly in work-based settings. Gillian is a foundation member of the Australasian Interprofessional Practice and Education Network (AIPEN) and Co-chair of the 2010 'All Together Better Health 5' international IPL conference.

Lisa Nissen

Lisa is an IPE researcher and pharmacy practice academic in the School of Pharmacy at The University of Queensland. She is a key member of the Faculty of Health Sciences IPE working party and project steering committee. She is also joint program director of HealthFusion Team Challenge, an Australia wide project to encourage best practice in student teams. Her interests include new and creative mechanisms for IPE teaching and learning including online delivery.

Mary Ellen Purkis

Mary Ellen Purkis is a nurse and is currently Dean of the Faculty of Human & Social Development at the University of Victoria in British Columbia, Canada. She completed her doctoral studies at the University of Edinburgh, conducting an ethnographic study of nursing practice in the field of public health. She has studied the practice of nurses in home-based care and has begun to focus more recently on community-based care of older adults experiencing dementia. Across these different sites of research, her interests in broad-based organizational change in health care service delivery have been foundational.

Natalie Radomski

Natalie Radomski is a Senior Lecturer in the Monash University, School of Rural Health and the Head of the Bendigo Regional Clinical School, Rural Medical Education Unit. Natalie's doctoral research is exploring interdisciplinary approaches to clinical practice and professional learning in primary health care settings.

Andrew Russell

Andrew Russell is a senior lecturer in the Department of Anthropology, Durham University, where he is a member of the department's Medical Anthropology Research Group and director of the MSc in Medical Anthropology. He was strand leader of Medicine in the Community, part of the Medicine programme at Queen's Campus, Stockton, for seven years from 2001-8 before being appointed director of the University's new community outreach and engagement programme. His research interests are in public health innovations and behaviour change. His most recent publication is a textbook for medical students, *The Social Basis of Medicine* (Wiley-Blackwell, 2009).

Dennis Sharpe

Dennis Sharpe Co-Directed the Centre for Collaborative Health Professional Education at Memorial University of Newfoundland, Canada for several years and is currently a Professor with the Faculty of Education. He chairs the post-secondary studies group and works with adult learners from a wide variety of occupational backgrounds, including those in the health professions. Recent involvement with interprofessional education has included co-leading a major Health Canada funded project *Collaborating for Education and Practice: An Interprofessional Education Strategy for Newfoundland and Labrador*, and work with the newly created Canadian Interprofessional Health Collaborative as a steering committee member.

Gail Whiteford

Professor Gail Whiteford is currently Pro Vice Chancellor (Social Inclusion) at Macquarie University, Australia. In her home discipline of occupational therapy she has held numerous senior roles over time as a research chair, scholar, manager and contributor to national and international professional bodies and journal editorial boards. She has undertaken work with the European Commission on two occasions and in 2009 was awarded the Canadian Association of Occupational Therapy's Merit Service award for her international contribution to the profession. Gail's research interests are focussed around inclusion, participation, practice scholarship and stakeholder driven research approaches.

INDEX

Q

R

S

T

U

V

W

Y